WISE

Also by Frank Tallis

NON-FICTION

Obsessive Compulsive Disorder: A Cognitive and Neuropsychological Perspective

Changing Minds: A History of Psychotherapy as an Answer to Human Suffering

Hidden Minds: A History of the Unconscious

Love Sick: Love as a Mental Illness

The Incurable Romantic and Other Unsettling Revelations

The Act of Living: What the Great Psychologists Can Teach Us About Surviving Discontent in an Age of Anxiety

Mortal Secrets: Freud, Vienna and the Discovery of the Modern Mind

FICTION

The Liebermann Papers (psychoanalytic detective series)
Adapted for television as *Vienna Blood*

WISE

Finding purpose, meaning and wisdom
beyond the midpoint of life

Frank Tallis

abacus
books

ABACUS

First published in Great Britain in 2026 by Abacus

3 5 7 9 10 8 6 4 2

Copyright © Frank Tallis 2026

The moral right of the author has been asserted.

All rights reserved.
No part of this publication may be reproduced, stored in a retrieval system, or transmitted, in any form or by any means, without the prior permission in writing of the publisher, nor be otherwise circulated in any form of binding or cover other than that in which it is published and without a similar condition including this condition being imposed on the subsequent purchaser.

A CIP catalogue record for this book
is available from the British Library.

Hardback ISBN 978-0-3491-4622-5
Trade paperback ISBN 978-0-3491-4623-2

Typeset in Dante by M Rules
Printed and bound in Great Britain by
Clays Ltd, Elcograf S.p.A.

Papers used by Abacus are from well-managed forests
and other responsible sources.

Abacus
An imprint of
Little, Brown Book Group
Carmelite House
50 Victoria Embankment
London EC4Y 0DZ

The authorised representative
in the EEA is
Hachette Ireland
8 Castlecourt Centre
Dublin 15, D15 XTP3, Ireland
(email: info@hbgi.ie)

An Hachette UK Company
www.hachette.co.uk

www.littlebrown.co.uk

Contents

Preface   1

1 Denial: The Quest for Immortality   11

2 Acceptance: Embracing Reality   35

3 Turning Points: Revelations, Awakenings and Callings   54

4 Soul Searching: The Psychology of Spirituality   77

5 Integration: The Essential Task   106

6 Circuits in Conversation: The Integrated Brain   128

7 Shadowlands: Negotiating Obstacles   147

8 Meaning: Existence and Purpose   160

9	The Subjective Hourglass: Time and the Perception of Time	176
10	Conclusion: How it Works	194
	References	227
	Acknowledgements	245
	Index	247

Preface

Look inside

'At one point, midway on our path in life, I found myself in a dark wood, the right way blurred and lost.' The first line of Dante's *Inferno* is powerful and engaging. Immediately, the reader is immersed in the story. What will happen next? The nineteenth-century French artist Gustave Doré produced an atmospheric engraving of this opening scene. It shows Dante, located in a cavernous nightmare of branches, foliage and serpentine stems, looking nervously over his shoulder. He stands next to a bank of exposed tree roots and ahead of him are tenebrous depths that recede into blank, featureless infinity. Bathed in a strange luminescence with no obvious source, he seems small and vulnerable, alone in a sinister universe of shadowy entanglements.

Dante's symbolism is intended to represent a common experience: reaching the middle years, feeling that one might have lost one's way, and recognising that decisions must be made to proceed along 'our path in life'. Like Dante, most of us have an intuitive understanding that the midpoint is highly significant.

Since the 1960s, psychological problems arising in the middle years have been given a special designation. The term 'midlife crisis' appeared for the first time in a paper written by the Canadian psychoanalyst and polymath Elliott Jaques. Jaques identified several symptoms associated with the midlife crisis, and these ranged from the relatively mild, such as insomnia and memory problems, to the severe, such as alcohol dependence and depression. The midlife crisis has since generated innumerable magazine articles and it is routinely employed as a plot device in novels and films. This kind of exposure has resulted in the slow erosion of its scientific credibility. Yet, there are many reasons why the middle years might become troubled: increased awareness of mortality, fewer occupational opportunities, accumulated regrets and perceived irrelevance in a culture that overvalues youth – to name but a few.

Psychotherapists have never suggested that the midlife crisis is a universal phenomenon. Nevertheless, a recent working paper produced by the National Bureau of Economic Research in the USA, based on a sample of half a million individuals from 'rich nations', found evidence consistent with Jaques' original description of the phenomenon. Relative safety, material comfort and access to good medical care do not protect many citizens living in the West from middle-aged angst.

Dante tells us that he entered the dark wood when he was midway along the path of life. He is of course referring to a notional rather than a mathematical midpoint. None of us are aware of when we are passing through the midpoint, because none of us know when we are going to die. For most people, it will very likely fall in the fourth or fifth decades. It is where the second half of life begins and, naturally, the second half of life presents very different challenges from those typical of the first half. How we negotiate and adapt to these challenges will be a key determinant of our ongoing mental health.

Dorothy L. Sayers (who in addition to being a very successful author of detective fiction produced a landmark English translation of *The Inferno* in the 1940s) explained the deeper meaning of Dante's first line by suggesting that once lost in the dark wood, a 'man' can only escape by descending into himself. After the turning point, the path proceeds as an inner journey, and it is only by choosing this inner path (as opposed to an external, worldly path) that one can hope to find a way through the darkness. For Dante, whose world view was shaped by fourteenth-century godliness, the 'right way' (also translated as 'the straightforward pathway') was strongly associated with religion and religious ideals. Only religion could provide answers to the big questions, invest suffering with meaning, and neutralise the threat of oblivion. The devout were (and still are) well equipped to make healthy adjustments in later life, because they expected to be rewarded with a blissful existence in paradise. Faith dispels existential unease.

Unfortunately, the panacea of religion has become less effective in the twenty-first century, particularly in the West. The majority find it difficult to believe in a perfect, omniscient God, and the average person is inclined to reject religious 'answers' because they seem implausible. Renunciation, prayer and atonement are no longer very appealing. They are too encumbered by outmoded concepts such as grace, unction and the remission of sin. If we wish to follow Dante through the dark wood, we must travel in roughly the same direction – that is, inwards – but we will probably find it easier to take a slightly different route.

On reaching the midpoint, many are drawn to the writings of philosophers, particularly the Stoics and existentialists, who urge us to cultivate acceptance when faced with the inescapable prospect of ageing and dying. Their guidance is predicated on logic rather than faith, and it is therefore more in accord with modern values. However, philosophy, even when carefully argued, is frequently experienced as an intellectual exercise. We can read an explanation of why we shouldn't fear death, we can accept its precepts and conclusions – and still feel frightened of dying. It seems that for intellectual truths to be translated into personal, *felt* truths, a closer connection is required between head and heart. Something must happen first. As the German philosopher Georg Wilhelm Friedrich Hegel attested, 'The owl of Minerva takes flight only at dusk.' The acquisition of wisdom takes time. It tends to appear rather late in life.

Psychologists who have written about personal development over the course of the human lifespan, most notably Carl Gustav Jung, tend to agree with Dante: the midpoint is frequently associated with uncertainty, and 'inner descent' is recommended as a means of achieving clarity and a renewed sense of purpose. Notions of 'inner descent' vary, and range from the systematic examination of thoughts, feelings and memories (as one might in psychotherapy) to engaging with the contents of the unconscious as they manifest in altered states and liminal experiences. Inner descent is encouraged not only because it promotes beneficial change, but also because the alternative, doing nothing, has been identified as a significant mental health risk. In some accounts of the life cycle (for example, the 'life-stages' model proposed by the psychoanalyst Erik Erikson), a failure to achieve healthy psychological adjustments after the age of sixty-five will result in persistent feelings of despair.

Increased awareness of one's internal world promotes closer intellectual and emotional integration, and this will have many positive consequences, including the ability to internalise philosophical truths. Such truths become the owned, *felt* truths of the wise, rather than just the mechanical reproduction of wise words.

One of the most consistent findings to emerge from the practice of psychotherapy over the last 140 years is that minds can be divided and that there is a relationship between the magnitude of these divisions and the amount of distress and dissatisfaction a person experiences. The classic confirmation of this relationship is hysteria, as described by Sigmund Freud in his early case studies. Freud's patients suffered from symptoms that were caused by unconscious memories, and these memories could only be retrieved – that is, raised into consciousness – with the help of psychoanalysis. Freud's treatment bridged a divide that had 'widened' between the conscious and unconscious regions of the mind.

A corollary of this general understanding of how minds work is that unity – or 'wholeness' – is beneficial. People who have achieved 'wholeness' have greater transparency. They can look inwards and see more of themselves, their inner vision is clearer, and they are less likely to be 'stressed' by internal contradictions; they are more self-knowing (a characteristic that we commonly ascribe to those who have attained wisdom and within whom philosophical truths resonate deeply); they are 'ontologically secure' (their sense of self is stable) and they experience life as a coherent series of connected events. By contrast, the 'ontologically insecure' are unsettled, unsteady, and tend to experience life as episodic or fragmented. Wholeness is also associated with 'ease of being', an important aspect of which is feeling 'at home' in one's body. The common expression 'to be comfortable in one's skin' exemplifies the largely intuitive understanding that minds and bodies can differ with respect to how well they are integrated.

There is a close relationship between the unconscious and the body. This is what Freud discovered when he was treating his 'hysterical' patients. Distressing memories in the unconscious can produce physical symptoms. Today, when unpleasant memories are repressed, we might not develop symptoms typical of hysteria in the nineteenth century – for example, phantom pains or inexplicable paralyses – but we frequently experience other forms of physical disturbance, such as elevated heart rate, muscle tension and stomach problems. Repression creates an inner division. 'Closing the gap' between conscious and unconscious regions of the mind – that is, achieving greater levels of wholeness – promotes somatic comfort, and a person who is snugly embodied is usually relaxed and spontaneous in the presence of others. Ease of being not only affects how we feel in our skins, but how we feel in social situations.

Wholeness is a concept that appears in the writings of psychologists whose theories vary significantly. It has been a feature of psychology from the late nineteenth century to the present. This suggests that when the human mind attempts to understand itself (its dysfunctionality and functionality) thinking in terms of underlying divisions and unity feels natural. People were thinking about the mind in this way long before the advent of modern psychology. For example, in the sixteenth-century Jewish mystical tradition Kabbalah, human qualities are represented as branches of a symbolic 'tree'. The evolution of the person over time involves the integration of these qualities – an ongoing process that gives life purpose.

Not everyone agrees that the mind can be divided and integrated. Some have rejected this framework because it involves visualising the mind as a 'structure'. The most famous structural model of the mind is Freud's trio of id, ego and super-ego, three agencies that are roughly equivalent to the unconscious, the autobiographical self and conscience. Freud's model is problematic – for some, at least – because it is a hypothetical 'object' that we cannot observe directly. When Freud introduced the structural model, he provided an egg-shaped diagram – with a partitioned interior – to help his readers imagine the mind 'objectified'. In reality, there are only brains, neurotransmitters and subjectivity. To talk about agencies such as the 'id' can be judged to be groundless. However, this kind of criticism misses the point somewhat. Structural models are *a way of thinking* about the mind and if they help us to understand what is going on in our heads then they have served their purpose.

Structural models are, in fact, much more than airy abstractions or conceptual tools. They can be mapped on to the brain. The ego, for example, is very probably supported by a complex neural system known as the default mode network. It has been suggested that the beneficial effects of psychedelic drugs are mediated by powerful experiences of ego-dissolution. Patients being treated with drugs like LSD or psilocybin remain conscious, but their ordinary, everyday sense of self is significantly attenuated. This temporary weakening of the ego creates an opportunity for the self to be 'renewed'. Rigid and unhelpful beliefs are more easily revised. In practical terms, someone with a tendency to see the world negatively might recalibrate their beliefs in favour of a more accurate and less biased view. This could, for example, result in reduced levels of depression and anxiety. Temporary weakening of the ego has been associated with improved mental health across a broad range of clinical conditions. Brain scanning studies have shown that psychedelics disrupt the default mode network, and when this happens, at least for the duration of the 'trip', the everyday, autobiographical self shrinks or disappears. Structural models – which divide the mind into parts – make sense, both psychologically *and* biologically.

Determined critics argue that 'wholeness' (a concept predicated on 'structure') is impossible to quantify and therefore of limited scientific value. This isn't strictly true. Scanning technology can be used to measure connectivity in the brain and this can be expressed in mathematical terms. Brains can be 'cross-stitched', as it were, either tightly or loosely.

The self-evident utility of viewing the mind as something that can be divided or unified has ensured the survival of 'wholeness' in the vocabulary of clinicians. It surfaces, in one form or another, in treatment approaches as diverse as integrative counselling and Lacanian psychoanalysis.

The term 'wholeness' is usually favoured by schools of psychology that have a 'spiritual' dimension. Again, critics suppose that this association devalues the concept; however, 'spirituality' (as understood by psychologists such as William James, Carl Gustav Jung and Abraham Maslow) has been reclaimed as a subject fit for scientific study since the emergence of sub-disciplines such as transpersonal psychology and neurotheology. Transpersonal psychology is concerned largely with altered states of consciousness and their subsequent effects on the person, and neurotheology seeks to identify the biological correlates of phenomena such as prayer, meditation and our sense of the sacred. These specialisms focus on the pragmatic benefits of 'spiritual' experience and no assumptions are made about their religious significance. As a result, much guidance concerning wholeness, personal growth and internalising philosophical truths relevant to maintaining mental health in later life (and previously summarily dismissed as 'New Age' or 'alternative') can now be reviewed without abandoning a scientific world view. A consistent finding that has emerged in several related literatures is that those who achieve good psychological adjustment beyond the midpoint of life are often 'spiritual'. This does not mean that they are religious, but rather that they have rejected materialism and have adopted a transpersonal outlook. They show minimal interest in accumulating possessions and feel strongly connected to the natural world and to others.

The title of this book – *Wise* – encourages the reader to make certain assumptions about the author. I would like to make it clear, from the outset, that I do not view myself as a particularly wise person, nor do I make any claims concerning the possession of 'special' knowledge. My objective, stated simply, is to explore how mental health can be best achieved (and maintained) in the second half of life. To this end, I have drawn on the work of several philosophers and psychologists whose writings are valued because they offer guidance concerning how we might live wisely. Similar ideas surface in books written in the ancient world as well as twenty-first-century America, which suggests, perhaps, that there are some fundamental constants. Indeed, there are a surprising number of correspondences. I have favoured the discussion of general principles over the provision of specific prescriptions. People are different. We have unique combinations of preferences and prejudices. It is more useful to consider frameworks that guide thinking than to offer precise instruction, because principles can be applied flexibly in ways that work for the individual. Where I discuss specifics – that is, the practical application of psychological theories – these discussions should be viewed as invitations to experiment. Sometimes, I illustrate points using clinical examples. These are real patients, but I have modified contextual details to ensure anonymity.

Life after the half point has many challenges: loss of direction, physical decline, pain, redundancy, dissatisfaction, compromised authority, bereavement – and all endured in the long shadow of death. Regardless of what has been achieved in the first half of life, no matter how much money you have, or fame or knowledge or love, you will still be obliged, one day, to stand in Dante's dark wood, uncertain, anxious, troubled, all too conscious of the shadowy depths that lie ahead.

What should you do?

This book explores what the wise can teach us about the acquisition of wisdom and it seeks to explain how neuroscience and related disciplines are confirming their insights. The core of this book concerns the accomplishment of a task – achieving 'wholeness' – which could well be the essential condition for good mental health in later life.

This book isn't a path through the woods, exactly. But rather, a signpost that shows where a path might be joined.

Let's start walking.

1

Denial: The Quest for Immortality

Abandon your immortality projects

The Epic of Gilgamesh is the oldest work of literature in the world. Several versions exist, but scholars frequently refer to the 'classic' or standard version which was written on clay tablets in the Akkadian language during the late second millennium BC. The Babylonians and Assyrians called Gilgamesh 'He Who Saw the Deep', a title which suggests the acquisition of hidden knowledge. Like many great stories, this venerable epic involves a voyage and a homecoming, a transformative journey. Gilgamesh, the King of Ùruk, slays an ogre and becomes obsessed with mortality after his friend, the wild man Enkidu, dies. He embarks on a quest to discover the secret of eternal life from Uta-napishti, an immortal. Uta-napishti reveals that there is a boxthorn on the seabed that has the power to rejuvenate. Gilgamesh ties heavy stones to his feet, sinks to the seabed, and finds the miraculous plant. He plans to eat it at night, but before he can do so it is stolen by a snake. Devastated, he returns home. As he approaches Ùruk, he admires its impressive walls – its greatness. His quest for biological immortality has failed, but there is still reputational immortality. Gilgamesh will not live for ever, but he will be remembered for as long as the ramparts and parapets of Ùruk remain.

Gilgamesh demonstrates that from earliest times, human beings have yearned for immortality. It is a preoccupation that finds expression in narrative traditions all over the world. The fountain of youth and the elixir of life have been staples of storytelling for millennia, and immortal characters appear again and again in a multiplicity of guises, as guardians, alchemists, elves, vampires, wanderers, time travellers. The quest for immortality is an abiding fascination that bridges ancient literature and the latest speculative fiction. Whether the means of achieving immortality is a plant that grows on the seabed or a digital personality archive, the motivation is the same. Gilgamesh communicates his feelings about mortality with a simple affirmation: 'I am afraid of death.'

The fact that human beings have been fantasising about immortality for at least three thousand years shouldn't be very surprising. Fear of death is intense and almost impossible to quell with rational arguments because the survival instinct pre-dates the evolution of higher mental functions such as reason. The structures in the brain which mediate primal fears do not possess language. They cannot be persuaded to 'think' differently in this respect. Socratic questioning can help you to modulate lesser fears, but the threat of extinction will cause the heart to pound so loudly your 'inner philosopher' will be silenced. The survival instinct is so fundamental, we share it with micro-organisms. Even bacteria protect themselves. Self-preservation is the prime directive, the first condition that makes everything else possible. Consequently, evolution has ensured that the survival instinct is compelling and indefatigable. It continues to influence our behaviour long after we have achieved our evolutionary purpose. Even when our genes have been safely transferred to the next generation, we still fear death – perhaps even more so. In the absence of severe depression, disability or pain, human beings never reach an age at which they decide that they have lived long enough and are now ready to die. The average person, if offered a magic potion on their death bed that could extend life for one more day, or even just one more minute, would take it.

Humans respond to the threat of death with the blind panic of a hunted animal. The limbic system, or mammalian brain, is activated, adrenalin is secreted into the bloodstream, and fear motivates fight and flight. Fight and flight are the two behaviours that have been favoured by natural selection to increase our chances of surviving attack by a predator. But death is the ultimate predator. It cannot be defeated or escaped. Moreover, our primal fear of death is complicated by intellect and imagination. Unlike animals, we can 'picture' the future. We can worry about fatal illnesses; we can envisage dying in a hospital; we can even create mental videos of our bereaved relatives grieving. Human beings are profoundly social animals, and the idea of never seeing those we love again is extremely distressing. The small sadness that accompanies every 'goodbye' contains a presentiment of finality.

Terror management theory is the modern term used by social and evolutionary psychologists to describe how human beings respond to the distress caused by the pairing of the survival instinct with knowledge of death. Conflict produces terror which is 'managed' by various forms of escapism, the most common historical precedent being belief in an afterlife. Although terror management theory is a relatively recent development, it was foreshadowed in the writings of many authors, most notably Sigmund Freud. When the unstoppable force of the survival instinct is resisted by the immovable object of death, terror is fuelled by the inexhaustible, circular energies generated by an irresolvable contradiction. *You must live. You must die.* Brains are perpetual motion machines that crank out existential dread.

We are always conscious, to a greater or lesser extent, of mortality. And when the noise of the world recedes, when we drift into states of quiet reflection or close our eyes at the end of the day, existential dread is likely to find its voice. The small hours have long been associated with coloratura performances, morbid arias that preclude sleep and make the darkness vertiginous. William James, the father of American psychology, was acutely aware that death is constantly with us. Employing a macabre image that he might easily have borrowed from Edgar Allan Poe, he wrote: 'the skull will grin in at the banquet'. Beneath our changing facial expressions, the fixed grin never relaxes. The death's head blends terror and mockery.

For those without faith, death is not only distressing because it represents personal negation. It is also distressing because it resonates with universal negation. What is the point of living if everything dies? What is the point of the universe if it is destined (as many physicists predict) to become an empty, frozen void? In Chekhov's short story 'Ward No. 6', the character of Dr Ragin, in the 'stillness of the night', discovers that death and cosmic nihilism are easily connected: '"Oh," he thought, "why isn't man immortal? Why the brain centres and convolutions? Why eyesight, speech, self-awareness, genius, if they are all doomed to pass into the earth and at last go cold with the earth's crust, and then whirl round the sun together with the earth for millions of years without rhyme or reason?"'

Some psychologists have concluded that the idea of death is so overwhelming, so swollen with cosmic horror, our thoughts on the subject never progress to the point of meaningful engagement. The existential psychotherapist Irvin Yalom has compared facing death to staring at the sun. We can't do it. We must turn away. Freud asserted that no one really believes in their own death. We are simply too 'defended'.

The identification of 'defences' was one of Freud's greatest contributions to psychology. When we encounter situations or have thoughts that make us anxious or uncomfortable, defences are deployed, and our anxiety and discomfort will diminish. The first defence mechanism that Freud identified was 'repression' (although many more were discovered and each of these mechanisms works in a different way). Freud's early patients, particularly those suffering from hysteria, exhibited symptoms that he attributed to troubling memories that had been 'pushed down' into the unconscious. Treatment involved retrieving these repressed memories using psychoanalysis.

Defences operate automatically like the expansion and contraction of our pupils in dim or bright light. When our gaze nears the sun, our pupils will contract to protect our retinas. Similarly, when reality becomes unbearable, our minds close a little, self-protectively, to reduce anxiety and discomfort. Defence mechanisms are not 'pathological'. When defences are operating optimally, they make it possible for individuals to function without being debilitated by anxiety. However, defences can become 'pathological' if they are deployed excessively. A massive mobilisation of defences *can* neutralise terror, but such a reaction, or overreaction, will very probably result in a damaging dilution or distortion of reality. Returning to the pupil analogy: the mind contracts to a pinpoint. Terror is no longer visible, but neither is much else. Be that as it may, extreme outcomes of this kind are rare, because even highly defended individuals experience some death-related anxiety. Very few people respond with indifference when they are informed that they have a terminal illness.

Although Freud was the first to emphasise the role of defences in general psychological functioning, it has always been recognised that human beings tend to avoid thinking about death if they can. Perhaps *memento mori* became fashionable among early Renaissance scholars for this reason. A grinning skull on one's table is less easily ignored than the skull beneath one's skin. We need to be reminded of our mortality so that we can make the most of life (whether that means seeking salvation for some or seizing the day for others). As Samuel Johnson once observed, death concentrates the mind 'wonderfully'. Puncturing defences can be a bracing antidote to complacency.

If psychological defences were completely effective, no one would fear death. Thoughts about dying could be excluded from awareness and intimations of death would fail to register. But defences are *not* completely effective. For most people, defences reduce fear, they do not extinguish it.

Around middle age defences are tested by frequent reminders of mortality. Aches and pains (signs of wear and tear) begin to accumulate; older relatives and acquaintances inform us of diagnoses that are potentially life-threatening (high blood pressure, high cholesterol, diabetes); the names of childhood heroes appear in obituaries. Of course, there are always exceptions. Defences can be weakened prematurely by early losses; however, the biology of ageing and the laws of population statistics normally delay the stressing of defences until the second half of life. For some, baleful portents trigger the deployment of new or reinforced defences, whereas for others, incremental stress of this kind will cause defences to fail or collapse. The majority discover that their defences have been weakened and that they are subsequently experiencing more thoughts about death and dying.

The 'midlife crisis' can trigger a sustained, disruptive and exhausting escape from morbid thoughts. Divorces rise when couples reach their forties. There are many reasons why this happens, but a strong desire to recapture some of the excitement of youth is clearly a significant contributory factor. The stereotype of the middle-aged divorced man with a new motorbike and younger girlfriend is well recognised and a gift to comedy writers. Sex draws its power as a defence not only from evolution, but also from our romantic ideals. Somewhere, in the unconscious, eternal love and eternal life are conflated. But passionate love doesn't last for ever. It lasts somewhere between three and seven years. Enduring love requires passion to be complemented by amity and commitment. The male midlife crisis isn't really a comedy. It is a tragedy. When men mistake motorbikes for magic boxthorns there are often unforeseen consequences. Divorced men – compared with divorced women – are at much greater risk of developing addictions and clinical depression.

The defence most relevant to death-related anxiety is denial. We can assume that this was the defence mechanism Freud had in mind when he said that none of us really believe in our own death. On the one hand, we know with absolute certainty that we are going to die. But on the other hand, we don't necessarily feel the inevitability of death in the core of our being. Denial is at work, offering resistance, impeding the transition of a discomfiting truth as it attempts to descend from the head and settle in the gut. A flicker of doubt always survives. *Will it really happen? Really? To others, maybe – but not to me.* Again, Chekhov noted this curious phenomenon in 'Ward No. 6', when Dr Ragin is talking to an aged postmaster. The postmaster says: 'Good gracious me, I say to myself, surely it's time you were dead, you old dodderer! But deep inside me, you know, a little voice whispers: "Don't you believe it, you will never die!"' This 'little voice', which, like Chekhov's postmaster, many of us hear occasionally, is no doubt encouraged by the fact that after every night of dreamless sleep (a state of personal absence that seems ostensibly indistinguishable from death) we are resurrected. It is hard to believe in decisive termination of consciousness because it is contradicted by experience. There is only one day in the entirety of our lives when we fail to resurrect – the day we die.

The Denial of Death is the title of a Pulitzer Prize-winning book by Ernest Becker that was published in 1973. Becker was a cultural anthropologist with an interest in recasting psychoanalytic ideas in the mould of 'existential psychology'. He was the son of Jewish immigrants, served as an infantryman during the Second World War, and witnessed the liberation of a Nazi concentration camp. For Freud, the sex drive is fundamental, whereas for Becker, it is fear of death: '*Consciousness of death* is the primary repression, not sexuality.' Becker supposed that our unique ability to anticipate death should be granted greater significance in any general theory of human behaviour. He believed that fear of death influences not only aspects of personal development, but also culture and the fate of nations. He is perhaps best known for introducing the term 'immortality project' to describe how legacies operate as defences by providing humans with symbolic permanence.

Immortality projects can take many forms. Gravestones and epitaphs are obvious examples, but books, aerospace companies, charities, concept albums, social media platforms and children can also be understood as immortality projects. They are all augmentations of the person, tokens of presence that continue to exist after the person has died. *My book will always be read, my business will never fail, my dynasty will last for ever.* Becker extrapolated from the individual to society and beyond. The pursuit of immortality projects can motivate whole civilisations. People identify with their cultures – and cultures clash. What we describe as 'wars' might be more accurately described as conflicts that arise between competing immortality projects. Individuals go to war to preserve a particular way of life. *Their* way of life, *their* tokens of permanence, *their* myths, legends, art, music and values. According to Becker, our defensiveness – our denial of death – has been the predominant cause of the very worst atrocities: torture, genocide, the dropping of nuclear bombs.

Although Becker introduced the term to describe a personal or cultural legacy, it has since found more general use as shorthand for any activity that reduces terror by denying death. 'Immortality project' is sometimes used to describe not merely an attempt to achieve symbolic immortality, but *actual* immortality. At present, among many theoretical alternatives, only 'suspended animation' is an option. There are now several companies offering to freeze and store brains at bargain prices. At some point in the future, it is assumed that it will be possible to safely thaw and reactivate frozen brains before transplanting them into new, purpose-grown bodies, or artificial, non-biological humanoid substitutes. Another form of immortality project (still in the very early stages of development) is whole brain emulation. Computer scientists believe that very soon it will be possible to convert brains into digital information. Thus, personalities will survive for as long as the information is stored. It is supposed that emulations could inhabit an infinite number of virtual worlds, including bespoke versions of paradise.

If immortality projects are a measure of defensiveness, then the citizens of western democracies have never been more defended. Technological advances have inspired shimmering mirages of deathless Utopias. Transhumanism is a relatively new 'philosophical' movement, and its prophets claim that the problems of the human condition will be solved by technology-based transformations and enhancements within a few generations. Some transhumanists have declared, somewhat optimistically, that the first immortals have already been born. Ray Kurzweil, one of the movement's most enthusiastic evangelists, has predicted a major transformative shift in our relationship with technology in the next decade: 'A key capability in the 2030s will be to connect the upper ranges of our neocortices to the cloud, which will directly extend our thinking. In this way, rather than AI being a competitor, it will become an extension of ourselves. By the time this happens, the nonbiological portions of our minds will provide thousands of times more cognitive capacity than the biological parts. As this progresses exponentially, we will extend our minds many millions-fold by 2045.' Kurzweil's vision of the symbiotic union of human and machine raises an interesting possibility: that the 'nonbiological portions' of the mind will outlive the 'biological parts'. Perhaps, in the foreseeable future, it will be difficult for doctors to declare a transhumanist 'wholly' dead, because most of his or her 'intelligence' will still be 'alive' in the cloud (although to what extent a disembodied auxiliary intelligence can be said to be 'alive' is questionable).

Transhumanism can be understood as an extreme immortality project; however, unless you have already arranged to have your brain frozen, the idea of attempting to defy death by harnessing the power of super-advanced technologies will probably feel somewhat removed and hubristic. Yet, most of us are already partial converts to transhumanism, because we have absorbed the ideals of a culture that supports the use of technology to preserve life and deny death, even when the life that has been preserved is devoid of qualities such as pleasure, meaning and connectedness. Old and terminally ill patients routinely consent to treatments that compromise mental functioning, produce distressing side-effects and have a vanishingly small chance of succeeding. Such treatments are offered because society expects its physicians to deny death, even when it would be more rational to concede defeat and offer – instead of questionable interventions – companionship, comfort and kindness. Today, we tend to die in ambulances, accident and emergency departments, or separated from loved ones by drips, tubes, oxygen masks and monitors, a technological exoskeleton that discourages human contact – the solace of hugging, kissing and hand holding. The outcome, however, is always the same. Death wins. The denial of death only serves to complicate dying. Even when patients are brain dead, we are reluctant to switch off their life-support machines. Death is denied even when denial is self-evidently futile. In fact, death is denied even when loved ones have been cremated or buried. The phenomenon of post-bereavement hallucination (which usually takes the form of a surviving spouse seeing and sometimes conversing with their deceased partner) is extremely common.

In the modern world, the denial of death is assisted by its concealment. It is easier to deny something that you never see. This is why Renaissance scholars owned skulls. To make death visible. Not so long ago, death was very much a part of life. A significant number of women died during labour. Different generations tended to live in the same building or neighbourhood, and most people died at home surrounded by friends and relatives. The number of deaths occurring in hospitals only began to exceed those occurring in homes around the middle years of the twentieth century. Corpses were not immediately removed from homes and deposited in mortuaries. It was relatively common for the dead to be embalmed and laid out in an open coffin. Prayers were offered for the repose of souls in parlours where it was possible to look directly at, or even touch, the dead. Under these conditions, outpourings of grief were not blocked by embarrassment or self-consciousness. No one attempted to gloss over or downplay death. By contrast, *we* can barely say the word. We prefer to employ euphemisms. People no longer die, they 'pass away' or go to 'a better place'. The dead are not dead, they have simply 'departed'. Victorian epitaphs often feature words like 'sleep' and 'rest', but death was so immanent in the nineteenth century, this kind of language served mainly poetic rather than defensive purposes. Infectious diseases such as smallpox, typhoid, tuberculosis, scarlet fever, influenza, croup, diphtheria and cholera killed so many adults and children, the denial of death was largely ineffectual.

When I was a small child, my maternal grandfather – a man born during the reign of Queen Victoria – died. He was the only grandparent I knew; the others had died before I was born. He was a carpenter from southern Italy and despite humble origins he was a fastidious dresser with aristocratic mannerisms. A proud man. Although he had received hardly any formal education, he would often lift me on to his knee and tell me about Galileo in broken English. He was particularly fond of retelling the apocryphal story of Galileo muttering under his breath 'But it moves' after having been forced by the Inquisition to concede that the earth is stationary. My last memory of my grandfather is of him laid out in his coffin. I can remember being carried, by my father, into the largest room of our house. The mirrors had been covered with purple drapes and the air was suffused with a cloying, heavy perfume. I peered into the coffin, and there was my grandfather, smartly dressed – as usual – and looking rather well. My throat tightened and I wanted to cry. Even so, I managed to control myself and my father said, 'Say a prayer.' I was never very good at remembering prayers, so I sub-vocalised a few lines and carried on looking at my grandfather. It's difficult to recall what I was feeling, exactly, but I fully understood that he was dead: that he would not be chasing me around the kitchen table again waving a stick, and that I wouldn't be hearing any more stories about Galileo. This scenario – exposing a small child to a corpse – didn't occur in rural Italy in the dim and distant past. It happened in London in the 1960s. Clearly, such practices are specific to certain faith groups, most notably Catholics. Nevertheless, over the course of my life I have seen this domestic ritual, which affords friends and family an opportunity to grieve and accept the reality of death, all but disappear.

Over half the world's population has been absorbed by cities, and urban living – particularly in developed countries – shields us from death. We are disconnected from nature and separated from life cycles. Seasonal changes are relatively inconsequential in buildings that have electric lights and central heating. The day can be artificially extended. The air is rarely tainted with the smell of decay, and we no longer need to kill when we are hungry. The meat, poultry and fish sealed in plastic containers on sale in supermarkets represent a further sanitisation of death. We no longer have to wipe blood from our hands or rip innards from a carcass. Only selected professionals – butchers and pathologists, for example – are obliged to handle dead animals.

I have another early memory connected with my grandfather. When I was four years old, my family visited my grandfather's village. It was an unsettling place, for me at least, because, if you looked down the central thoroughfare, you could see a volcano belching smoke. This was very different, and considerably more threatening, than anything I'd seen in north London. I was taken by relatives (keen to entertain within their modest means) to see a cow being slaughtered. I can remember standing in a barn in which the atmosphere was charged with communal excitement. A lean man raised a sledgehammer and knocked the animal unconscious. Its legs buckled and it collapsed – heavily. A long ventral incision was made with a knife, and the animal's steaming guts tumbled out. A lake of dark blood expanded, and I can remember children paddling in it. The smell was strong and unpleasant. But there was laughter, conversation – a sense of occasion and festive camaraderie. After all, *this* was life. Small communities are united by necessity. If you want to eat and survive, something must die. There isn't scope for debate. Opinions converge.

Ernest Becker decried what he called the 'Babel of views', the cacophony of opinion – characteristic of modern life – that shows a marked tendency to degenerate into trivial bickering and loss of judgement. 'One of the reasons, I believe, that knowledge is in a state of useless over production is that it is strewn all over the place, spoken in a thousand competitive voices. Its insignificant fragments are magnified all out of proportion, while its major and world-historical insights lie around begging for attention. There is no throbbing, vital centre.' These words were written before 1973, but Becker could easily be describing social media: echo chambers, widening social divisions, intolerance, fads, and the neglect of much that is meaningful. It is an environment that allows a phenomenon like climate change denial to flourish – arguably the most extreme example of Becker's thesis. The denial of death on an apocalyptic scale.

Becker's thoughts on death and the human condition are uncompromising. Probably too uncompromising for most contemporary readers. He writes extensively about the indignities of embodiment, particularly 'shitting', with something close to relish. Yet, his brutal honesty serves a purpose. He is not interested in platitudes, because they diminish us. He does not offer us bland reassurances, because they can only provide temporary relief from existential anxiety. On the final pages of *The Denial of Death*, Becker comes close to stating the very essence of his philosophical position: 'I think that taking life seriously means something such as this: that whatever man does on this planet has to be done in the lived truth of the terror of creation, of the grotesque, of the rumble of panic underneath everything. Otherwise it is false.'

We must paddle in blood and feel it thickening between our toes. We must stare at the sun. Death is a fact of life.

Immortality projects can be as tangible as the walls of an ancient city. But they can also be subtle and insidious. In *Travels* with *Epicurus: Meditations from a Greek Island on the Pleasures of Old Age*, the author Daniel Klein shares an unusual epiphany. During a routine dental check-up, he was informed that due to age-related atrophy of the jaw he needed to have some teeth extracted and replaced with implants. He accepted the proposal without hesitation. Later he began to have doubts. Treatment would involve a minimum of seven visits spread over a year. He would have to travel to the surgery, experience pain, restrict his food, and spend thousands of dollars. 'In my early seventies did I really care if I presented to the world an old man's goofy smile? And even more to the point, with my years of clear thinking and reasonable mobility dwindling as quickly as my jawbone, did I honestly want to dedicate an entire year to regular visits to an oral surgeon?' Klein concluded that his automatic acceptance of treatment was symptomatic of a much larger problem. He, along with the rest of western civilisation, had been swept up in 'an epidemic of denial'.

Cosmetic surgery can erase wrinkles, Viagra can restore sexual performance, hormones can be replaced. The current global anti-ageing products market is valued at $40 billion and the revenue forecast for 2028 is $60 billion. ALTOS, a biochemical technology company (funded mostly by Jeff Bezos and established in 2022), aims to discover a technique for reversing human ageing. Another tech billionaire, Bryan Johnson, has vampirically transfused blood from his seventeen-year-old son into his own body, hoping to be revitalised. Self-help book titles aimed at older readers typically encourage the idea that prolonged health, vigour and youthful vitality are credible goals. Octogenarian rock stars are applauded when they perform in front of large stadium audiences, because they appear to confirm what everyone wants to believe. Eighty is the new sixty – sixty is the new forty – forty is the new twenty.

A combination of medical help, good nutrition, regular sleep, intellectual stimulation and exercise *can* delay physical and mental deterioration. But for many, adopting healthy habits isn't about prolonging the capacity to enjoy life. It is about denying death. In the same way that the collective immortality project of war harms humanity as a whole, so it is that personal immortality projects harm the individual.

Denial is essentially self-deceit – a lie that becomes less convincing over time. Even the most entrenched falsehoods cannot support the cumulative weight of reality. Ageing proceeds inexorably. Lung capacity decreases, teeth stain and break, sweat glands stop working, swallowing becomes difficult, bowels seize up, joints swell, arteries harden, muscles waste, and the brain shrinks. In advanced old age, brain tissue mass is about the same as that of a seven-year-old child. The longer reality is denied, the more likely it is that critically weakened defences will collapse. Instead of benefiting from an extended period of gradual adjustment, the individual will be suddenly shocked into awareness of death's imminence. The probable outcome will be combinations of depression, anxiety and panic.

Perhaps the most subtle manifestation of denial is the curiously obliging mathematics we employ when calculating how much time we have left to live. Years stretch to accommodate achievements, travel, retirement plans and grandchildren. We can only estimate when we are going to die, and the probabilistic vagueness of the prospect tends to disperse into an even vaguer sense of open-ended possibility. In the manner of Zeno's famous paradox, if we use up half the time we have left, we still have the other half remaining. And once we have used up half of that – the subsequent balance can be divided again. Our relationship with death is asymptotic. Our subjective mathematics always includes a term for infinity. The curve never meets the line: the sand keeps flowing in the hourglass, but the upper chamber never empties.

Defences are powerful and should not be underestimated. They can compromise insight regardless of one's sophistication and intelligence. The neurosurgeon Henry Marsh has written about volunteering for a research project that required him to have a brain scan: 'I had blithely assumed that the scan would show that I was one of the small number of older people whose brains show little sign of aging ... I ran many miles every week and lifted weights and did manly press-ups. But when I eventually looked at my brain scan, all this effort looked like King Canute trying to stop the rising tide of the sea.' Marsh's brain showed signs of ischaemic damage and small-vessel disease. 'As I looked at the images on my computer's monitor, one by one, just as I used to look at my patients' scans, slice by slice, working up from the brain stem to the cerebral hemispheres, I was overwhelmed by a feeling of complete helplessness and despair.' Even a man who has spent his life confronting death can be *so* defended that when those defences crumble, he is overcome by 'complete helplessness and despair'.

Psychologists have identified two types of coping: problem-focused and emotion-focused. The former is applicable to problems that can be solved. For example, someone dissatisfied with their job can seek alternative employment. Many difficulties, however, cannot be overcome by actions. Major surgery, for example, is unavoidable. In this situation, emotion-focused coping is more appropriate. If it is not possible to change a situation, all you can do is attempt to modify your emotional response to that situation. In western democracies, ageing and dying seem to have been misclassified as soluble problems. We doggedly persist in our efforts to remain youthful and postpone death. This obstinacy is probably fortified by a certain amount of narcissism and entitlement. Since the 1960s, the citizens of developed nations have been encouraged to think of themselves as unique and special, to follow their dreams and reach for the stars. Exceptionalism is almost always associated with the idea of dispensation. *Rules might apply to others, but not to me.* Apart from the over eighties, almost everyone currently in the second half of life has been raised in a climate of exceptionalism. Consequently, post-war generations have found it relatively easy to exempt themselves from ageing and death. The natural inclination that Freud identified, to be sceptical about one's own demise, has been greatly amplified.

Denial of death is profoundly problematic for many reasons, and ultimately, all immortality projects fail. Pursuing immortality is delusional, a retreat from reality, and narcissistic. The person who seeks to live for ever might never live at all – or at least, live incompletely. Denial of death robs life of its urgency. It encourages complacency, superficiality and procrastination. Immortality projects are entanglements – traps that hinder healthy development. They prevent us from making the psychological adjustments that are essential if we are to cope (as well as our circumstances allow) with ageing – and ultimately dying. Instead of letting go, as a person lets go of consciousness before sleep, the individual who has denied death and invested in immortality projects lets go with the reluctance of someone hanging from the edge of a cliff by their fingernails.

Earlier, a distinction was made between knowing something intellectually and knowing something in one's gut – at the very *core* of one's being. It is a distinction that merits further emphasis, because it will be a recurring theme in this book. Inner divisions make it possible to know, and not know – simultaneously. It is possible to grasp an idea, but not feel its truth very deeply. Indeed, to assimilate knowledge, to absorb knowledge, to make truths *our* truths – to own them and to live them – requires 'work'. In the language of cognitive psychology, assimilation of knowledge requires 'depth of processing'. It is one thing to concede that the denial of death is futile and that immortality projects will fail. But it is quite another thing to 'embody' the truth of these propositions.

The capacity to know – and not know – underlies Freud's assertion that no one truly believes in their own death. Intellectual understanding isn't necessarily complemented by heartfelt understanding. Ernest Becker doubted that complete engagement (cerebral and emotional, conscious and unconscious) with the prospect of oblivion is possible. He supposed that minds are too fragile to survive exposure to such a merciless absolute: 'I believe that those who speculate that a full apprehension of man's condition would drive him insane are right, quite literally right.' We can work on ourselves, reflect and meditate, attempt to internalise something of the reality of death, but a protective residue of denial will always remain, indeed *must* remain, because reaching out and touching the void will drive us mad. This is clearly an extreme position. Many people face death knowingly and sanely with enormous courage; however, Becker's supposition serves to remind us that achieving 'full apprehension' of negation is complicated by powerful resistances.

Michel de Montaigne, the much-loved sixteenth-century writer of expansive and digressive essays, was able to overcome his fear of death after experiencing an altered state of consciousness. Until that time, he had been obsessed with dying, which was probably the cardinal symptom of a longstanding ruminative depression. As he approached the midpoint of life, he experienced several losses – his best friend, his father, his younger brother – none of which helped him to accept his mortality. He tried following the advice of Stoic philosophers, who suggest that frequent reflection on death and dying can engender a state of calm readiness. But practising this mental discipline made Montaigne even more anxious. At the age of thirty-six, Montaigne was the victim of a serious riding accident. He fell from his horse and his servants believed that he was dead. Indeed, he was 'taken for dead for two good hours'. As Montaigne was being carried home, he began to inhale and make movements. He was roused from insensibility and immediately vomited a 'bucketful' of blood. He was self-aware, but in a state 'closer to death than to life'. Later, he recalled: 'To me it seemed as though my life was merely clinging to my lips.' The experience was 'free from unpleasantness' and Montaigne was tempted simply to surrender to the pull of oblivion. It was like 'that gentle feeling which is felt by those who let themselves glide into sleep'. He seems to have remained in an ambiguous state of being and non-being for some time. He was responsive, but his movements were mechanical, as though his 'soul' had become detached from his body.

When he finally recovered, Montaigne was a changed man. He was no longer troubled by mortality, and he began writing his extraordinary essays. The principal subject of these essays is not death, but life. Gustave Flaubert once explained to a friend how best to approach Montaigne's oeuvre: 'Don't read him as children do, for amusement, nor as the ambitious do, to be instructed. No, read him *in order to live*.'

For Montaigne, dying (or at least being as close to death as can be imagined) was transformative. The episode convinced him that philosophy – grappling with the problem of death intellectually – is a largely sterile undertaking. Something additional is required. A powerful experience had changed his *feelings* about death. He had fully apprehended the reality of death and he hadn't (as Becker might have expected) lost his mind. Quite the contrary. As a result, death was less frightening, and he could devote all his energies to understanding what it means to be alive. Summarising Montaigne's metamorphosis, biographer Sarah Bakewell writes: 'From being the gloomiest among his acquaintances, he became the most carefree of middle-aged men, and a master of the art of living well.'

Montaigne's description of his near-death experience makes no reference to God or religious sentiment. His account is entirely psychological. An altered state of consciousness cured his morbidity. Montaigne condensed the wisdom he had acquired into a sentence that resembles an aphorism: 'to inure yourself to death all you have to do is to draw nigh to it'. We could translate this aphorism into the language of psychoanalysis: 'to come to terms with death, all you have to do is abandon your defences'. Although Montaigne had been obsessed with death all his life, obsessing about it hadn't brought him – in any meaningful way – 'closer' to death. If anything, obsessing about death had locked his mind in a particular attitude that prevented him from making further progress with respect to accomplishing a 'fuller apprehension' of death. His near-death experience had been, by contrast, direct, fluid and immersive, and consequently a powerful catalyst of change.

In the same way that there is knowing and *knowing*, there is also thinking and *thinking*. Montaigne's eventual disillusionment with philosophy hints at perhaps the most perverse manifestation of unconscious defensiveness: thinking about death to avoid more meaningful engagement with death. Paradoxically, thinking about a distressing subject – at a refined altitude – can prevent the activation of emotions. What purports to be sober, reflective engagement is in fact a form of dissociation. Death becomes as impersonal as calculus. Psychoanalysts call this defence 'intellectualisation'. A related defence is 'generalisation', which involves thinking about topics as purely abstract generalities, rather than specific 'instances' that are relevant to the person.

I am reminded of the equally paradoxical clinical phenomenon of patients who talk excessively to limit the number of penetrating questions a therapist can ask. The motivation is usually unconscious and talking becomes a means of avoiding the kind of discussion that will ultimately necessitate confronting a difficult truth. Genuine scrutiny can be deferred indefinitely by means of continuous empty disclosure. Avoidant talking in therapy has many equivalent behaviours that serve the same purpose. For example, the full diary that locks a person into a busy routine and leaves no time for meaningful self-reflection.

The feature of Montaigne's near-death experience that seems to have changed him most was the experience of letting go. Ordinarily, the idea of letting go of life generates dread. As we have already established, billions of years of reproductive biology and natural selection have shaped a survival instinct that is satisfied with nothing less than immortality. Montaigne's altered state of consciousness allowed him to contemplate oblivion with sublime equanimity – 'I felt myself oozing away so gently, and in so gentle and pleasing a fashion'. Hardly anyone feels this relaxed about dying in a normal, waking state. The survival instinct makes us fight to stay alive. We are genetically programmed to dig our fingers into the cliff edge.

Our attachment to life is so strong, our Darwinian compasses set so fixedly on a course for eternity, that we rarely stop to consider whether we would want to live for ever or what living for ever might mean.

Many years ago, I saw a young man for psychotherapy who suffered from a delusional obsession that God would punish him by placing him in a box for eternity. What would it be like? Eternity in a box. Think about it for a moment. The end of history, the end of the solar system, the second law of thermodynamics gradually unravelling the fabric of the universe. The inexorable dissipation of energies until the last star becomes a spent remnant. Trillions upon trillions of years passing, and you are still in your box; trillions more, and you are *still* in your box, alone in the darkness, where you will remain, for ever and ever and ever. For a social, pleasure-seeking animal, this is probably the worst hell imaginable. A boundless nightmare. But it is a nightmare that casts the folly of our attachment to immortality into sharp relief.

Life gets duller as you get older. The lens of the eye yellows and retinal cells lose their sensitivity. A child's summer is brighter than an adult's summer. In fact, all the senses lose sensitivity with age and pleasurable experiences become less intense. Orgasms, for example. Moreover, by late middle age, most people's tastes and preferences are well established and confined by limitations. For example, there are only a finite number of pre-Raphaelite artists to discover or classic jazz albums to collect. Over time, we habituate to many of life's pleasures because a significant part of pleasure is novelty. Even the super-rich, who are free to indulge in outrageous hedonism, get depressed and find themselves agreeing with Hamlet:

> *How weary, stale, flat and unprofitable*
> *Seem to me all the uses of this world!*

In fiction, immortals are often depicted as decadent sophisticates. They have seen and done everything. Their sighs communicate infinite boredom. If you could live for ever, eventually everything would become boring. Your world, perhaps the entire universe, would feel much the same as being placed in a box. Eternal entrapment. Perhaps you would yearn for an ending. Oblivion, rest, peace.

It is possible to counter this argument with transhumanist rhetoric. A whole brain emulation could be modified so that nothing is boring. But how many modifications can a person undergo before he or she is no longer a person? An immortal consciousness abstracted from the brain and uploaded into virtual reality might be such a radical transformation that the person – or what we would recognise as the person – effectively no longer exists. The same question can be raised concerning all forms of immortality project that rely on technological translations, enhancements and augmentations. A frequent response to minor ailments or pharmacological side-effects is 'I'm not feeling myself today'. Even the slightest physical or mental perturbation can disturb our habitual sense of self.

The second half of life is challenging, and the individual must adapt to these challenges. Unlike other animals, human beings are driven to survive, but they are also aware of their own mortality. Awareness of mortality generates existential anxiety which is managed with defences, and death is denied. Some of these defences are subtle and are not recognised or understood as defences. Unfortunately, the denial of death prevents engagement with reality and interferes with beneficial psychological adjustment. Immortality projects are obstacles, and should be abandoned.

As Dylan Thomas observed, although 'wise men at their end know dark is right', we struggle with the idea. Most will find themselves burning and raving 'at close of day', raging against 'the dying of the light'. Thomas's poetic heroism is stirring. But how many of us want to die burning and raving? How many of us want to grow old shaking our fist at an invincible adversary who is making giant strides towards us? Or even worse, how many of us want to be startled by the grim reaper's grin because, one way or another, we have been fooling ourselves that we are immortal?

2

Acceptance: Embracing Reality

There is more, perhaps, to acceptance than just accepting

It was obvious that their relationship was about to end. The middle-aged comedian's wife had fallen passionately in love with one of her colleagues and her position was clear. As far as she was concerned, there was nothing more to say and she was eager to move in with her new lover. The comedian was devastated. In fact, he was so depressed that his friends thought he was contemplating suicide. Even though couples therapy hadn't been successful, the comedian wanted to continue seeing me on his own. He still had things to say, even if his wife didn't. His misery was made more pitiful by his profession. He must have made countless jokes about relationships and marriage. Yet, his cynical, edgy act was at odds with his true nature. Beneath his stage persona he was conservative and sentimental. He believed that love must conquer all – that love will overcome any obstacle and, in the end, if love is *true*, it will *always* be reciprocated.

Unfortunately, dogged repetition of his romantic convictions didn't bring him any closer to a happy ending. 'I want us to be together so much. I want to spend Christmas with her – every Christmas – I want lights on the tree and presents and kids and puppies and—' He suddenly stopped. A crooked smile appeared. 'I sound like a fucking country and western song.' He sighed and added with heavy emphasis, 'But it wasn't to be.' There was a subtle change in atmosphere. His shoulders relaxed and his features softened. 'No. It wasn't to be.' After all the torment and grief, the heartache and anger, he had finally realised that there was nothing he could do to get his wife back. She loved someone else. He seemed to draw himself together, and as his spine straightened and his chin lifted, his expression suggested dignified forbearance. Usually, acceptance is a gradual process, but it is not uncommon during therapy to witness moments like this: sudden insight, ennobling transformations.

A few years later I learned that the comedian had remarried and that he was the proud father of a baby girl. I imagined him hugging his wife and child beneath an elaborately decorated Christmas tree, next to a pyramid of presents, surrounded by puppies. Naturally, I added a country and western soundtrack and a host of slide guitars.

Accepting what *isn't to be* or *can't be* is essential for mental health. If we are willing to accept frustration and failure more readily, we can redirect our energies in more profitable directions. We can abandon our otherwise exhausting attempts to forestall the inevitable. Almost every spiritual and intellectual tradition that aspires to alleviate suffering recommends the cultivation of acceptance. This shouldn't be surprising because acceptance is underwritten by indestructible logic. Why seethe and rage over circumstances that one can do nothing about? Why compound an already unhappy situation with futile protests and boiling emotions?

We live in a culture that applauds instrumentality, self-determination and the pursuit of advantage. Acceptance is no longer regarded as desirable. Children are routinely told that they are special and can achieve anything regardless of their abilities or circumstances. Adults are preoccupied with empowerment and our cinematic heroes are superhuman. Acceptance has acquired overtones of defeatism. This is highly relevant for those who have passed the midpoint of life, because ageing is nothing if not the cumulative imposition of limitations on the person until a final temporal limitation is imposed. It makes sense to cultivate acceptance, because as we get older, there is a great deal that we are obliged to tolerate and endure.

Acceptance is strongly associated with Epicurean and Stoic schools of philosophy, both of which, although dating back to the fourth century BC, appeal to contemporary readers because they are comparatively modern in outlook. They are rational and their objectives are explicitly 'psychotherapeutic'. Epicurus asserted that one shouldn't postpone the study of philosophy 'because the search for mental health' – literally, hygiene of the soul – 'is never untimely or out of season'. There is a passage in Epictetus that can be read as a succinct guide to good clinical practice. The Greek Stoic says that whenever you encounter someone who is tearful, have ready the reflection that they are not upset by what has happened, but by their view of what has happened. Obviously, you can't change the past – the past is fixed, by definition – but you can change your perspective. Unlike immutable historical events, appraisals can be modified. You can review where you stand in relation to misfortune. When supporting someone who is distressed, Epictetus suggests that one should never be dismissive, but instead offer sympathy and words of comfort – while simultaneously maintaining a degree of emotional detachment. Be empathetic, he suggests, but not so empathetic that you find yourself lost in someone else's suffering.

The American clinical psychologist Albert Ellis was inspired by Epictetus's repeated insistence that 'It is not events that disturb people, it is their judgements concerning them.' This insight became the underlying principle of Ellis's Rational Emotive Therapy, the first of several 'cognitive' therapies that have since become the dominant therapeutic modality. Cognitive therapies work by identifying and correcting biased thinking. A person who is socially anxious might habitually misinterpret facial expressions. A frown (produced by someone who is concentrating) could be interpreted as a sign of impatience or hostility and then the socially anxious person will feel uneasy or even threatened. The object of therapy is to correct 'automatic' thinking – sometimes called 'thoughtless thought' – and to replace it with accurate thinking. In accord with Epictetus's dictum, it is not the social encounter that is disturbing, but the anxious person's judgements concerning the social encounter.

In the previous chapter it was suggested that awareness of death generates existential anxiety, which is usually modulated by psychological defences. The outcome of excessive defensiveness is detachment from reality. Epicurus and the Stoic philosophers offer ways of thinking about death that can potentially reduce anxiety and make the deployment of defences less necessary. In addition, a truly accepting person, one who is fully prepared to embrace the realities of ageing and dying, will be much less likely to dissipate time and energy on hopeless attempts to remain 'forever young'.

Epicurus and the founder of Stoicism, Zeno, were contemporaries and in the ancient world they were perceived as rivals; however, from our twenty-first-century coign of vantage, the two schools of philosophy they established appear more complementary than contradictory.

The life story of Epicurus is included in *Lives of the Eminent Philosophers* by Diogenes Laertius. He was born on the island of Samos, lived in various places when young, and eventually settled just outside Athens where he established and led a community of philosophers known as 'The Garden' for forty years. The community survived for another forty years and thereafter Epicurus became something of a cult figure. His most famous devotee was the first-century BC Roman poet Lucretius. The aim of Epicureanism is *ataraxia*, a state of tranquillity achieved by conquering anxiety and controlling one's desires and appetites.

Epicurus declared, 'nothing is sufficient for the person who finds sufficiency too little' – an aphoristic observation that locates the cause of dissatisfaction firmly in the person. It is also germane to our subject. After the material goals of the first half of life have been accomplished, to what extent does the accumulation of more things really make us happy? If we are prepared to *accept* less, to live more, then perhaps life would be more enjoyable. We should not become enslaved by ownership. This prescription is equally applicable to the more abstract possession of time. Our marked tendency to invest in immortality projects suggests that human beings are unable to accept the sufficiency of the average lifespan. Refusal to accept that we cannot *have* unlimited time is a cause of unhappiness.

Epicurus's thoughts on death arose directly from his materialism. Human beings are constructed from atoms and when a person dies these atoms disperse and consciousness is extinguished. He argued that if we cannot sense anything when we die then 'death is nothing to us'. Epicurus's followers found his materialism consoling, not only because of its authoritative logic, but also because it disposed of supernatural terrors (such as post-mortem descent into the underworld). Non-existence was a reassuringly uneventful alternative.

Human beings have immense difficulty grasping non-existence. When we try to think about death, we inappropriately think of *being* dead, when in fact death is the end of being. The nullity of death is total: 'so long as we are existent death is not present and whenever it is present we are non-existent'. Existence and death separate naturally, like oil and water, and a thorough appreciation of this mutual exclusivity will reduce our anxiety. Death is 'of no concern either to the living or to those who have completed their lives. For the former it is non-existent, and the latter are themselves non-existent.'

Because our brains have evolved to represent 'things' rather than 'non-things', a full appreciation of Epicurus's notion of nullity might be beyond the intellectual capacity of many otherwise highly intelligent people. We tend to think of life as a line (indeed, we often envisage life proceeding along a 'lifeline') which comes to an end, and beyond the 'end of the line' we imagine total blackness or a void. In other words, we put something there. We do the same when we try to mentally recreate the big bang. Inaccurately, we think of a dot of light appearing in a pre-existing void and its subsequent expansion simulates the birth of the universe (in fact, it took about three hundred thousand years for light to appear). Physics has nothing to say about what happened 'before' the big bang, because there was *absolutely* nothing. Which is why we find the question 'Why is there something rather than nothing?' so profoundly taxing. If something (the universe) had come from something else (an empty expanse) that wouldn't be quite so remarkable. The 'nothing' that preceded the birth of the universe is so voracious that it even swallows the idea of precedence. Time did not exist. All relative concepts, such as emptiness, darkness and cold, become entirely meaningless. There were no complementary polarities – fullness, light and heat. When Epicurus says that death is nothing, the nothingness he is referring to is comparable to the almost inconceivable nothingness that 'preceded' the big bang. We think of life as a line sandwiched between two voids. But for Epicurus – subjectively – there is only the line, and it isn't sandwiched between anything. The nothing he is asking us to imagine is *total* nullity. A 'nothing' that can't be filled with *any* of our concepts of nothingness, because there is nowhere to put them. If we could *truly* grasp non-being, at this level, then the idea of dying wouldn't be quite so distressing. Death would, as Epicurus suggests, be nothing to us.

There are several reports of Epicurus's death, and all of them suggest that even though he was in great pain, he died like an ideal Epicurean. His equanimity is evident in a letter he wrote to his friend Idomeneus: 'On this happy day, which is also the last day of my life, I write the following words to you. The symptoms of my strangury and dysentery are continuing and have not lost their extreme seriousness. But offsetting all this is the joy in my heart at the recollection of the conversations we have had.' His life had been a good life. He had enjoyed many pleasurable conversations with his dear friend Idomeneus. And yes, he was suffering, but he accepted the indignities of the human condition, and he was ready to let go. Diogenes tells us that Epicurus got into a hot tub, asked for some wine, 'exhorted his friends to remember his teachings and passed away'.

The Stoic philosopher Seneca also died in a bath, albeit in more trying circumstances. He was born the same year as Jesus Christ, in Córdoba, Spain, and his family were wealthy and distinguished. He became a public official and, later, a courtier; however, the Roman court was a treacherous workplace. The emperor, Caligula, ordered Seneca's execution – we still don't know why, exactly – but he was saved by an illness that was incorrectly reckoned to be fatal. Caligula's successor, Claudius, banished Seneca because he had allegedly conducted an adulterous affair with Julia Livilla, the sister of Caligula and Agrippina. Eight years later, Agrippina married her uncle Claudius and summoned Seneca back to Rome where he was appointed as tutor to her son, Nero. At the age of sixteen, Nero became emperor after Agrippina arranged for Claudius to be poisoned. Seneca realised that sustained contact with Nero, a homicidal lunatic, was likely to end badly. Nero is still remembered for outstanding acts of sadism – burning Christians to light up his garden at night, for example. In due course, Seneca tried to extricate himself from courtly obligations. He informed Nero that he was old and unwell; he had outlived his usefulness and, to improve the tyrant's mood, he gifted him his estate. After a failed plot against the emperor, Seneca was suspected of protecting conspirators and Nero demanded that he, Seneca, take his own life. Seneca accepted his fate so calmly, with such sublime dignity, that those around him were reduced to tears. Using a blade, he cut his body in several places, but his blood didn't flow. He then tried expediting his demise with poison. This didn't work either. In the end, Tacitus informs us, 'he was carried into a vapour-bath, where he suffocated'.

Seneca has been accused of being a hypocrite. While espousing Stoic values he lived a life of luxury and was seemingly attracted to power. It is possible, of course, that he always intended to use his position and influence to do good. If so, he failed to appreciate the fatal impossibility of his task until it was too late.

Many Stoic philosophers exhibit an acute awareness of the passage of time, but this characteristic is particularly evident in Seneca's writings. His work speaks directly to those who have passed the midpoint of life and who are therefore more conscious of the fact that their time is running out. Perhaps Seneca's sensitivity to time was heightened by his hazardous circumstances. A Roman courtier could never be entirely confident in the morning that he would still be alive at the end of the day. Although, in a sense, this is probably true for all of us.

Seneca asserted that time is our most precious possession, yet we tend to value money much more than time. We rarely waste money, but we frequently waste time. Seneca's thoughts on temporal profligacy have acquired new relevance in the twenty-first century, because today we have countless opportunities to squander time. The modern world is full of shallow distractions, the equivalent of what Seneca called 'preoccupations'. He observed that 'living is the least important activity of the preoccupied man'. We haemorrhage time on social media, become entranced by entertainments that are so insubstantial we can barely remember them the next day, and find sustained attention (the prerequisite of vital engagement) increasingly difficult. Seneca's corrective to imprudent use of time is the practice of a strict mental discipline: we should reflect on our own mortality every day and treat each day as if it is our last. These prescriptions are intended to keep our attention focused on meaningful priorities and to prevent our precious time being expended on trivial 'preoccupations'.

Although Seneca pre-dates Freud and Becker by nearly two thousand years, one could argue that his advice is helpful because it weakens the kind of defences that deny death and facilitate immortality projects. We are strongly advised to combat complacency, and Seneca suggests that we do this by thinking about death not as something distant and abstract, but close and real. We should not think of death as a single event located in the future. 'This is our big mistake,' Seneca wrote, 'to think we look forward toward death. Most of death is already gone. Whatever time has passed is owned by death.' We die a little every day and once we pass the midpoint of life we are mathematically more dead than alive. This is an impressive example of intellectual legerdemain, a cognitive 'trick' that recasts death as a solicitous companion who leads us gently to non-being. It is a way of turning 'nothing' into something we can think about. Death is not the sudden descent of a curtain, the arrival of a hooded figure with a scythe, but a form of continuous subtraction. A similar sentiment was expressed by the Czech novelist Milan Kundera, except in relation to memory: 'the act of forgetting is a form of death always present in life'. We remember only a tiny fraction of existence. We have forgotten most of what it is like to be alive, long before we die. Oblivion starts seeping into our heads as soon as we are self-aware.

Like Epicurus, Seneca supposes that reflecting on the absolute nullity of death will reduce anxiety; however, he attempts to reduce our anxiety further still by reframing nullity as something familiar, something, in fact, that we have already come to terms with. Seneca declares: 'It will be the same after me as it was before me.' He amplifies his point: 'Wouldn't you think a man an utter fool if he burst into tears because he didn't live a thousand years ago? A man is as much a fool for shedding tears because he isn't going to be alive a thousand years from now. There's no difference between the one and the other – you didn't exist and you won't exist – you've no concern with either period.'

For many Stoics, ageing is a more pressing problem than death because although it is possible to be old, it is not possible to *be* dead. Seneca wrote that old age can be understood as 'a kind of incurable sickness'. There are no treatments – magical or mundane. Even so, old age *can* be 'full of pleasure', providing one is realistic and one has the right attitude.

There is a popular quotation, often attributed to the writer Kingsley Amis (but probably derived from a classical source), which asserts that being young and sexually active is like being chained to a maniac and that losing one's libido in old age can be a liberating experience. Seneca agrees: 'How nice it is to have out-worn one's desires and left them behind!' There are some things, such as sexual obsession, ambition or vanity, that – as we age – become redundant, irrelevant or simply absurd, and their disappearance is experienced not as a loss, but as a relief. Moreover, Seneca suggests that old age can be viewed not so much as an ending, but as a culmination: 'It is the final glass which pleases the inveterate drinker, the one that sets the crowning touch on his intoxication and sends him off into oblivion.'

Although Seneca likened old age to an illness, he reminds us that it is only living things that sicken. 'You will die,' he declares, 'not because you are sick but because you are alive.' We can only die because we have experienced the extraordinary and massively improbable privilege of being alive.

The greatest Stoic to follow in Seneca's immediate philosophical wake was Epictetus. In fact, their lives overlapped by roughly ten years. Epictetus was born a slave and for almost half his life he lived as a slave. His master was Nero's secretary, Epaphroditus, who according to some sources was an exceptionally cruel man. We know that Epictetus was 'lame' and it is possible that this was because of an injury inflicted by Epaphroditus. An early Christian author tells us that Epaphroditus twisted Epictetus's leg. Epictetus endured the pain with impressive calm and pointed out that if Epaphroditus didn't stop, the leg would break. Epaphroditus didn't stop and, somewhat predictably, the leg broke. 'Didn't I warn you?' said Epictetus. His response shows that he was Stoical long before the world recognised him as a Stoic.

Epaphroditus released Epictetus from servitude, a practice relatively common among city dwellers, when Epictetus was probably in his thirties. Thereafter, Epictetus dedicated himself to the study and teaching of philosophy. In AD 93 the emperor Domitian banished philosophers from Rome, because of their alleged Republican sympathies. Epictetus travelled to the Roman colony of Nicopolis on the Greek mainland where he settled and continued to study and teach.

Apart from a few fragments there are no texts that can be directly attributed to Epictetus. But what we *do* have is a record of his lessons and reflections collected by his students, most notably Arrian (also a historian, public servant and military commander).

Epictetus, like Epicurus, understood that philosophy can be therapeutic. He urged his disciples to think like psychologists – 'the mind and its functions require the bulk of our attention' – and he found medical analogies useful: 'The philosopher's lecture-hall is a hospital. You shouldn't walk out of it feeling pleasure, but pain, for you aren't well when you enter it.' The latter observation bears interesting comparison with what is known about the process of psychotherapy. Psychotherapy isn't painless. The recovery of unpleasant memories and the stirring up of at least some distressing emotions can, ultimately, be helpful.

Having been born a slave, Epictetus was acutely aware that life is, to a greater or lesser extent, circumscribed. Everyone is subject to some form of limitation (not just slaves) and all freedoms are subject to qualifications. What happens to us is largely out of our control. Even our bodies are out of our control. You can't decide to stop urinating or ageing because they are inconvenient. Epictetus declared that the principal task in life is to identify what can and can't be controlled. Chief among those things that we can control are certain aspects of mental functioning. We can choose – within reason – how we see the world and how we respond to events that affect us. Epictetus uses lameness (his students would have been aware that he limped) to underscore his point. Lameness, he says, 'is the body's problem, not the mind's' – 'an impediment to the leg, but not to the will'. You might not be able to alter your infirmity, but you can certainly alter how you respond to your infirmity.

Epictetus agreed with Seneca about death. It is something we should think about every day. If we are in a state of readiness, then hopefully we will die without having to cope with the additional complication of distress. 'I must die. But must I die bawling?' In Book One of the *Discourses*, he seems to have prepared himself so well that he has become almost indifferent to death. 'I have to die. If it is now, well then I die now; if later, then now I will take my lunch, since the hour for lunch has arrived – and dying I will tend to later.' Why let death spoil a good meal? It sounds like hubris, but Epictetus, the pedagogue, is surely using a concrete example to dramatise a general proposition. We are all waiting to die, and while we are waiting, various forms of 'lunch hour' arrive, and we should not let the inevitability of death spoil our experience, whatever it might be – eating, talking, reading, or just looking at clouds drifting overhead.

Of course, facing death is made considerably more difficult by our attachments. We fear death not only because when we die we will cease to exist, but also because the prospect of dying reminds us that our enjoyment of people, places and things must come to an end. The eastern answer is non-attachment. If we are non-attached, then we can let go more easily. Although non-attachment might be a realistic goal for a Buddhist monk, it is considerably more challenging for the average westerner. We are social animals who need to love and be loved. Our emotional attachments are an important part of who and what we are. Epictetus offers an alternative. He suggests that rather than trying to be non-attached, we should try to reduce our sense of ownership. This will help us to accept not only our own demise, but the demise of others. 'Under no circumstances ever say "I have lost something", only "I returned it". Did a child of yours die? No, it was returned. Your wife died? No, *she* was returned.' We should resist treating lives – our own life and the lives of others – like possessions. For Epictetus, a former slave, the connections between ownership and suffering, however indirect, were self-evident.

'But I don't think of my partner as a possession. Or my child.'

Your initial response to Epictetus's exhortation might be sceptical. 'I don't think of my closest relationships in the same way as I think about owned objects – like cars, necklaces or smart phones.' Indeed, it would be ridiculous to suggest that losing a child is in any way comparable to losing a handbag or a golf club; however, whenever we form strong emotional bonds, the notion of ownership is present as an 'undertone' and it *does* influence our behaviour. Infidelity is not tolerated in marriages. Even the polyamorous struggle to master feelings of jealousy in the context of otherwise loving relationships. Proprietary entitlements are implicit in romantic declarations: 'Please be mine – be mine for ever'. We don't want our partners to be intimate with others, and by the same token, we don't want them cosying up to the void either. Tension frequently arises in families when children enter adolescence and start to assert their independence; mothers and fathers find it difficult to relinquish ownership – 'We're losing our baby'. When children become high-achieving adults, many parents experience vicarious pleasure because they have appropriated a measure of credit.

Epictetus sets a high benchmark – the complete renunciation of ownership. This is unrealistic for most of us. We have been shaped by evolutionary pressures to be jealous and possessive. That is what we are. Nevertheless, Epictetus's supposition that ownership contributes a quantum of grief to the totality of mourning merits reflection. We can attempt to moderate our feelings of ownership, and modest mitigations might, at some point in the future, be helpful. We could, perhaps, edge a little closer to Epictetus's ideal and make efforts to accept the idea that lives (including our own) are much more like loans than rightful possessions. After all, it is more natural in a constantly changing universe to expect things to be given and taken away, than to be gifted in perpetuity.

Epictetus was the poorest of all the Stoic philosophers. The richest was Marcus Aurelius, who became Roman emperor in AD 161. He is perhaps the only convincing example of a Platonic philosopher king. His reign was troubled by border wars and in 169 he travelled to a military outpost, close to modern Vienna, where he wrote his famous *Meditations*. John Sellars, a reader in philosophy at the University of London, has described the *Meditations* as 'a late middle-aged man doing his best to cope with the demands of life'. This 'coping' involved a great deal of self-examination, and Marcus Aurelius understood his own mind as a vaguely Freudian combination of 'higher' rational parts and morally weaker 'lower' parts. He even behaves – on the page – like a psychoanalyst, addressing himself as 'you' and offering himself observations and interpretations. Like many middle-aged people, he has clearly reached a turning point and he has chosen to look inwards for answers. His language suggests inner travel, because he describes the attainment of his desired contemplative state as if it is a destination – specifically, a 'fortress', where his soul can heal, and where he can acquire wisdom.

Paradoxically, retreating behind the walls of an inner sanctum enlarged Marcus Aurelius's purview. He became increasingly aware of the scale of the universe – 'the whole earth is a mere point in space' – and the vastness of 'immeasurable time'. He developed a consciousness-raising exercise, which quite literally involves raising consciousness (albeit in imagination) to a great height to achieve a humbling, cosmic perspective: 'Take a view from above – look at the thousands of flocks and herds, the thousands of human ceremonies, every sort of voyage in storm or calm, the range of creation, combination, and extinction. Consider too the lives once lived by others long before you, the lives that will be lived after you . . .' His purpose is to combat egocentricity, and he asks himself: 'how many have never even heard your name, how many will very soon forget it[?]'.

By the second century AD, acceptance had been discussed by many Stoic philosophers, but Marcus Aurelius still manages to enrich our understanding of the concept by placing it in the broader context of causes and effects. 'Whatever happens to you was being prepared for you from everlasting, and the mesh of causes was ever spinning from eternity...' Ultimately, whatever happens to you and whatever you decide to do, you always find yourself in a present moment that is the outcome of a 'thread of destiny' that can be traced back to 'ancient causes'. You can only ever be where you are – so you might as well accept it. We are being offered a justification for Stoicism grounded in the solid reality of Newtonian physics.

Marcus Aurelius argues that this formulation confers universal significance on every individual. We are links in a causal chain, part of an unimaginably complex interconnected network of causes and effects, and the universe would be incomplete without us. 'You should meditate often on the connection of all things in the universe and their relationship to each other. In a way all things are interwoven and therefore have a family feeling for each other: one thing follows another in due order through the tension of movement, the common spirit inspiring them, and the unity of all being.' This, then, is who we really are. Not inflated, fatuous egos, but essential parts of a cosmic totality. Every individual contributes to the coherence of the whole, and Marcus Aurelius asserts that the whole 'is maimed if you sever even the tiniest fraction of its connection and continuity'. Animals constitute a tiny fraction of all the matter that exists, but if animals are uniquely conscious and intelligent, then a global extinction event would undoubtedly 'maim' the universe. This vision of connectivity is also pro-social. Employing an illustrative example from the natural world, Marcus Aurelius observes: 'What does not benefit the hive, does not benefit the bee either.' In the end, in an interconnected system, all forms of harm are ultimately self-harm.

By stressing individual indispensability, Marcus Aurelius also hints at an intriguing possibility. We are always looking for meaning in the universe, but perhaps it is us who supply the universe with meaning. Perhaps we – and all other conscious life forms – are the means by which the universe comes to know itself.

If causes and effects always deliver us into the present, and we can only live in the present moment, then when we die – Marcus Aurelius argues – the present moment (more than anything else) is what we lose. 'The present moment is equal for all; so what is passing is equal also; the loss therefore turns out to be the merest fragment of time. No one can lose either the past or the future – how could anyone be deprived of what he does not possess?' Moreover: 'both the longest-lived and the earliest to die suffer the same loss. It is only the present moment of which either stands to be deprived.' Regardless of whether you live for thirty years or three hundred years, all that can ever be lost is the present moment. Quality of experience should be valued more than longevity because the present moment is all we have, and what we lose when we die is, in fact, only the 'merest fragment of time'.

This assertion requires qualification. Although it is true that we can live only in the present moment, we know that when we die, we will lose a great deal more than a 'fragment of time'. We fear death because it extinguishes the autobiographical self – our stories and our memories. Even so, Marcus Aurelius still makes it easier for us to contemplate death by showing us that our purchase on existence was always quite weak. We are tethered to reality by a filament. For some, envisaging death as the easy, effortless snapping of a thread will be comforting. It is an image that suggests instant release. The surrender of a final moment of time and our connection with the world, painlessly broken.

The Stoic philosophers did not write exclusively about death and time. They had much to say concerning a broad range of topics, for example, nature, friendship, adversity, duty and responsibility. However, for those who have passed a notional midpoint of life, Stoic reflections on death and time are particularly relevant. In clinical settings, it is usually older patients who raise the subject of mortality, and when *my* older patients expressed their fears, I would sometimes respond by paraphrasing the Stoics, hoping, of course, that a little ancient wisdom would provoke shifts of perspective and new ways of thinking. Sometimes this worked – sometimes it worked a little – and sometimes it didn't work at all.

Why is it that some people can make use of Stoic counsel, and others can't? It will be recalled that Michel de Montaigne didn't find reading the Stoics very helpful (see chapter 1). He needed a transformative experience to overcome his fear of death. Stoicism – and the 'cognitive' therapies it inspired – are vulnerable to the same criticism. The Stoics assume that thoughts and feelings are closely related and that changing our thoughts will change our feelings. There *is* a relationship between thoughts and feelings, certainly, but it is a relatively loose one. Correcting inaccurate thinking can help patients to manage depression, for example, but that doesn't mean that inaccurate thinking *causes* depression. Indeed, many critics believe that negative thinking is simply a symptom of a more fundamental mood disturbance and that if we could treat the underlying mood disturbance more effectively (with drugs or transformative experiences) we wouldn't have to concern ourselves with 'cognitive restructuring'. Thinking would spontaneously self-correct. It is possible that the relationship between acceptance and Stoic reasoning is equally loose. We can rehearse mental manoeuvres that make us feel more accepting, and this will be partially effective, but to be truly accepting may require something to change within the person at a much deeper level.

Epicurus observed that 'living well and dying well are one and the same discipline'. How we live, and by implication how we develop and grow, will affect how capable we are of profiting from philosophical insight, and ultimately, perhaps, whether we die in a state of calm preparedness or terror. It is possible that philosophical insight is a necessary but *not sufficient* condition for the attainment of *ataraxia*. An ingredient is missing.

What might this be?

What do we have to do to internalise wisdom – to embrace reality and become truly accepting? Many great thinkers since Epicurus and the Stoics have attempted to answer these questions and we will be exploring their work in subsequent chapters.

Epicurean and Stoic philosophers are generally good role models. They die well. They accept that they must die, step calmly into baths, and deliver dignified farewell speeches. The third-century BC Stoic Chrysippus did not die in a dignified manner, but his irregular end is perhaps the most powerful vindication of Stoicism to be found in a competitive field. There are conflicting accounts of the death of Chrysippus, but scholars tend to favour the 'donkey and figs' version, probably because it is the most uplifting. Amused by the sight of a donkey eating figs, Chrysippus began to laugh. He found the sight so funny that he couldn't stop. He urged the owner of the donkey to give the animal some wine to aid its digestion and continued laughing, harder and harder, until finally, overcome by the blissful hilarity of everyday life, he died.

Who wouldn't want to die laughing?

3

Turning Points: Revelations, Awakenings and Callings

Be receptive to subtle feelings

The Hero with a Thousand Faces was written by Joseph Campbell and published in 1949. It is a compendium of myths and legends from 'every corner of the world'. Campbell identified several recurring elements – for example, certain character types and incidents – and he concluded that all myths are versions of a fundamental monomyth about a hero's journey that can also be understood as a symbolic account of psychological development. The hero is in fact *everyone* and the hero's story, in whatever form it comes to us, is a life lesson. Myths are not only narrative entertainment, they are also distilled folk wisdom and repositories of collective learning.

According to Campbell, the starting point of the hero's journey is 'the call to adventure'. Perhaps the most mundane example of 'the call' is a mistake, or blunder; a blunder that reveals an unsuspected 'world' or draws the hero into a closer relationship with things that have previously been neglected or poorly understood. Campbell thought that this feature, common to many of the stories he studied, could be interpreted psychoanalytically. According to Freud, there are very few innocent blunders. Mistakes are usually the result of repressed desires and conflicts. They are not accidents, but motivated outcomes that arise under conditions where the motive is not available (at least initially) to consciousness. For example, we forget to send emails containing bad news and we lose relevant paperwork when we don't want to attend a difficult work meeting. The mistake or oversight allows us to avoid emotional discomfort in the present moment (if not in the future).

Mistakes frequently precede reflection and growth. We often get locked into comfortable routines and complacency can impede progress. Something must happen to 'shake us up', to make us more alert to possibilities. If we are not courageous enough to make certain decisions, a blunder might *necessitate* change. The unconscious 'creates' a crisis that encourages transformation. Much of psychotherapy is concerned with helping people to reconstruct their lives after a seemingly chance event has disrupted entrenched but unsatisfactory patterns of behaviour.

The 'blunders necessitating change' that I encountered most often in clinical practice took the form of mistakes made at work. I saw many patients – men and women in senior roles – who had, quite inexplicably, made a catastrophic error or a series of minor errors that proved to be cumulatively catastrophic. Once, I saw a middle-aged man, Ben, an employee of a high-street bank, whose mistakes at work had resulted in a 'crisis of confidence' so severe he had to be hospitalised. Employing the traditional 'catch-all' term, the occupational health consultant had said that Ben was having a 'nervous breakdown'. Prior to Ben's sudden loss of competence his performance at work had been very good. Which was why, six years earlier, he had been promoted to a senior position with weighty responsibilities. Ben told me that he was eager to get back to work, but the more he talked about his job, the more obvious it was that he hated it. Ben was from an immigrant family and his mother and father had suffered considerable hardship in the past. He had grown up in a home environment where work was discussed as a life-and-death matter. A man who couldn't find work would starve, and so would his family. It was unthinkable, for someone from Ben's background, to entertain the idea of resigning from a secure, well-paid job. Ben *couldn't* resign – so his unconscious resigned for him. His mistakes and his breakdown were 'provocations'. They created conditions that allowed Ben to think the unthinkable.

Even minor mistakes can be informative. The poet Philip Larkin's extraordinary poem 'As Bad as a Mile' explores the revelatory potential of throwing an apple core at a bin and missing. This small disappointment is retroactive. Where did this failure begin? The poet's sense of failure is displaced backwards in time, to when his hand was 'unraised' and 'The apple unbitten in the palm'. The fact that Larkin threw an apple core is significant. It implies that all failures are connected to earlier failures, and ultimately to the primordial failure that led to the expulsion of humanity from the garden of Eden. Minor mistakes can have epic subtexts.

Life is full of minor hitches and mishaps. Forgotten cakes burn in ovens, and keys, when dropped, land in cold vomit. Trivial snags and glitches can produce a disproportionate sense of frustration, anger, or even despair. One of my patients, a man in his sixties who had had an ostensibly charmed life of fame and good fortune, was referred to me after a suicide attempt. The trigger, so he said, was that his pen had fallen behind his work desk and he couldn't retrieve it. This trifling inconvenience had activated a chain of hitherto repressed memories. If he had been more willing, prior to his suicide attempt, to consider what his mounting sense of frustration in response to minor mishaps might signify, then perhaps he wouldn't have been quite so overwhelmed when he watched his pen disappear in the gap between his desktop and the wall.

When you miss the bin or watch the pen disappear or smell the cake burning – and sigh – listen carefully. Is your sigh weighted with memories? What would happen if your consciousness sank with your sigh? If you allowed it to drag you down into your depths – where would it take you? What would you find?

Another 'call to adventure' that Campbell identified is the appearance of a herald. These harbingers take many forms, but animals are especially common in myths and fairy tales: frogs, birds, or elusive forest creatures such as a hart. Campbell linked the appearance of heralds with 'the awakening of the self'. If understood as symbols, these creatures represent the unconscious mind impressing upon the conscious mind the need for action.

In real life, a herald can be anything that leads to the awakening of the self. Campbell suggests that heralds have about them an 'atmosphere of irresistible fascination'. If you are receptive, you will sense that something significant is happening. What must be faced 'is somehow profoundly familiar to the unconscious – though unknown, surprising, and even frightening to the conscious personality'. It could be a curiously deep conversation with a stranger, a figure in a painting that makes the eyes prickle with incipient tears, or the discovery of an old letter that makes you feel restless. Contact with a herald has consequences. Life feels different. What was formerly satisfying might start to feel unsatisfying, and after the encounter, Campbell says, 'even though the hero returns for a while to his familiar occupations, they may be found unfruitful'. The deep conversation echoes in memory, the figure in the painting haunts imagination, the old letter continues to whisper and agitate from beneath a pile of documents in a drawer. Typically – in myths – the hero responds, crosses a threshold and the adventure begins.

Campbell's monomyth has the following structure: the hero is called, descends into a literal or metaphorical underworld, faces challenges or trials, and returns, transformed, often after receiving a gift (which can be interpreted as representing wisdom). According to Campbell, myths are *essential* learning, an incalculably precious resource. They have survived for thousands of years and continue to fascinate us because they encode important truths about the human condition. Campbell asserted that mythology is psychology. In fact, mythology is a form of universal psychology.

The hero's journey, as described by Campbell, is very closely related to Carl Gustav Jung's theory of individual development. Jung was interested in how people change throughout the entirety of their lives, but his writings about personal evolution in the second half of life contain some of his most interesting speculations. He was also one of the first psychologists to consider how personality develops beyond middle age. Similarities between Campbell and Jung are to be expected, because Campbell was greatly influenced by Jung's analytical psychology, and Jung was an avid student of Campbell's specialism – comparative mythology. Jung proposed that from around the fourth decade, personal growth is optimised by a process that involves undertaking an inner journey, descent into the psychological underworld – that is, the unconscious – and return in possession of the gift of wisdom. We will consider how Jung thought this journey could be accomplished in chapter 5.

'Often in actual life,' Campbell wrote, 'and not infrequently in the myths and popular tales, we encounter the dull case of the call unanswered; for it is always possible to turn the ear to other interests.' The call may come, but not everyone responds. Myths that include a neglected call, or perhaps a preliminary rejection before the call is heeded, are cautionary. They imply that a failure to develop, to move on, will have negative consequences. These cautionary examples translate into common-sense advice for those who have passed the midpoint of life. As you get older, your body changes, your needs change, and your context changes. You can't cling to outmoded ways of being. Adjustments *must* be made, or you will find yourself living a life that doesn't match the reality of your physical condition and circumstances. Those who seek to remain 'forever young', for example, will feel more and more strain as they attempt to defy the inevitable effects of time on their muscles, internal organs and bones.

There are of course many other potential mismatches. For example, identification with being handsome or beautiful while the face in the mirror sags and wrinkles.

Campbell interpreted *refusing the call* in much the same way as he interpreted blunders – that is, psychoanalytically. Freud believed that human beings progress through several stages of development, from infancy to adulthood, and that certain psychological problems arise when people get stuck or fixated at one stage, when they should be moving to the next. Usually, when Freud wrote about fixation, he was referring to specific instances likely to result in infantile or childish needs resurfacing in adulthood; however, it isn't necessary to think of fixation in such narrow terms. Attitudes can become fixed, patterns of behaviour can become fixed, and by middle age we are usually wary of experimenting beyond our comfort zones. We appear to be living in the present, but really, we are living in the past. A call to adventure is easily refused, because it is experienced as an inconvenience, an unnecessary complication.

Complacency is frequently observed in the clinic. Even when

middle-aged patients are living in circumstances that could be described as humdrum, they will resist change. When their stronghold of self-justification is tested with Socratic questioning, they will still respond with threadbare folk wisdom and platitudes: 'Better the devil you know', 'Let sleeping dogs lie', 'Don't rock the boat'. Without growth, there is stasis, or, even worse, retreat, withdrawal, shrinkage, stagnation. Reluctance to 'move on', to embrace the new, is most evident in our dealings with technology. The writer Douglas Adams has amusingly documented how our attitude to technology changes as a function of age. Anything in the world when you're born is normal; anything invented when you are between fifteen and thirty-five is exciting; but anything invented after you are thirty-five is 'against the natural order of things'. Excitement curdles into suspicion and fear.

The philosopher Henri Bergson – a highly original and inexplicably neglected thinker – asserted that life 'flows' forwards and everything changes. This is 'the natural order of things', therefore we should be wary of inertia, habit – 'petrification'. In *Le Rire*, which was published in 1900, Bergson issued a warning to those who have reached the midpoint of life: 'It seems possible that, after a certain age, we become impervious to all novel or fresh forms of joy, and the sweetest pleasures of the middle-aged are perhaps no more than a revival of the sensations of childhood, balmy zephyrs wafted ever more faintly by an ever-receding past.'

In 'actual life' (as Campbell termed it) the call manifests as a thought, feeling or experience that catalyses change. At some deep level the person realises that change is necessary and the adventure, the inner journey, begins. Because the call originates in the unconscious, it is often allusive and subtle. In 'actual life', we don't come across deer and follow them into forests, but we do follow intuitions, gut feelings and hunches. Even random events – seemingly trivial random events – can trigger change, if we are receptive. Campbell suggests that small things, a 'chance word, the smell of a landscape, the taste of a cup of tea, or the glance of an eye may touch a magic spring'. He is identifying a certain kind of *readiness*: a readiness to detect signs, to explore chains of association, and to speculate about meaning and significance.

Perhaps the finest literary example of a person exhibiting this kind of readiness appears at the beginning of Marcel Proust's semi-autobiographical *In Search of Lost Time*. The author tastes a madeleine, he is unexpectedly moved, and he stops to reflect. 'I feel something start within me, something that leaves its resting-place and attempts to rise, something that has been embedded like an anchor at a great depth; I do not know yet what it is, but I can feel it mounting slowly.' Proust recognises that remote memories – 'palpitating in the depths of my being' – have been stirred by the taste of the madeleine and that these memories are trying to *follow* the flavour into his 'conscious mind'. He is tempted to 'leave the thing alone' and go back to thinking about his usual worries and hopes, when suddenly he remembers an old grey house, a town square, a parish church, and country roads. His head fills with vivid childhood memories which trigger a process of self-examination.

What is most significant about Proust's 'madeleine moment' is that he is describing an involuntary process. He is not trying to remember anything. In this respect, involuntary memories are comparable to artistic inspiration. They are like 'visitations' from the unconscious and have the capacity to surprise; they can jolt us out of complacency and draw us inwards along unexpected associative pathways of self-discovery.

Our minds channel a ceaseless flow of impressions, thoughts, images and commentary that psychologists, philosophers and literary theorists describe as 'the stream of consciousness'.

Typically, we focus on some mental content (particularly if it is relevant to an ongoing task) and ignore the rest. A great deal of the stream of consciousness is seemingly nonsensical, irrelevant or obscure, and often there is no obvious stimulus for a particular recollection. For example, while having a shower, one might remember sitting at a desk in primary school. Why this memory rather than any other memory? While compiling a shopping list, a colleague you haven't thought of in decades might – apropos of nothing – suddenly insinuate herself between the apples and the toothpaste. Even more intriguing are arbitrary feelings: inexplicable shifts in mood, curious glimmers of hopefulness unattached to any incident, fleeting moments of unprovoked sadness. Readiness or willingness to consider ordinarily ignored mental content is a basic requirement of psychoanalysis. Freud urged his patients to report anything that passed through their minds, however trivial, embarrassing or ridiculous. The psychoanalytic session is a space in which distractions are limited so that random thoughts, dreams, odd sensations and seemingly insignificant memories can become the focus of attention. According to Freud, this is a reliable way of achieving the deepest level of self-understanding.

Of course, one cannot stop to reflect on every mental event, otherwise one would never have the time to do anything else. Modern living, which tends to be goal-directed, pressured and hectic (especially if one has a demanding job, a young family, or both), has a momentum which is largely incompatible with stopping and wondering. And when we do stop, we tend to crave easy and accessible diversions: television, radio, shopping, podcasts. Since the introduction of smart phones, it has become increasingly difficult for people to enjoy moments of open-minded, meditative calm. When people have completed their necessary tasks, they no longer sit and do nothing. They occupy themselves scrolling down social media feeds or surfing the net. There are no longer intervals in the day when the mind is simply idling. Under such conditions the call to adventure will almost certainly be missed. The fragrances we detect and the cups of tea we drink will never, as Campbell colourfully suggested, 'touch a magic spring'. By contrast, indigenous cultures (who live life at a more sedate pace and are generally less distracted) frequently exist in a state of readiness to identify signs and portents – a characteristic that is viewed by the denizens of industrialised nations as primitive, superstitious and childish. They are presumed to be intellectually inferior.

The problem with shifts of feeling of this kind is that they frequently have an ineffable quality. They are elusive and difficult to describe. Which is why people tend not to reflect on them for very long. Language – in the first instance – is insufficient. We can't find the right words to 'fix' the experience and make it tractable. The impression of something important having just happened gradually fades and the moment is forgotten. If the 'shift' happens in the presence of others, ineffability discourages discussion. People are reluctant to start free-associating to work out the meaning of their inner stirrings and perturbations. The preliminary phase of such an interrogation – searching, faltering, vague – can sound like self-indulgent gibberish. Yet, this is precisely what is required to achieve insight. Ineffability is an indicator that one is experiencing more than a commonplace emotion. If one can sense significance, but can't explain why, this suggests depth – meanings located below the threshold of awareness. When people *do* allow themselves to pick up an associative thread, with the intention of following it into the unconscious, they often discover that their self-examination is becoming increasingly consequential. What started as something that felt like 'groping' hopelessly in the dark will begin to yield results – small indications of unsuspected promise. However, the nature of what we are trying to uncover within ourselves can be exceedingly subtle. Indeed, so subtle that how we look at what we discover can influence whether we see it or not.

When I was ten years old, I came across an image of the northern lights in a school science book. It was a very uninspiring pen-and-ink drawing, with hardly any detail. Even so, the idea of curtains of light suspended in the night sky made such a profound impression on me that I immediately thought: *At some point in my life, I really must see this.* Fifty years later, I found myself standing in the Arctic circle, my extremities numb with cold, gazing up at what looked to me like the work of a cosmic artist scattering patterns of phosphorescent powder across the celestial dome. Shimmering veils swirled into existence, twisted into magnificent complex structures, and then dissolved into nothingness. I stood there, knee deep in snow, transfixed, in a state of joyful awe. Yet, the northern lights are an extremely fragile phenomenon. A full, bright moon had risen, and its 'glare' bleached half the sky. It was necessary to look in the opposite direction to continue enjoying the spectacle. Sometimes, you need to dim one source of light to make another visible. Sometimes, you can only see in the dark.

Our enlightenment values – in particular, the veneration of reason – are difficult to reconcile with the works of Campbell and Jung or the practices of indigenous peoples. We are suspicious of intuitions and discomfited by paradox. Campbell described the unconscious using rich, poetic language. He conjured visions of a vast kingdom of fire-seeds, jewels and stars, giving light 'in the bosom of immortal night'. However, if you carry the torch of reason into the unconscious, you won't see very much. Everything vanishes, like the northern lights in the glare of a full moon.

The kind of psychology that takes myths, intuition, symbols and the unconscious seriously has always been denigrated by 'mainstream' university departments as unscientific – a regression to the primitive. But as we shall discover, this orthodox view has recently been called into question. Several contemporary psychologists and neuroscientists have argued that by rejecting the perspectives of thinkers such as Campbell and Jung, our understanding of the mind and the human condition has become greatly impoverished. Our knowledge of who we are is incomplete. And if we do not know who we are, if our self-understanding is fragmentary, we may find that we are unequal to the challenges of later life.

When I was practising as a clinical psychologist (I'm now retired from clinical practice), patients would occasionally arrive for their weekly session and announce that they no longer needed my help. They had benefited from an experience that had unexpectedly changed their perspective. I am not referring to spontaneous remission. A relatively high percentage of individuals suffering from psychological problems, such as depression, will naturally improve over time. This is why studies designed to test the effectiveness of specific therapies usually include a 'waiting list' control group who receive no treatment. An outcome study must demonstrate that subjects in the treatment group have shown significant improvements compared to subjects who have been simply waiting for treatment, many of whom, if diagnosed with depression, are likely to recover without any contact with a mental health professional over a period of three to six months. The patients I am referring to here were different. They hadn't improved gradually over time, and they attributed their recovery to a specific transformative experience.

Very little research has been conducted on transformative experiences, and psychotherapists rarely have an opportunity to discuss them because as soon as patients start feeling better they usually stop coming for psychotherapy. The transformative experiences described by my patients ranged from the profound (for example, the felt presence of a deceased loved one) to the seemingly unremarkable (observing a flock of birds and simultaneously feeling less troubled). Invariably, these experiences were difficult to describe and volunteered with a degree of nervous apprehension. Intensely personal experiences with hints of the paranormal are easy to ridicule.

Transformative experiences of this kind probably overlap with what some psychologists (especially those associated with humanist and transpersonal schools of psychology) have called 'revelatory experiences'. These are experiences in which something comparable to Campbell's *unsuspected world* or *aspect of the world* is revealed. They are usually associated with a shift of consciousness and leave the person with a strong sense of having been *shown* something or *told* something of significance. Moreover, revelations of this kind are commonly perceived as coming from somewhere beyond the self. For psychologists, the most likely source of these 'communications' is the unconscious. A sub-category of revelatory experiences (designated with language reminiscent of Campbell) are 'calling experiences'. The principal feature of calling experiences is that they tend to influence the direction of an individual's life in a tangible way. Perhaps the most widely recognised instances of receiving a 'call' are vocational. Indeed, the English expression 'to have a calling' implicitly acknowledges that individuals do not always choose their professions, as such, but rather are *called* to them, which – as with all revelatory experiences – suggests inducement from an external source. Once again, the calling, when it happens, is perceived as super-ordinary. Although calling experiences are under-researched, what evidence we have shows that those who follow vocational 'callings' also report finding their work deeply satisfying and personally meaningful. Answering the call was a good decision.

Is it wise to act on one's feelings? To be guided by hunches? A person who chooses to steer his or her life in a different direction based on such vague indications could be described as impulsive or even reckless. For decades, psychologists have made a relatively sharp distinction between thoughts and feelings. Thinking is effortful, slow and accurate, whereas feelings (more commonly referred to as emotions in academic circles) are automatic, fast and inaccurate.

From an evolutionary perspective, both have survival value. When we have enough time, we can solve problems by thinking things through. But when we don't have enough time – in a potentially threatening situation, for example – it is better to act quickly. Fear (the outcome of a fast but possibly inaccurate evaluation of threat) motivates escape from danger. In the ancestral environment, avoiding predators was significantly more consequential than overreacting. An early human who habitually paused to think about whether an approaching large animal was dangerous or not would almost certainly die young.

Given that feelings are 'quick and dirty', it has been generally supposed that the best way to make decisions, particularly if one has the luxury of time, is to think carefully about costs, benefits, objectives and consequences. This is correct – but conditionally so. When decisions are complex, acting on a feeling might be superior to rational thinking and the only *real* option.

Few people ever use a spreadsheet (with costs and benefits laid out in neat columns) to determine whether they should get married. People in western democracies decide to get married because they are in love. Although love is powerful, it is notoriously difficult to define. When attempting to explain their decision to get married, most people resort to the standard vagaries of high romance: 'It felt like we were destined to be together – like it was just meant to be.' If one attempted to make such a decision rationally, one would have to consider every relevant factor and assign each of these a value. After identifying obvious areas of importance, such as physical attraction and sexual compatibility, the process quickly becomes problematic. What else should one consider? And where should one stop? Taken to its logical extreme, this method of rational accounting might include the impact of marriage on opportunities for pastry consumption or train travel. Charles Darwin tried to work out whether he should get married by listing costs and benefits and he ended up with two columns that included absurdities such as 'less money for books' and 'better than a dog'. Clearly, it is impossible to account for every factor and every consequence. Most people when presented with complex situations that require a decision simply do what feels right. There is a growing body of evidence showing that when presented with complex problems, people frequently make better decisions intuitively compared to decisions made after painstaking deliberation. I am not suggesting that trusting feelings is always right. Hunches and intuitions can be wrong. However, as a post-enlightenment culture, we tend to underestimate the value of attending to what our feelings are telling us.

When we act on our feelings we are not acting irrationally. The unconscious can process vast amounts of information – much more information than can be processed consciously – and the result of this processing is a continuous emotional contribution to consciousness that to a greater or lesser extent influences behaviour. Evidence demonstrating the superiority of intuition over deliberation has been gathered largely by studying experts making complex decisions. These studies seem to show that experts can consult their extensive and specialised internal libraries unconsciously, and what they then feel – negative or positive affect – serves as a 'precis' that prompts them to make the right decision. If this wasn't the case, there would be no relationship between outcomes and levels of expertise.

The Case of the Getty Kouros – which sounds pleasingly like the title of a Sherlock Holmes short story – has become a much-referenced example of this phenomenon. It is discussed in academic papers on intuition as well as in best-selling popular psychology books. A kouros is an ancient Greek statue of a male youth. Around two hundred have been recovered and they are extremely valuable. In the 1980s, the J. Paul Getty Museum in Los Angeles was offered a seven-foot kouros that, unlike most, was in excellent condition. The kouros was on loan to the museum for a year and numerous state-of-the art, high-tech methods (for example, mass spectrometry and X-ray fluorescence) were used to establish its authenticity. The museum was satisfied with the test results and the kouros was acquired and exhibited. However, long before the art dealer who had approached the museum was paid almost $10 million, there were several experts who were uneasy about the purchase. None of them could articulate precisely what was bothering them, but they had in common a 'feeling' that the kouros 'didn't look right'. Their objections were vague and nebulous, and their 'criticisms' were not sharp enough to puncture and deflate the persuasive authority of the scientific reports. When a former director of the Metropolitan Museum of Art in New York was shown the kouros, the first word that popped into his head was 'fresh'. The head of the Acropolis Museum in Athens glanced at the kouros and 'knew', instantly, that it had 'never been in the ground'. In due course, it was discovered that the kouros was of questionable provenance and its authentication documents – when re-examined – were found to be counterfeit. The kouros was removed from display. A photograph of the kouros continued to be included in the Getty catalogue but the accompanying text read: 'About 530 BC, or modern forgery'.

It should be noted – in passing – that the distinction made between slow, accurate thoughts and fast, inaccurate feelings has been, until recently, somewhat overemphasised. The unconscious is active over time and feelings can be the result of slow as well as fast processing. Our moods – which can last for weeks or months – are also instructive. They too can be understood as meaningful communications, the result of ongoing, unconscious evaluations and judgements.

Nietzsche once wrote, 'There is more sense in thy body than in thy best wisdom.' His use of the word 'body' is significant, because he is suggesting that embodied, unconscious knowledge is superior to conscious knowledge. The link between unconscious knowledge and the body is exemplified by the idea of 'gut feeling', which has acquired increasing scientific legitimacy, now that the enteric nervous system is better understood. The gut has between two and six hundred million neurons – more than can be found in the brains of many animals that we commonly regard as intelligent – and it contains roughly 95 per cent of the body's serotonin (which is one of the most significant neurotransmitters involved in the regulation of feeling states). In addition, the gut transmits more information to the head than the head transmits to the gut. It seems unlikely that such a complex system has evolved simply to digest food and burp. The gut is effectively an auxiliary brain. I have spoken to experienced gastroenterologists who clearly think about the gut as a secondary personality. A patient might be sane, but unfortunately, they possess a gut that is 'mad'. The gut can respond to the world 'neurotically' creating physical problems – for example, bloating, diarrhoea and constipation. From the outside, it looks like the patient's life is being sabotaged by an interfering, independent agency, operating inside the body.

The heart also has its own nervous system – the intrinsic cardiac nervous system or ICNS – which is frequently referred to as the 'little brain' of the heart. The principal function of this 'little brain' is to make continuous adjustments to ongoing mechanical and electrical activity; however, more controversially, it has also been suggested that the 'little brain' may have a role to play in the processing and decoding of intuitive information. The little brain has around forty thousand neurons and it sends 'feeling information' via afferent nerve fibres to a subcortical structure called the medulla. From the medulla the information is relayed 'upwards' to the higher cortical centres. Given the close relationship between the 'little brain' of the heart and the 'big brain', it has been suggested that the 'little brain' can influence aspects of perception and decision-making.

Surely it is significant that the two parts of the body that have long been associated with intuition and 'deep feeling', the gut and the heart, are also the locations of relatively 'independent' neural networks – the 'enteric' and the 'intrinsic cardiac' nervous systems. The degree to which these auxiliary brains are poorly integrated into the general functioning of the totality of the nervous system may reflect – at least in part – divisions within the self; divisions that effectively compromise intuition. If we are unable to make use of our 'gut feelings' and what we 'feel in our hearts', then perhaps we will find ourselves increasingly adrift, coasting through life without the aid of subliminal guidance when we get emotionally confused or lost.

I would like to stress at this point that I am not in any way building a case against rationality. Because of our predilection for dichotomies, it is all too easy to misconstrue anything said in favour of intuition, gut feeling and the 'heart-felt' as a repudiation of rationality. Our engagement with reality should *always* be rational; however, at the same time, we should not conflate intuition with irrationality. More importantly still, we should not allow our rational outlook to interfere with or obstruct or hinder our receptivity to hunches and gut feelings. We are continuously making use of knowledge that we cannot articulate. Most people can tie a shoelace, but hardly anyone can describe how it's done. A small child can catch a ball without consciously calculating its trajectory using appropriate mathematical formulae. We can *know*, but *not know that we know*.

The idea that there is much to be gained from 'listening' to one's feelings overlaps with Campbell's view that we can learn a great deal by attending closely to myths. If we are going to receive a 'call to adventure', then it will more than likely manifest in our lives as some kind of emotional tremor. Like Proust, we might discover that something ordinary is accompanied by disproportionally deep stirrings and a sense of immanence.

The middle years and the years that follow are frequently associated with dissatisfaction and adjustment difficulties. Typically, the standard response to psychological distress is that one should *do* something. There is no shortage of advice: eliminate ultra-processed foods from your diet – join a gym – trace old friends. Advice of this kind is well meaning and beneficial, but it can also be precipitate. 'Staying' with one's dissatisfaction while resisting the urge to escape it can allow underlying causes to clarify. And few people hear Campbell's call with music blasting out of a loudspeaker while they sweat and gasp on a treadmill. There is a lot to be said for doing nothing – at least for a while. American clinical psychologist Lisa Miller has described some forms of depression as a 'call of the soul'. Calls need to be received and considered before replies can be meaningfully articulated.

In the West, we have difficulty with paradoxes, whereas in the East, essential truths are situated quite comfortably between polarities. Taoism teaches that certain forms of inactivity are more productive than activity. The concept of *wu wei* is often invoked – action through inaction or 'effortless action'. For the western mind, this kind of thinking can appear so abstruse that it is effectively meaningless. But most people have had the experience of doing less and achieving more. When trying to find the solution to a difficult problem, disengagement can be the optimal strategy. If one lays a problem aside the answer often presents itself spontaneously. This effect has been demonstrated repeatedly in laboratory settings by cognitive psychologists.

The idea that disengagement from problem-solving can be helpful is usually attributed to Graham Wallas – a pioneer of social psychology, an educator, and the author of *The Art of Thought*. He suggested that problem-solving involves four stages: preparation, incubation, illumination and verification. Typically, people think about a problem; then, for a while, they do nothing or something else; an answer suddenly presents itself – and subsequently this answer is applied or tested. Incubation is the most intriguing of Wallas's stages. What is happening, exactly, when a problem is set aside, and the person appears to be distracted or doing nothing? Wallas believed (and most modern cognitive psychologists would agree) that during the incubation stage, thinking continues below the awareness threshold, and that the eureka moment occurs when an answer, reached in the unconscious, ascends into consciousness. We are all familiar with a commonplace analogue: 'the tip of the tongue' phenomenon. When you can't remember a name or fact, but you *know* that you know it, it is usually best to do nothing or something else. Paradoxically, this is more likely to result in success.

Campbell associated the arrival of heralds in myths with the 'awakening of the self', a designation that resonates strongly with what the British transpersonal psychologist Steve Taylor refers to as 'awakening experiences'. According to Taylor, an awakening experience is 'a temporary expansion and intensification of awareness that brings significant perceptual, affective and conceptual changes'. Awakening experiences, like calling experiences, have a profound impact on the person. They cast the world in a new light and recalibrate the individual's relationship with reality. Awakening experiences are complex, but the three most common characteristics that Taylor has identified are: elation (which transcends fear and anxiety), intensification of perception (or hyper-real experience), and a sense of connection (to humanity and the universe in general). These core features are sometimes supplemented by deep feelings of love or compassion, altered time perception, an impression of access to knowledge (otherwise hidden or obscure), and inner quiet or peace. Taylor has established three principal triggers: psychological distress, contact with nature, and spiritual practices. These triggers underscore some of the points made above. Psychological distress can be understood as a meaningful transitional state. Lacunae in life – such as immersion in nature – can reduce 'noise' to the extent that subtle mental events can be detected (and subsequently allowed to develop). And finally, cultivating receptivity – as might be achieved through practices such as yoga or meditation – will increase the likelihood of aspects of the self becoming more accessible to consciousness (like Proust's madeleine raising his childhood from the depths of memory).

Lisa Miller has conducted some fascinating research into the relationship between depression, spirituality, the brain and 'awakened awareness'. Her departure point was the discovery that the spiritually committed adult offspring of depressed parents are considerably less likely to develop depression than their less spiritually inclined peers. Although adult offspring from high-risk families (that is, families including a parent who suffers from depression) were known to exhibit thinning of the cerebral cortex, Miller and her colleagues found that if spirituality was important to them, the opposite was true. They exhibited cortical *thickening*. This suggests, perhaps, that those most at risk of depression are also endowed with a compensatory capacity to benefit from spiritual enrichment. A subsequent fMRI scanning study sought to investigate the specific neurological correlates of spiritual experience. While being scanned, experimental subjects listened to scripts based on accounts they had already given of numinous experiences. It is generally accepted that thinking about a prior experience will reliably increase blood flow to the same brain areas that were active during the *actual* experience. A distinctive pattern of activation and deactivation was revealed. Specific structures and areas of the brain associated with ego awareness and body boundary perception became deactivated, whereas structures and areas associated with certain forms of attention and relational bonding became active.

The attentional system that becomes active when encounters with the numinous are recalled is the ventral attention network, which – Miller suggests – makes us 'see that the world is alive talking to us'.

Miller's investigations have led her to propose two forms of awareness: 'achieving awareness' (a form of focused attention which facilitates the accomplishment of goals) and 'awakened awareness' (a broader form of attention that makes us alert to serendipitous surprise and meaning). Both are important for general functioning, but it is 'awakened awareness' that is more likely to engender mental states that protect against depression.

When we enter the state of awakened awareness, Miller writes, 'we literally *see more*, integrating information from multiple sources of perception. Instead of seeing ourselves as independent makers of our path, we perceive ourselves as *seekers* of our path. We look across a vast landscape and ask, *What is life showing me now?*' Miller uses a geographical metaphor to express the essence of her formulation. We are seeking a path again – with Dante, with Joseph Campbell – embarking on a journey, and there is the prospect of return, laden with gifts. 'This awakened awareness,' Miller continues, 'allows us to perceive more choices and opportunities available to us, feel more connected with others, understand the relationships between events in our lives, be more open to creative leaps and insights, and feel more in tune with our life's purpose and meaning.'

Too good to be true?

Maybe not.

4

Soul Searching: The Psychology of Spirituality

Spirituality is important for your mental health even if you don't believe in God

She was approaching her fortieth birthday and according to her GP's referral letter she was suffering from depression. As the assessment session progressed, I began to doubt the accuracy of this diagnosis. She was happily married and worked as a business administrator, her circumstances were relatively benign and, although she regularly experienced episodes of low mood, she failed to report many of the symptoms that would ordinarily result in a formal diagnosis. Like so many of my psychotherapy patients, she seemed dissatisfied rather than 'clinically depressed'. She felt uneasy, unfulfilled, and complained of constantly being 'on edge'. When pressed, she admitted that she was troubled by a nagging sense of pointlessness. We became philosophical. Did life have a purpose? Soon we were circling the numinous without explicitly mentioning 'God' or 'spirituality'.

I asked a simple, open question: 'What would make things different for you?'

After a brief, thoughtful pause, she replied: 'Well, if I knew that there was life after death, something more, anything really, I'm sure that would change how I feel.' She had absolutely no interest in religion. Faith wasn't an answer – 'Why would you believe anything without evidence?' She had always been interested in the possibility of spirit communication, because at least theoretically, one might receive a message from a deceased relative or friend that 'proved' (to the recipient's satisfaction) post-mortem survival. Nevertheless, she had never consulted a medium for a 'reading' because she supposed that most so-called 'sensitives' were probably charlatans or con artists. 'If there was somewhere to go,' she said, 'somewhere . . . somewhere respectable – if that's the right word – I'd definitely, *definitely* try it. But I doubt there is such a place, and besides, who's got the time to go looking?'

We discussed her views on spiritualism in some detail and she was surprised that I was willing to explore the topic. As our session neared its end, I did something that I imagine most of my colleagues would disapprove of: I gave the administrator the name of an organisation dedicated to spiritual development where mediums could be consulted. It was, to the best of my knowledge, the most 'respectable' organisation of its kind in the country (a registered charity with trustees and a long history).

The next time I saw the administrator she was smiling broadly. She sat down and said: 'I was going to cancel but I thought I should come and tell you what's happened – and I wanted to say thank you.' She had consulted a medium and the experience had been transformative. The prospect of exploring her 'spiritual side', an aspect of herself that she had previously neglected, filled her with excitement. Perhaps life had a point after all? As far as she was concerned, she had found the perfect solution to her malaise.

I feel obliged to justify my behaviour because I do not believe that mediums contact the dead and I could reasonably be accused of fobbing my patient off with superstitious nonsense. Firstly, I don't *know* that mediums can't contact the dead, I'm just not persuaded by the evidence and think it is extremely unlikely. Secondly, my patient wanted something quite specific, and I knew precisely where she could get it. I didn't feel comfortable withholding information simply because I have a different (and not necessarily superior) world view. And thirdly, I made it clear that if her malaise returned, then she could always make another appointment to see me. In fact, I never saw her again.

Spirituality is loosely associated with ageing. When death approaches and existential anxiety increases, people tend to 'find' God. Even so, as Christianity has declined in the West, immortality projects have replaced prayer. Churches have emptied, and many have closed. Yet, having a faith has many benefits. Being part of a large religious community guarantees social support and reduces feelings of loneliness. Helping others gives congregants a sense of purpose. Regular participation in rituals maintains a general sense of connectedness. Belief in an afterlife (repeatedly reinforced by collective affirmation) reduces fear of death. And so on. Freud claimed that religion is an 'illusion', a defence against existential terror and therefore, ultimately, a distortion of reality injurious to mental health; however, he failed to consider how incidental factors such as higher levels of social engagement might *improve* mental health.

Philosophers and psychologists have written about a major spiritual crisis arising in the twentieth century. It is a crisis that has not only failed to resolve, but also appears to be deepening with every passing decade. Many social scientists have argued that unprecedented levels of dissatisfaction, depression and despair are the inevitable consequence of the decline of religion.

When people are detached from the numinous, it seems that they do not flourish.

The idea of 'flourishing' has been used by psychologists to describe a state of well-being characterised by positivity and good social functioning. Four major determinants of flourishing have been identified: family, work, education and religious community. Regular attendance of religious services is associated with increased longevity and better survival rates after individuals have been diagnosed with cancer. There are also considerable mental health benefits – for example, reduced depression and a greatly reduced risk of suicide. Such findings have reversed a common misconception, that being religious makes one vulnerable to developing a mental illness. This misconception arose largely because delusions and hallucinations are often religious in nature. Although it is true that a religious person will probably be more likely than a non-religious person to experience religious delusions and hallucinations, this does not mean religious conviction *causes* conditions such as 'schizophrenia'.

Religion and spirituality overlap, but they should not be treated as equivalents. A religion usually has a creed – a set of key principles or beliefs – holy texts, observances, rituals and symbols that bring devotees closer to God (or at least whatever concept they have of divinity or the sacred). Spirituality is less circumscribed and associated with questing, seeking answers to ultimate questions, and the pursuit of meaning. Personal experience, especially altered states of consciousness, encounters with nature and revelations (which can be understood as moments of profound insight), are highly valued by those who describe themselves as 'spiritual'.

Perhaps because spirituality is less encumbered than religion by histories of intolerance and doctrinal differences it is often perceived as being more 'acceptable' by westerners who have become disaffected with materialism but do not wish to adopt a faith. This preference is exemplified by the popularity of mindfulness meditation which has been detached from its Buddhist context and repurposed as a psychotherapy – albeit a psychotherapy with inescapable 'spiritual' resonances. Patients are not expected to become Buddhists, but they are encouraged to question assumptions about the nature of selfhood. For example, do our anxious thoughts define us? Or can we separate these thoughts from a more fundamental, observing self?

Over the past thirty years, social scientists have demonstrated that spirituality and religion can be disentangled; however, they have shown more interest in identifying the psychological benefits of spirituality than religion. A key study, published in the *American Journal of Psychiatry* in 1997, was conducted by the American psychiatrist Kenneth Kendler and colleagues. Using as his subjects 1,902 female twins from the Virginia Twin Registry, Kendler demonstrated that it is possible to distinguish between spirituality and religious conformity (which he termed 'personal conservatism'), and he found that high levels of spirituality were associated with a range of mental health benefits – for example, low levels of depression and decreased risk of addiction. Statistical models were employed to determine the degree to which spirituality could be attributed to genetic or environmental factors, and it was found that spirituality was 29 per cent heritable. Of course, this also means that spirituality in Kendler's sample was 71 per cent environmental. Nevertheless, the figure of 29 per cent is significant. Interpreting this kind of data is always contentious, but notwithstanding the usual caveats, Kendler's results appear to show that spirituality is (at least in part) rooted in biology. We are, as it were, born with a spiritual 'instinct'.

Lisa Miller, whose concept of awakened awareness was discussed in the previous chapter, found that when a mother and child are both concordant for spirituality – as opposed to non-concordant pairings – the child is 80 per cent less likely to suffer from depression. Miller highlights the significance of this discovery by sharing her initial reaction: 'It was the largest protective effect I'd seen anywhere in the resilience literature.' Depression can be understood as a mental illness. However, Miller suggests that what we call 'depression' might really be what happens when a genetically determined 'spiritual hunger' is continuously frustrated. The materialistic world view has clearly encouraged the widespread denial of this fundamental spiritual need, contributing, perhaps, to the seemingly inexorable rise in our depression statistics. Suicide statistics are also rising, although in specific populations (young men, for example). Clearly, depression is a complex state, and not every instance of depression can be 'repackaged' as spiritual frustration; however, Miller and many other researchers like her are now demonstrating that spirituality *can* and *should* be considered as a factor highly relevant to mental health.

The scientific study of spirituality has an uneven history, and it has only recently become established as a valued specialism in university departments. This is surprising because it is generally agreed that the entire field rests on a foundational work that is an undisputed masterpiece. *The Varieties of Religious Experience: A Study in Human Nature* by William James is a volume of lectures originally delivered at the University of Edinburgh in 1901 and 1902. These fascinating addresses – with titles such as 'Religion and Neurology', and 'The Religion of Healthy-Mindedness' – were so warmly received that when James came to the end of his final presentation the audience sang 'For He's a Jolly Good Fellow'. James's treatment of psychological and physiological aspects of religious experience proceeds in the absence of any assumptions about the existence of an underlying 'religious' reality. He is 'agnostic' and interested in outcomes rather than absolutes. Given James's impartiality and the nature of his project, it has been argued that we should think of *The Varieties of Religious Experience* as 'The Varieties of Spiritual Experience' – a substitution that better reflects not only James's objectivity but also trends in contemporary research.

William James was born in New York City in 1842. His grandfather, known as 'Old Billy', was a poor Irish immigrant who lived the American dream and became so wealthy that he could number among his many possessions the city of Syracuse. He owned almost all of it. James's father, Henry senior, after a period of somewhat irregular living, became a student of theology and later a writer on related subjects. He entertained New England transcendentalists, and Henry David Thoreau (the author of *Walden*) was one of his dinner guests. The philosopher Ralph Waldo Emerson was William's godfather, and his younger brother was the novelist Henry James.

There is an arresting photograph of William James as a young man that shows a startlingly different figure from the more familiar Harvard patrician he was destined to become. James, in his early twenties, is wearing a wide-brimmed cowboy hat, baggy trousers, a loose jacket and sunglasses. He is a Victorian, yet there is nothing stiff or formal about his pose. In fact, he looks like an adventurer in a steam-punk novel – a comparison that isn't too whimsical because the photograph was taken in 1865 on an expedition up the Amazon during which he survived storms, capsizing canoes and predatory big cats; became so attached to a spider monkey that he described the animal as his 'best friend'; and watched dancing girls with 'splendid soft black hair' whose movements left traces in the air of 'the most wildly melodious perfume'.

James studied medicine and graduated in 1869. He began teaching physiology at Harvard in 1873 but became increasingly interested in psychology. He established a psychology laboratory (used mostly for demonstrations) and wrote a benchmark textbook, *The Principles of Psychology*. James wanted to understand *all* mental phenomena, even those that many considered unfit subjects for scientific study, such as spirit communication. He believed that one should investigate what one sees, and clearly there is much more to be 'seen' in the human mind than just processes (such as perception) and capacities (such as memory). In the end, he wasn't convinced that there was sufficient evidence to support the claims of mediums; nor was he won over by evidence that purported to prove the existence of the paranormal. However, he remained interested in what were then still relatively new and exciting areas: religious experience, psychotherapy, hypnotism, and the unconscious.

When James wrote *The Varieties of Religious Experience*, he had specific aims that he expressed in one of his letters. Firstly, he wanted to demonstrate that experience rather than dogma was the 'real backbone' of 'religious life', and secondly, 'to make the hearer or reader believe ... that, although all the special manifestations of religion may have been absurd (I mean its creeds and theories), yet the life of it as a whole is mankind's most important function'. If religious experience is mankind's *most important* function, what is it important for, exactly? James's pragmatic answer is psychological adjustment. In fact, a form of psychological adjustment that is particularly beneficial for those who have reached middle age or old age. His thinking is highly original, and it foreshadows aspects of Jung's analytical psychology, humanistic psychology, transpersonal psychology, and even certain branches of contemporary neuroscience.

James acknowledges that although some people tolerate the trials of life without being greatly troubled, others are vulnerable and suffer. Human beings, he says, are prone to 'world sickness', a malaise caused by the accumulation of failures, blunders and misdeeds. Consequently, it doesn't take much to make the average person feel depressed: 'a little cooling down of animal excitability and instinct, a little loss of animal toughness, a little irritable weakness and descent of the pain-threshold, will bring the worm at the core of all our usual springs of delight into full view, and turn us into melancholy metaphysicians'. We can try to lift our spirits with distractions – money, love, the pursuit of fame – but James asks: 'Can things whose end is always dust and disappointment be the real goods which our souls require?' James uses the word 'soul' to denote the essence of a person's being, rather than an immaterial part of the person. Worldly distractions might muffle existential terror, but they are never enough to extinguish it. We are always dimly aware that at the 'Back of everything is the great spectre of universal death, the all-encompassing blackness.' Ultimately, 'Old age has the last word.' James weakens our defences by personalising his rhetoric. He reminds us that 'every individual existence goes out in a lonely spasm of helpless agony'.

In chapter 3, it was suggested that distress, although unpleasant, can sometimes herald beneficial change. Low mood can be debilitating and remove a person from the everyday world of routines and shallow distractions, thus creating an opportunity for painful but nevertheless productive reflection. An episode of depression can be a turning point. James was one of the first psychologists to acknowledge that 'mental illness' can be understood as a stage in a person's psychological progress, rather than an interruption or an obstacle. He cites the example of Leo Tolstoy, who at the age of fifty experienced a crisis related to a loss of meaning. The resultant depression was so deep he became suicidal. However, one day in early spring, while Tolstoy was alone in a forest, listening to 'mysterious noises', he had what seems to have been an awakening experience that triggered his recovery. His dormant 'juvenile force of faith' was revived, and he realised that his refined and conventional life was 'no life, but a parody of life'. He embraced a simpler and more authentic way of living – dressing like a peasant, working in the fields and adopting a code of universal love.

James concludes that Tolstoy's 'crisis was the getting of his soul in order, the discovery of its genuine habitat and vocation, the escape from falsehoods into what for him were ways of truth. It was a case of heterogeneous personality tardily and slowly finding its unity and level.' Expressions such as 'heterogenous personality' and 'unity and level' reflect a way of thinking about the mind that not only helps us to understand why we become unhappy or anxious – or lose meaning – or feel crushed by the weight of our failures, blunders and misdeeds, but also suggests a fundamental reparative mechanism.

The 'world sickness' that James described is ultimately attributable to conflicts and divisions within the self. A mind can pull in many directions, sometimes simultaneously. Moreover, the links between different parts of the mind can become attenuated, or even break. It is possible to desire purity, for example, but at the same time struggle to overcome animal instincts. James quotes from St Augustine, who described having two contending 'wills' that disturbed his soul. Similarly, divisions can widen between the conscious and unconscious strata of the mind. 'There are persons,' says James, 'whose existence is little more than a series of zig-zags, as now one tendency and now another gets the upper hand.' The unhappy and dissatisfied are characterised by 'a certain discordancy' – 'an incompletely unified moral and intellectual constitution'.

James proposes that healthy psychological adjustment involves 'the straightening out and the unifying of the inner self'. For some people, this 'unifying of the inner self' proceeds spontaneously and without difficulty. 'The higher and the lower feelings, the useful and the erring impulses ... end by forming a stable system of functions in right subordination.' However, for those who do not achieve inner unity, a form of rebirth is necessary to make them whole. Typically, a crisis or an awakening experience will trigger this second nativity: 'sick souls', James says, 'must be twice-born in order to be happy'. Although James employs the term 'conversion' (a term heavily laden with religious connotations) to describe the process that leads to the reintegration of divided and conflicted selves, the reader is reminded that he does so without metaphysical prejudice.

James is particularly interested in the role of the unconscious in spiritual awakenings and rebirth. He prefers the term 'subconscious' to unconscious – and there are certainly 'technical' reasons why one might favour the former rather than the latter – but for present purposes the two words can be regarded as synonymous. James supposes that much of what we call spiritual experience might be the result of unconscious mental activity. Moreover, demonstrating remarkable freedom of thought and willingness to speculate, he suggests that it is conceivable that the unconscious could serve as a kind of portal through which transpersonal aspects of reality might create impressions on awareness: '*if there be* higher spiritual agencies that can directly touch us, the psychological condition of their doing so *might be* our possession of a subconscious region which alone should yield access to them'. Furthermore, 'The hubbub of the waking life might close a door which in the dreamy Subliminal might remain ajar or open.'

What are the characteristics of those who have achieved James's state of inner unity? In a purely religious context, such people are usually described as saintly; however, we can just as easily think of them – stripped of their halos or *tilakas* or *sudreh* and *kushti* – as wise. James itemises their attributes: a sense of participation in a wider life beyond selfish interest, connection, acceptance, elation associated with altered states of consciousness, and 'a shifting of the emotional centre towards loving and harmonious affections ...' These correspond closely with the cluster of pro-social and Stoic virtues that contemporary social scientists associate with healthy ageing. We will be taking a closer look at the scientific literature on wisdom and ageing in due course (chapter 10).

Spirituality is a core feature of human experience and every civilisation that has ever existed has engaged in worship. Clearly, a detailed analysis of a phenomenon that is so monumentally significant, so central to being human and so broadly consequential should yield – in addition to a deeper understanding of purely spiritual matters – a host of more general, psychological insights. This was most certainly the case with *The Varieties of Religious Experience*. It is ostensibly about 'religion', but it is full of stimulating asides and thought-provoking reflections on the unconscious, the causes of unhappiness, vulnerability and – most relevant here – what must happen dynamically and structurally within the mind if we are to emerge from a mid- or late-life crisis on to what James poetically described as 'the smooth waters of inner unity and peace'.

Although James was an outstandingly original thinker, the idea that psychological problems are ultimately related to divisions in the mind (and that healing those divisions restores mental health) was very current when he delivered his lecture series in Edinburgh. Freud had already proposed that traumatic and inaccessible memories buried in the unconscious could cause neurotic unhappiness. His treatment, psychoanalysis, involved the excavation of those memories. Patients improved (so he thought) because lost parts of themselves were being reintegrated into a newly restored whole. James was fully aware of Freud's work in 1901 and he mentions him, and several contemporaries who had similar ideas concerning mental illness and recovery, in *The Varieties of Religious Experience*.

Although Freud and James were in broad agreement with respect to certain dynamic and structural features of the mind, their attitude to religion was quite different. As we know, Freud thought religion was an elaborate defence, a delusional system – a form of immature self-deceit that retards psychological growth and distorts reality. James was more nuanced. He rejected religion too, especially dogmatic religion (with its 'absurd manifestations'), but he thought that spirituality was so fundamental to being human that it couldn't be dismissed. He also held the pragmatic view that spiritual experience should be given serious consideration if it is associated with psychological health. Outcomes are more important than absolutes.

Perhaps James was more open-minded than Freud because he had had a few direct experiences of raised consciousness. While travelling in Switzerland, James was so moved by a scene of natural beauty that he was overcome by a 'torrent of adoration' that somehow connected the landscape, love for his wife, and 'virtue'. The apprehension of these connections is reminiscent of Marcus Aurelius, who, it will be recalled, suggested that 'all things are interwoven'. To love one's wife – an indispensable part of the universe's totality – strengthens one's connection with the universe, and conversely, to 'adore' the universe (exemplified by the majesty of nature) strengthens one's connection with one's wife. James also experimented with nitrous oxide, and under its influence he felt that deep but ineffable truths had become accessible to him. In his first published description of the effects of inhaling the gas, he wrote: 'The keynote of the experience is the tremendously exciting sense of an intense metaphysical illumination.'

James's approach to spirituality attracted many distinguished admirers. The philosopher Bertrand Russell, who wrote *Why I am not a Christian*, was an exceptionally rigorous thinker who declared that he neither believed in God nor immortality nor the greatness of Jesus Christ. He was effectively an atheist, although being a logician, he felt obliged to describe himself as agnostic because he could not prove the non-existence of God. Eight years after reading *The Varieties of Religious Experience*, Russell wrote *Mysticism and Logic*, in which he asserts that 'there is an element of wisdom to be learned from the mystical way of feeling, which does not seem to be attainable in any other manner. If this is the truth, mysticism is to be commended as an attitude towards life, not as a creed about the world.' Like James, who rejected religious dogma but believed that spirituality was 'mankind's most important function', Russell criticised Christianity but acknowledged 'metaphysical' pursuits as the inspiration for 'whatever is best in Man'.

In his autobiography, Russell describes an episode of 'mystic illumination' that echoes James's 'metaphysical illumination'. It was triggered by seeing Evelyn Whitehead (the wife of the philosopher Alfred North Whitehead) in extreme pain. 'Suddenly the ground seemed to give way beneath me, and I found myself in quite another region.' She was 'cut off from everyone and everything by walls of agony'. Russell was overcome by a profound recognition of the unendurable 'loneliness of the human soul' which could only be penetrated by 'the sort of love that religious teachers have preached'. The Whiteheads' three-year-old son was in the room and Russell, wishing to spare him the grim spectacle of his mother's 'paroxysms', took him by the hand and led him away. After five minutes of altered consciousness, Russell 'became a completely different person'. No longer an imperialist, but a pacifist with a strong desire to find a philosophy to make life endurable. Reflecting on the experience five decades later, he wrote: 'The mystic insight which I then imagined myself to possess has largely faded, and the habit of analysis has reasserted itself. But something of what I thought I saw in that moment has remained always with me, causing my attitude during the first war, my interest in children, my indifference to minor misfortunes, and a certain emotional tone in all my human relations.'

Five minutes of receptivity, openness and sensitivity to subtle perceptions had shaped his entire outlook, created inner cohesion, harmonised his pro-social attitudes, and made him more accepting. It is an extraordinary claim, but one which is supported by current research into awakening experiences (see chapter 3).

Even though James's *The Varieties of Religious Experience* has always been highly regarded, it had little impact on the development of mainstream psychology which became increasingly focused on variables that could be directly observed and quantified. This lack of influence is probably attributable to bad timing. The Victorians, many of them very eminent scientists, had been conducting investigations into mediums, hauntings and psychic phenomena for several decades; however, by 1900, enthusiasm for this kind of research had begun to wane due to disappointing results. Religious experience was yet another arcane subject likely to frustrate empiricists. For those who still wished to explore the unknown, Freud was offering an attractive 'occult' alternative: namely, the unconscious – a fascinating inner realm of dreams and primal memory that could be understood using the 'scientific' method of psychoanalysis.

For the first half of the twentieth century, psychological thinking was dominated by psychoanalysis and behaviourism. Although ostensibly very different, these two approaches overlap insofar as both understand human beings primarily as 'organisms' that are shaped by environmental contingencies. We seek pleasure (or reward), we avoid pain (or punishment), and how we act in the future will be greatly influenced by what we have learned in the past. Psychoanalysis and behaviourism are *deterministic*. After the Second World War, dissatisfaction with these two schools expedited the emergence of what came to be known as the 'third force' – a group of dissenting voices who are now classed as representatives of 'humanistic' psychology. Humanistic psychologists were influenced by existential philosophy and the spiritual belief systems of India and China, and they rejected the deterministic reductionism of psychoanalysis and behaviourism. Human beings, they asserted, are not biological automata constrained by learning experiences. They are free to make choices (many of which are guided by 'higher' values). Human beings pursue aesthetic ideals, try to find meaning and purpose; they feel compassion, love, have moments of profound insight, commune with nature, and have deep spiritual feelings. These are not marginal characteristics, but *defining* qualities that must be acknowledged in any complete account of the human animal. At the same time, humanistic psychology adopted a very Jamesian attitude with respect to its interest in outcomes rather than absolutes and its efforts to collect supporting evidence. The profile of humanistic psychology was raised in the 1960s because it resonated strongly with counter-culture values. Third force thinking was subsequently absorbed into the intellectual mainstream, and modern transpersonal psychology can be viewed as a branch of humanistic psychology that has become increasingly specialised in the twenty-first century.

Much of the research agenda of contemporary transpersonal psychology has been inspired by the work of the pioneering humanist psychologist Abraham Maslow. Maslow was born in New York, the son of Jewish immigrants, and raised in extreme poverty; however, he spent a great deal of time in public libraries and soon identified education as a means of improving his prospects. After a brief flirtation with law, he became interested in the mind and subsequently studied psychology at the University of Wisconsin. When he was still relatively young, he received a grant that allowed him to spend the summer of 1938 with the Northern Blackfoot on a reservation in Alberta. It was a life-changing experience. Maslow believed that shared 'tribal' values (non-acquisitiveness, prioritisation of community, concern for the well-being of future generations) had shaped a society that, as far as he could see, was relatively free of crime, violence and greed. Maslow's anthropologically enlightening summer persuaded him that human beings are basically good (rather than destructive and selfish), and exposure to an alternative way of life led him to question the moral integrity of western materialism. For the Northern Blackfoot, status was earned by demonstrations of virtue rather than the accumulation of wealth. In due course, Maslow became a professor of psychology at Brandeis University in Massachusetts, where he remained from 1951 to 1969 – the period during which he produced his most influential work.

Today, Maslow's name frequently appears alongside his famous 'hierarchy of needs' – a triangular diagram of human 'motives' that is now so recognisable it has become a popular internet meme. Although Maslow is the undisputed originator of the hierarchy, he described its 'structure' using words only; the diagram itself (sometimes referred to as 'Maslow's Pyramid') was in fact the creation of a management consultant. Maslow argued that we are motivated according to our needs and that these needs are satisfied serially with respect to their urgency. Thus, we are highly motivated to find water, food, shelter and warmth, before seeking, for example, the satisfaction of our aesthetic needs. If you are hungry, you will look for a restaurant, not an art gallery or a concert hall. Basic needs (for example, safety) are usually satisfied before less compelling needs (for example, sex). Maslow wasn't quite as rigid as is sometimes supposed concerning the step-by-step ascent of his hierarchy – we don't always consider safety before sex, for example – but the progressive satisfaction of needs according to situational demands is so much a part of everyday experience that few people would query the general principle. Moreover, what Maslow chose to include in his hierarchy – things like 'belonging' and 'self-esteem' – have considerable prima facie validity. Given that much of the first half of life is concerned with satisfying fundamental needs, such as the acquisition of skills, finding employment and forming a durable intimate relationship, we can assume that the majority tend to postpone the satisfaction of higher and more 'philosophical' needs until after the middle years.

At the pinnacle of Maslow's hierarchy is 'self-actualisation'. According to Maslow, our most elevated need is to self-actualise. Essentially, what this means is that after our physical and social needs have been met, we are motivated to realise our full potential, to find fulfilment in accordance with our unique dispositions. Self-actualised people have many characteristics; however, it should come as no surprise (given the material covered in previous chapters of this book) that ranked highly among these traits are an accepting attitude, connectedness (especially in the context of relationships) and a general openness to experience. Because self-actualised individuals function optimally, it is assumed that they enjoy good mental health.

While undertaking research on higher needs, Maslow had discovered that self-actualised individuals are more likely than non-self-actualised individuals to report episodes of raised consciousness. He called these episodes 'peak experiences'. Like 'self-actualisation', peak experiences are loosely defined and possess many characteristics; however, in the present context, some key features deserve particular emphasis: ego transcendence, richer perception, loss of fear, and 'fusion of the person and the world'. Maslow's pioneering work on peak experiences supplied the initial impetus for ongoing research into the nature of revelatory, awakening and calling experiences (discussed in chapter 3).

Maslow's hierarchy 'embodies' the idea of upward evolution; human beings have the potential to satisfy needs in ascending order – deficiency needs (I'm hungry) and then growth needs (My life lacks meaning) – until they become self-actualised, at which point the fully functioning person is likely to have peak experiences. However, the relationship between personal development and peak experiences is probably circular rather than linear. Peak experiences will almost certainly potentiate further development by 'the straightening out and the unifying of the inner self' that William James equated with spiritual rebirth (or conversion). An episode of raised consciousness will inevitably encourage new ways of attending and being – shifts of perspective that are likely to engender Stoic and pro-social attitudes. Maslow shared James's view that mental health is associated with integration and wholeness. Indeed, he presupposes that self-actualisation is a facet of an integrated hierarchy and that a self-actualised person is whole (as opposed to divided by defences and conflicts).

In addition to peak experiences, Maslow identified another form of 'unitary consciousness' that he designated 'plateau experiences'. Whereas peak experiences are relatively short, plateau experiences are prolonged and reflective rather than ecstatic. The defining feature of the plateau experience is a sense of gratitude or wonder evoked by what is usually perceived as quotidian. In other words, the sacred, poetic or symbolic are apprehended in everyday things. The poet William Blake seems to have been familiar with plateau experiences. His famous couplet (from 'Auguries of Innocence') 'To see a world in a grain of sand, And a heaven in a wild flower' inverts our usual perspective and discovers cosmic significance in the ordinary. Maslow believed that, unlike peak experiences, which tend to be spontaneous, plateau experiences can be willed into being. In fact, just before he died he was writing in his journal about the possibility of devising 'unitive' and 'sacralizing' exercises. Of course, Maslow was not being entirely original in this instance.

For Zen Buddhists, everyday activities such as sweeping, cleaning and gardening, when undertaken in the right frame of mind, frequently acquire a sacred dimension.

'Maslow's hammer' is the term used to describe how the adoption of a particular perspective will alter or bias perception. On more than one occasion he expressed this idea axiomatically: *when all you have is a hammer, everything looks like a nail.* In a sense, how you look at the world alters what you see. But the same is true when you look inwards. A prerequisite of psychological development and good psychological adjustment is the cultivation of a certain attitude – a sensitivity to the subtle and elusive.

Over time, Maslow began to suspect that self-actualisation might not be the summit of personal evolution, but instead a transitional or 'bridging' state that can, in some cases, facilitate elevation to an even higher level of being – *transcendence.* 'Transcenders' are more generously endowed with the qualities associated with self-actualisation, and altered states of consciousness are more central to their existence. They transcend ego more readily and with greater frequency; however, they are not necessarily happier than self-actualisers, who Maslow described, somewhat provocatively, as 'merely healthy'. Transcenders are more prone to sadness because they are acutely aware of the suffering of others. Once again, we find 'depression' reconceptualised, not as a symptom but as an aspect of spiritual growth – a form of inescapable philosophical sorrow. (We will encounter this phenomenon again when we take a closer look at the neural foundations of psychological integration in chapter 6.)

On 28 March 1970, a few days before his sixty-second birthday, Maslow wrote an entry in his journal that appears to suggest that he had reached a state of enviable equanimity with respect to his own mortality. 'I had thought that I'm at the peak of my powers & usefulness now, so *whenever* I die will be like chopping down a tree, leaving a whole crop of apples yet to be harvested.

That *would* be sad. And yet acceptable. Because if life has been so rich, then hanging on to it would be greedy & ungrateful.' Several characteristics of the wise are evident in these few short lines: inner peace, acceptance, gratitude, a sense of connection with others, continued investment in the future, a touch of melancholy, and a willingness to let go. A few months later, while jogging in Menlo Park, California, he had a heart attack and died.

As Maslow had hoped, the metaphorical tree may have been chopped down, but its destruction provided others with a rich harvest. He had not only revived James's project – the pragmatic study of raised consciousness – he had also brought the study of transcendent experience into the scientific mainstream. Only a year after Maslow died, a paper titled 'A Cartography of the Ecstatic and Meditative States' by the experimental psychologist Roland Fischer was published in *Science*. Fischer's opening sentence is unusually evocative: 'In this age so concerned with travel in outer space as well as inner space, it is strange that, while we have detailed charts of the moon, we have no cartography of the varieties of human experience.' Maslow's work almost certainly prepared the way for many scientists who, like their forebear William James, were convinced that a truly comprehensive psychology must necessarily embrace the spiritual or transcendent. But – and this cannot be stressed enough – their willingness to embrace the spiritual was never at the expense of empiricism or neuroscience.

One of the first studies to attempt to identify the neurological substrates of spiritual experience was conducted by Andrew Newberg (a professor at Thomas Jefferson University) and colleagues. Tibetan meditators and Franciscan nuns had their brains scanned using single-photon emission computed tomography. Subjects (all of whom meditated or prayed every day and had been doing so for many years) had developed the ability to voluntarily achieve a 'mental state of deep unity'. Tibetan meditators reported that they felt connected to 'everything' whereas the nuns reported that they felt a closer connection to God. In both groups, entering a state of deep unity was associated with inhibition of the superior parietal lobe – a brain region that mediates the representation of the boundary between the body and its surroundings. Clearly, this finding is consistent with the subjective experience of self-transcendence which typically involves the feeling that consciousness has expanded beyond its familiar sphere. There is also some evidence to suggest that when the inferior parietal region (which is positioned slightly lower than the superior region) is damaged after brain surgery, and therefore less active, recovering patients are more likely to report episodes of mystical unity.

A compelling description of the self dissolving into universal totality was recorded by the English author and seeker of truth Paul Brunton, who served in a tank regiment during the First World War, became a bookseller, visited India in the early 1930s, and meditated with the revered spiritual master Sri Ramana Maharshi: 'I find myself outside the rim of world consciousness. The planet which has so far harboured me disappears. I am in the midst of an ocean of blazing light ... it stretches away into untellable infinite space, incredibly alive ... my heart is remoulded in rapture.'

Our understanding of the neurobiology of spirituality has also been informed, albeit indirectly, by research into the effects of psychedelic substances on the brain – a scientific endeavour that gained momentum in the 1960s, but for political and cultural reasons temporarily ground to a halt by around 1970.

Psychedelic compounds have been used in religious rituals for millennia. We know this from cave paintings (many of which resemble hallucinations induced by ingesting psychedelics) and the presence of psychedelic alkaloids on excavated objects and skeletal remains. From earliest times, shamans and priestesses have used substances like psilocybin (magic mushrooms) and mescalin (from the peyote cactus) to dissolve the autobiographical self and merge with a greater reality. A study conducted by psychopharmacologist Roland Griffiths and colleagues at Johns Hopkins Hospital in Baltimore, published in 2006, found that subjects who were given psilocybin were, even after fourteen months, still rating their experience as one of the most meaningful and spiritually significant events of their lives. Another distinguished psychopharmacologist, Robin Carhart-Harris, a professor in the Department of Neurology at the University of California, San Francisco, has suggested (with supporting evidence from brain scans) that psychedelics produce their effects by disrupting or suppressing the 'default mode network' – a large-scale neural system that many neuroscientists believe is the biological substrate of the everyday self.

Clinical trials have been conducted using psychedelics on patients suffering from a broad spectrum of psychological problems, and preliminary outcomes range from promising to impressive; however, psychedelics might be particularly helpful in palliative care settings. From the 1950s to the early 1970s, research had been undertaken showing that psychedelics can reduce existential anxiety and despair in advanced stage cancer patients. The most persuasive contemporary study, published in 2016 and conducted, once again, by Roland Griffiths and colleagues at Johns Hopkins Hospital, found that psilocybin can produce substantial and sustained decreases of general anxiety and depression in patients with life-threatening cancer diagnoses, along with a significantly reduced fear of dying. It appears that one or two experiences of raised consciousness can be enough to replace existential anxiety with Stoic acceptance.

Why do psychedelics have transdiagnostic efficacy? Individuals suffering from depression, anxiety, PTSD, obsessive compulsive disorder and addictive problems all respond well to psychedelic medication. Carhart-Harris and colleagues have suggested that psychopathology is associated with rigid expectations and beliefs, and they explain the universal efficacy of psychedelics by proposing a model of change that utilises the idea of 'canalization' – a construct originally formulated by the British evolutionary scientist Conrad Hal Waddington in the 1940s. According to Carhart-Harris, one can think of psychopathology as a canalised (or entrenched) feature of the mind. This conceptualisation of mental illness can be translated into a topographic representation – the eponymous 'Waddington landscape'. Imagine a surface with 'valleys' of varying steepness and depth. A ball bearing would roll down some of these 'grooves' more easily than others and we can think of these as paths of least resistance – habitual routes to unhappiness. The Waddington landscape has been revived, because it is a potentially useful 'bridging construct' that can be employed to connect psychology, biology and computational neuroscience.

Carhart-Harris and colleagues have proposed that psychedelics have the effect of making the Waddington landscape temporarily more plastic. Psychedelics 'heat' the 'terrain', allowing it to be 'flattened', and when the landscape 'cools' psychopathological entrenchments are less deep and steep (that is, less likely to produce severe symptoms). Carhart-Harris writes: 'Here, we invoke the analogies of "wiping the slate clean", "starting afresh" or "rebirth".' The 'flattening' of a pathologically canalised mental landscape provides a model that can explain not only the success of psychedelic therapy for ostensibly very different conditions, but also the spiritual transformations described by William James – the enlightenment of 'sick souls', the 'straightening out' of those who must be 'born twice' to find happiness.

In 1959, the Hollywood film star Cary Grant admitted to the press that, under medical supervision, he had taken LSD. The experience was life-changing. His instinctive grasp of what might have happened in his brain to produce this transformation is remarkably consistent with the 'flattening' of a Waddington landscape: 'We come into this world with nothing on our tape. We are computers, after all. The content of that tape is supplied by our mothers, mainly because our fathers are off hunting or shooting or working. Now the mother can teach only what she knows, and many of these patterns of behaviour are not good, but they're still passed on to the child. I came to the conclusion that I had to be reborn, to wipe clean the tape.'

Ecstatic worship was a feature of the mystery cults of ancient Greece and Rome. These cults offered initiates a direct experience of the divine; however, to experience the divine, it was necessary to 'dissolve' the everyday self. Dionysus was worshipped with ecstatic dances that usually took place beyond the city limits. Given that Dionysus is the god of wine, the breakdown of inhibitions and uncontrolled behaviour was very much a part of Dionysian ritual. Initiates, or bacchants, removed their ordinary clothes, dressed in animal skins, and – abandoning everything emblematic of civilisation – travelled to uncultivated areas where they would dance wildly, sing and, in effect, 'lose' themselves. It was in this state of ego dissolution – with their tapes 'wiped clean' – that they would meet their god.

Dionysus was a masked god, a god who adopted many disguises. Ecstatic worship unmasked Dionysus and revealed the reality behind appearances. Intense encounters of this kind – on the slopes of Mount Parnassus or today, in a modern treatment centre – are almost always experienced as a form of rebirth. A changed person sees a changed world. But it isn't only the person who is reborn. Subjectively, the entire universe is 'reborn' too.

*

I have a friend, Phil, whom I met for the first time at a non-religious memorial service. Attending funerals and memorial services becomes a more frequent occurrence as one gets older. Phil is eighty-four years old. He learned to fly a Tiger Moth aircraft when he was still at school, was subsequently accepted in the inaugural intake of a new flying college set up by British European Airways and the British Overseas Airways Corporation, and qualified as a pilot. It is difficult to have a long career in aviation without ever having to deal with a life-threatening situation. Once, when Phil was a junior co-pilot on a commercial aircraft, it filled with smoke. The captain, thinking it was on fire, initiated an emergency descent. But the crew couldn't see anything. The plane probably went into a spiral dive and Phil thought he was about to die. Fortunately, he is quite short. He could sit much further forward than most pilots. He pressed his face against the instrument panel, became icy calm, looked at each reading one by one and carried out all the required actions. The plane landed safely. To say that he is a level-headed person is something of an understatement. Eventually, he became a senior pilot manager in the British Airways Flight Operations Department.

In October 1986, when Phil was forty-six years old, he was eating his dinner with his wife and daughter. He felt something 'burst' in his chest. He then found himself in what he describes as a 'vast black velvet space', floating towards a very bright and incredibly beautiful white light. He had no sense of possessing a physical body; nevertheless, his perceptual world felt intensely real. He sensed infinity, peace, warmth, harmony and love. The sublime tranquillity of the experience was disturbed by a thought: he was about to die without telling his wife that he loved her. Somehow, his consciousness shifted, he was able to declare his love, and he was immediately returned to his prior condition of disembodied suspension. At this point he had absolutely no fear and he was ready to die.

Suddenly, he felt cold. He became aware of an oxygen mask clamped on his face and the presence of paramedics. He was lifted on to a stretcher, placed in an ambulance, and rushed to the intensive care unit of a hospital where tests were carried out. When he was fully conscious, he wondered if he had had a heart attack and whether he would be allowed to fly again. A specialist ascribed his collapse, rather vaguely, to a 'vasovagal incident'.

In due course, he learned that while he was floating in the velvety blackness his wife had given him the kiss of life and started CPR. She had been unable to find a pulse for ten minutes. Although Phil discussed his near-death experience with his family, he didn't talk about it to anyone else for some time. Near-death experiences are frequently attributed to hypoxia, but part of Phil's training involved being placed in a pressure chamber and slowly deprived of oxygen. Phil knows exactly what hypoxia feels like, even to the point of losing consciousness, and his near-death experience was nothing like it.

Until October 1986, Phil had what he considers to be a 'normal' pragmatic view of death, which – so he says – is shared by many pilots; however, since that time, he has experienced minimal levels of existential anxiety. And there were other consequences of his near-death experience. He became acutely aware of the interconnectedness of all living things. Gradually, he became a calmer, more tolerant person, and although he had always disliked violence, he now found it increasingly abhorrent (even when depicted in TV dramas and films).

Unlike many people who have had a near-death experience, Phil's fundamental beliefs concerning post-mortem survival and the existence of God were unchanged. He has never been a 'believer' and describes himself as agnostic. As far as he is concerned there is insufficient evidence to justify belief in God, but he also finds the certitude of militant atheists extreme. He is a perfect Jamesian pragmatist, much more interested in practical outcomes than speculative absolutes – deeply grateful for having had a transformative experience and quite content to enjoy its psychological benefits without jumping to any unmerited or irrational conclusions.

Getting old hasn't troubled Phil greatly and compared with many octogenarians he remains astonishingly engaged and curious. He seems to be interested in just about everything. Ernest Becker suggested that death is so terrifying and reality so overwhelming that the average human being would become unhinged if they lowered their defences. Phil doesn't fear oblivion and finds the vastness and complexity of the universe inspiring: 'When my body decays, the atoms of which it is made will continue in the great cycle of life on earth. I also find it very comforting to know that all the atoms in my body, in the life forms around me, and in the earth itself, were made in stars. Isn't that a beautiful thought?'

Spiritual experiences are strongly associated with good psychological adjustment. An episode of raised consciousness, either experienced spontaneously or artificially induced by taking a psychedelic drug, can accelerate the beneficial 'straightening out and the unifying of the inner self' that James identified in *The Varieties of Religious Experience*. The mind becomes more flexible, divisions are healed, rigid beliefs change, and new perspectives are revealed.

But not everyone is happy with the idea of opening the 'doors of perception' with the aid of a magic mushroom. And not everyone will feel a deep connection with the cosmos when they look up at a starry sky. What else can one do to unify the inner self? Is there an alternative to 'peak experiences' or taking psychedelics? Carl Gustav Jung spent years grappling with the problem of integrating the self and he developed a 'method' that makes use of the three aspects of mental life which constitute the title of his famous autobiography: *Memories, Dreams, Reflections*. Moreover, he came to believe that integration was not only relevant to the second half of life, but also, for most people, the essential task – the prerequisite for combating nihilistic despair and achieving satisfactory psychological adjustment. Expressed differently, he discovered another path through Dante's 'dark wood'.

5

Integration: The Essential Task

Listen to your unconscious

The Swiss psychiatrist Carl Gustav Jung has become an indispensable cultural reference point. His oeuvre, which frequently marries western and eastern ways of thinking, found a broad and sympathetic readership in the 1960s. He was even included in the crowd of celebrities gathered behind the Beatles on the cover of *Sgt. Pepper's Lonely Hearts Club Band*. Notwithstanding his iconic status, Jung has always been a controversial figure. For some, he is wisdom incarnate, but for others, he is just an eccentric who mistook an episode of mental illness for enlightenment.

Freud and Jung were both interested in psychological development over time, but whereas Freud focused principally on the early years, especially between birth and puberty, Jung was clearly more absorbed by mental evolution in the second half of life. Jung began his career as Freud's intellectual heir-apparent but over a relatively short period of time their relationship deteriorated, and they ceased all communication. There are many reasons why these two giants of twentieth-century psychology became estranged; the most significant was that Jung could not accept Freud's sexual reductionism. Sex and sexuality were central to Freud's theoretical accounts of neurotic illness and personality. Jung's 'psychology' was less 'embodied' than Freud's, and like William James he considered spirituality too important to ignore. Consequently, his general theoretical framework and associated treatment method, 'analytical psychology', acknowledges metaphysical aspects of mental life and prefigures humanistic and transpersonal psychology.

Freud asserted that the mind is divisible into conscious and unconscious parts. The conscious part is experienced as the autobiographical self and the unconscious part contains personal memories, many of which are repressed or inaccessible. Jung added a third and deeper stratum: the collective unconscious. This is a repository of inherited predispositions, memories and symbols which Jung associated with 'mental templates' for certain character types and motifs that frequently appear in dreams, stories, art and hallucinations. He called these templates 'archetypes' and he believed they are formed from memory traces of recurring transgenerational experiences. For example, from earliest times, during periods of conflict, certain individuals have shown great courage in battle, and memories of their fearlessness and valour have been transferred from one generation to the next. These memory 'residues' have coalesced to form a prototype of the warrior-hero in the collective unconscious. Archetypes should not be confused with their manifestations. The archetype of the warrior-hero is a 'disposition' – an abstract ideal – which potentiates the creation of heroic figures appropriate to their cultural context. A Native American hero will differ from an ancient Greek hero, but they are both expressions of the same archetype. Archetypes are comparable to moulds, stored in the unconscious, but filled by conscious material. Jung supposed that an archetype resembles the axial system of a crystal, 'which as it were, performs the crystalline structure in the mother liquid, although it has no material existence of its own'.

At its deepest level, the collective unconscious is identical in all human beings. Freud also believed in ancestral memory, and he wrote about a version of the collective unconscious that he called the 'mass unconscious'; however, this construct plays a relatively minor role in his general formulations.

Archetypes can influence ideas, how we feel, and what we do. For example, Jung suggested that archetypes pattern instinctual behaviour. Thus, maternal instinct is, in a sense, organised by the 'mother' or 'earth mother' archetype. Although this idea sounds somewhat fanciful, it isn't really very different from what most neuroscientists and evolutionary biologists believe. Maternal behaviours have been selected by evolutionary pressures because they are essential if the human infant is to survive. They are a skill set, refined over many generations, that are assumed to have a neurological substrate. This substrate can be thought of as the physical aspect of the archetype. Richard Dawkins has described the human genome as a palimpsest, a transcript of embodied past interactions. In a recent interview published in *New Humanist*, he said: 'A living organism, over time, becomes a kind of archive, giving us insight into its ancestral history. The body, behaviour and genes of every living creature can be read as a book.' It is interesting that even 'traditional' biologists sometimes use language that sounds quite Jungian, even though they would undoubtedly reject the collective unconscious.

The idea of 'ancestral memory' (which for much of the twentieth century was considered incompatible with modern genetics) is now finding modest support among psychotherapists who specialise in the treatment of transgenerational trauma and biologists conducting laboratory-based animal studies of transgenerational learning.

Rachel Yehuda, a professor of psychiatry and neuroscience at Mount Sinai School of Medicine, New York, was one of the first to study 'inherited trauma' in the offspring of holocaust survivors. She identified several psychiatric vulnerabilities and a neurobiological marker (low cortisol levels) which suggest that traumatic sequelae can pass down several generations. Psychotherapists specialising in the treatment of trauma claim that the descendants of traumatised ancestors develop trauma-related symptoms that cannot be explained by having heard accounts of traumatic family histories. Moreover, meaningful connections can often be made between ancestral experiences and the symptoms of descendants. For example, a patient with an ancestor who lost all his or her material possessions might present with the symptoms of compulsive hoarding. This has led some psychotherapists to conclude that a form of continuous 'working out' or 'working through' is in progress – a labour shared by grandparents, parents and children.

Epigenetics is the study of how experiences affect our genes. What was once regarded as heresy, or at best a 'research curiosity', has since become an exciting area of mainstream biology. It is now uncontroversial to suggest that events can produce heritable and stable genetic effects. Typically, environmental factors 'switch' certain genes 'on' or 'off'. Evidence from animal studies (which are more controlled than human studies) is strongest; however, epigenetic pathways that might dispose individuals to develop psychiatric problems are being identified. In a 2015 article in *The Neuroscientist* titled 'Epigenetic Basis of Mental Illness', psychiatrist Eric Nestler and colleagues concluded that 'While epigenetic studies of mental illness remain at early stages, understanding how environmental factors recruit the epigenetic machinery within specific brain regions to cause lasting changes in disease susceptibility and pathophysiology is revealing new insight into the etiology and treatment of these conditions.'

Jung's notion of the collective unconscious has always been considered suspect because of the absence of an explanatory mechanism. How can residues of experience be inherited? Ultimately, Jung favoured a metaphysical account. Although epigenetics does not – by any means – prove that complex memories are transmissible from one generation to the next, recent advances have undoubtedly weakened resistance to the idea. Over the past ten years there has been a noticeable increase in references to Jung in scientific and philosophical publications (particularly those related to the psychedelic renaissance). This trend was perhaps presaged by the British biologist Rupert Sheldrake's theory of morphic resonance – proposed in 1981 – which is a much disputed but testable account of 'formative causation' that can be interpreted as a 'radical affirmation' of Jung's collective unconscious.

After his relationship with Freud had come to an end, Jung suffered a serious mental breakdown; however, rather than an 'illness' he viewed his symptoms as a natural, indeed logical response to critical events, and subjected his moods and disturbing thoughts to careful analysis and interpretation. By attending to material that had risen from the unconscious in the form of dreams, or even hallucinations, he was able to overcome his confusion and find new meaning, purpose, clarity and direction. He believed that his illness could be understood as part of a process of growth and development that he called 'individuation'. Jung used the word to describe the evolution of the person towards uniqueness. However, brief definitions of this kind reveal nothing of the concept's 'spiritual' complexities.

Individuation is a lifelong process, but Jung was particularly interested in how it proceeds in the second half of life. According to Jung, we typically spend the first half of life facing *outward* and pursuing material goals, whereas the second half of life is more reflective and *inward*-looking. This shift of focus, from external to internal, is reminiscent of the spiritual paths described by William James and Abraham Maslow. The need to 'individuate' is comparable to the need to become 'whole' or to self-actualise. It is like a drive that motivates the individual to achieve his or her full and singular potential. The work of individuation involves healing inner divisions and integrating polarities – for example, reconciling reason and emotion, or the conscious and unconscious divisions of the mind. Typically, it is those aspects of the person that have been most neglected in the first half of life which need to be nurtured and integrated in the second. Moreover, it is assumed that a person who is better integrated is also better equipped to cope with the challenges of later life.

Jung was reading *The Divine Comedy* as his mental state began to deteriorate. Like Dante, he found himself feeling lost, midway through life, peering into the darkness of his own unconscious – the equivalent of the shadowy wood in the first canto of *The Inferno*. Dante wasn't alone for long. After a few pages, he meets the shade of the Roman poet Virgil, who from that point onwards acts as his guide. Jung also acquired a guide, the hallucinatory being that he called Philemon, an archetypal sage or old man figure who first appeared to Jung in a dream. Jung realised that this apparition wasn't real, but rather a personification of 'superior insight' that had risen from the depths of his being.

As his crisis evolved, Jung kept a detailed record of his dreams, visions and reflections in a series of journals known as the black books. These provided the source material for *The Red Book*, a substantial volume that takes as its general theme spiritual alienation in the modern world and recovery of the 'soul' – although in analytical psychology Jung conflates the religious idea of the soul and the psychological concept of the self. Thus, *The Red Book* can also be read as an exploration of how we lose and find ourselves.

Jung was aware that his travel diary of the unconscious was an irregular piece of writing, and that admitting to consorting with archetypal figures was likely to damage his reputation as a doctor and scientist. Later, he confessed that he had translated his insights and experiences into the sanitised language of psychology, because if he hadn't, he would more than likely have been judged insane and his work would have been dismissed as the ravings of a lunatic. Jung didn't write about his crisis until late in life, but when he did, his disclosures were frank and comprehensive. His autobiography, published in 1962 (a year after his death), contains accounts of what he called his 'confrontation with the unconscious'. *The Red Book* is the 'raw data' of this 'confrontation' and it wasn't published until he had been dead for forty years.

The visions Jung recorded in *The Red Book* read like passages taken from a fantasy novel: 'I am walking alone in a dark forest and I notice that I have lost my way. I am on a dark cart track and stumble through the darkness. I finally come to quiet, dark swamp water, and a small old castle stands at its center [*sic*]. I think it would be good to ask here for the night's lodgings. I knock on the door, I wait a long time, it begins to rain.' Jung is admitted by a servant wearing old-fashioned clothes, is taken to meet a venerable scholar, and is visited in the night by the scholar's beautiful captive daughter. The language of *The Red Book* is mostly declarative, almost biblical. It is – according to Jung – the 'style of the archetypes'. For example: 'Then we saw him coming high across the mountains on a chariot made of the bones of the dead.' Or: 'How shall I ever walk under your sun if I do not drink the bitter draught of slumber to the lees?' It is somewhat ponderous and overblown.

The visions Jung includes in his autobiography are described in less pompous language, but they are equally lurid and fantastic. 'Before me was the entrance to a dark cave, in which stood a dwarf with a leathery skin, as if he were mummified. I squeezed past him through the narrow entrance and waded knee deep through icy water to the other end of the cave where, on a projecting rock, I saw a glowing red crystal.'

The Red Book can be placed in a western tradition of writing that documents travel through inner space, and that probably begins with Thomas De Quincey's *Confessions of an English Opium-Eater* and its sequel, *Suspiria de Profundis*. De Quincey, like Jung, described voyaging across hallucinatory landscapes and encounters with an extraordinary cast of 'archetypal' figures. From the mid-nineteenth century onwards, following De Quincey's example, many doctors began experimenting with drugs and there are numerous accounts of their equally 'fantastic' inner journeys. Jung doesn't advocate the use of opium to facilitate inner voyages, but rather certain practices – and interpreting dreams ranked highly among those he identified.

Although dreams are associated with the unconscious, we are *conscious* of at least some of our dreams – otherwise we wouldn't remember them. When we sleep, however, the rational, conscious part of the mind is largely inactive, so it is assumed that what we remember reflects unconscious mental activity. When we dream, a little consciousness is preserved during sleep, but it is reduced to the status of a passive observer. Because dreaming resembles being awake (in so far as we enter situations and meet people) we think of dream events taking place in a dreamworld – that is, a location (albeit a rather confusing one where the usual laws of logic do not apply). Again, it has been customary, since Freud's time, to think of this location as a destination – somewhere one can visit to gain insights and learn.

All animals (apart from a few and controversial exceptions) sleep. Because the sleeping animal is in an extremely vulnerable state, sleep must have been selected by evolutionary pressures because it is of immense value. We can be confident that sleep is *so* valuable, its benefits outweigh the cost of being easy prey.

Sleep has many functions – for example, physical repair and memory consolidation – but clearly we also sleep to dream, and contemporary research suggests that dreaming has its own special functions, such as the regulation of emotion, preparation for challenging situations, and problem-solving. Indeed, it appears that for those who make the effort to remember and reflect on their dreams, there are tangible gains: for example, the ability to see the world afresh, and greater creativity. Jung believed that if 'used' correctly, dreams can change the way we think about ourselves. Ideas and feelings find unique expression in dreams and sometimes certain types of knowledge cannot be accessed in any other way. For those in crisis, for those who feel in some sense stuck, dreams offer alternative possibilities if conventional problem-solving has failed.

We spend about a third of our lives asleep. Unlike indigenous societies, dreams are almost universally ignored in western democracies. It is as though we have decided to live only a part of life, rather than its totality. Jung believed that attending to dreams (and considering what they might mean) makes us whole. Engagement with the unconscious completes us. The counter-argument is that we only remember a fraction of our dreams, so perhaps they aren't that important from an evolutionary point of view. But this is like arguing that legs aren't important for lions because they spend a lot of time lying down.

Jung discovered that it wasn't necessary to wait for sleep to engage with the unconscious. He could choose to be receptive; he could empty his mind and create a mental vacuum that would suck up content from below. The mental state he recommended bears interesting comparison with the productive emptiness and inactivity – the non-doing – valued by Taoists. Eventually, he refined a technique that he called 'active imagination', which involved visualising personifications, places and situations, and allowing narratives to unfold. Most of us have fantasies that develop effortlessly – unconsciously. Indeed, it is a common experience to become absorbed by a fantasy which continues, as though we are passively watching a film, until we are obliged to reconnect with reality by environmental demands. Jung believed that fantasies – which can sometimes become so vivid that they are more like visions – should be cultivated and interpreted in much the same way as dreams. He found that with practice, he could talk to figures that appeared in his fantasies, and that they would reply as if they were not figments, but independent, living entities. They told him things that were inaccessible to ordinary consciousness. *The Red Book* contains passages laid out on the page like a play to better represent these dialogues.

In addition to dream analysis and active imagination, Jung experimented with a range of other techniques intended to access the unconscious and usually neglected aspects of the self. A person might, for example, draw, paint or sculpt. A mood or vague impression might be explored artistically, but with critical faculties temporarily muted or suspended. This kind of therapeutic art should be freely associative, like doodling, allowed to evolve with minimal conscious interference. Many artists aspire to a state described by the travel writer and poet Gérard de Nerval as the 'overflowing of dreams into real life'.

A particular class of freely associative drawings that became important to Jung were circular abstractions. He realised that the ones he had produced resembled mandalas (meditation aids associated with Tibetan Buddhism). Jung made a distinction between his conscious self and his greater *self*, his totality, and his mandala drawings could be understood as symbolic representations of the greater self. They can be used diagnostically. For example, inspection of a mandala might reveal asymmetries – evidence of lopsided development. A symmetrical mandala, in which elements are balanced, is indicative of ongoing successful individuation. It is an expression of unity, integration, the reconciliation of opposites.

Although Jung's recipe for personal development may seem esoteric, when reformulated for pragmatists it becomes readily apprehensible as common sense. The demands of career and family frequently lead to the neglect of certain aspects of the self in the first half of life. However, in the second half of life there may be many opportunities to develop and express those neglected aspects of the self. This process of recovery of neglected parts (feelings, intuitions, interests, wants) and subsequent integration can be accelerated by engagement with almost any activity that facilitates access to parts of the self that would otherwise remain divorced from the general totality of the person.

It is not uncommon for people to reach a point in life after which they start expressing a certain amount of regret for what might have been: 'I wish I'd studied drama instead of finance'; 'Why did I listen to my parents?'; 'If I hadn't married so early things would have been different.' Our decisions channel life along particular courses that must necessarily exclude alternatives. Obviously, you can't do everything. It is interesting that a whole genre of film and literature has evolved that explores alternative storylines that diverge after a single decision or event. The phrase 'Sliding Doors moment' (derived from the 1998 film) has become a proxy term for bifurcation points and the connotation that sometimes even trivial contingencies (for example, catching or missing a train) can have major consequences. The popularity of this genre is probably attributable to widespread self-recognition. We are all aware that our lives are shadowed by potential but unrealised surrogates – lives that could have been, but never were. A conspicuous feature of retirement is what appears to be an attempt to recover something of what was lost or sacrificed: painting, yoga classes, photography, walking, tennis, book clubs, voluntary work. From a Jungian perspective, post-retirement activities could be viewed as more than just pleasing occupations. They are, perhaps, the expression of a deep need to restore balance, to nourish the parts of the self that have wasted away through neglect. They can be understood as efforts to reclaim something of the person that might have been, but could not be, because 'getting on with life' usually requires a narrow and exclusive focus.

When Jung was in his fifties, he identified a phenomenon that he called synchronicity. Life is full of coincidences. For example, one might think of an old school friend while on holiday and then find them sitting in the foyer of one's hotel; one might dream of a Siamese cat and wake to find one sitting at the end of one's garden. Clearly, the first event (the thought or dream) does not cause the other (the appearance of the school friend or the cat). But they seem to be meaningfully related. Jung believed that many of life's coincidences are significant and not attributable to chance alone. He came to the highly speculative conclusion that certain coincidences were being 'influenced' by archetypes. Thus, many coincidences can be interpreted and understood as another form of unconscious communication. They can prompt reflection and add momentum to the individuation process. The philosopher and computer scientist Bernardo Kastrup has stressed that we should not think of archetypal influence as *causal* with respect to synchronicities. Jung supposed that he had discovered an entirely new *acausal* principle. Kastrup writes: 'The archetype is not a causal agency, but the *natural template* according to which both the human psyche and – if Jung is correct – the physical world *spontaneously* organize themselves.'

The idea that archetypes create confluences of mind and matter is reminiscent of magical thinking. Primitive societies, deluded patients and small children believe that thoughts and events are connected. Yet synchronicity, a concept that often keeps close company with the uncanny, aroused the curiosity of the world's pre-eminent scientists. Jung discussed synchronicity with Albert Einstein and Wolfgang Pauli – both winners of the Nobel Prize (in 1921 and 1945). Indeed, Pauli can almost be counted as one of Jung's collaborators. He suggested that synchronicity could be clarified by probabilistic mathematics, which prompted Jung to review his thinking about the nature of archetypes.

At the age of thirty, Pauli had a somewhat premature midlife crisis. He divorced, his mother committed suicide, he drank excessively, and his relationships with women were unsatisfactory. Even though his emotional state was deteriorating, he was still performing intellectually at the very highest level. Around this time, he proposed the existence of a new particle – the neutrino. Pauli arranged a consultation with Jung, who didn't accept him as a patient, and instead referred him on to one of his female pupils. Jung thought that if Pauli saw a young woman for therapy this would be helpful, given his problems relating to the opposite sex. Pauli attended therapy with Jung's pupil for five months, analysed his own dreams independently for three months, and finally found his way back to Jung who, after further discussion, agreed to treat him. Pauli's subsequent analysis with Jung lasted for two years and the outcome seems to have been very successful. About eight months later, the two men began what was to become an extensive correspondence.

Pauli was extraordinarily sympathetic to Jung's way of thinking, which encompassed the rational and the intuitive, the material and the spiritual. Although as a physicist he was, of course, an extremely rational man and his work explored the material world at its most fundamental level, he was also entirely open to the idea that there might be a greater reality than material reality, and that apprehension of this greater reality would very likely necessitate a different type of knowing, the kind of knowing associated with dreams, active imagination and acausal correspondences. Mind and matter might have a common 'metaphysical' ground, which could potentially explain synchronicity. Pauli was not religious, but he was 'spiritual' in the Jamesian sense of the word. He looked back with great affection to the seventeenth century, a time in which the 'magical-symbolical' and 'quantitative-mathematical' descriptions of the world coexisted.

Pauli believed that at its best western civilisation develops in a way that resembles Jungian individuation. In 'Science and Western Thought', he suggested that science and mysticism are complementary opposites (comparable to conscious and unconscious divisions of the mind). He wrote of 'the destiny of the occident continually to keep bringing into connection with each other these two fundamental attitudes, on the one hand the rational-critical, which seeks to understand, and on the other the mystic-irrational, which looks for the redeeming experience of oneness'. A failure to achieve wholeness is a potential threat to civilisation. The rational-critical, unchecked, divorced from the greater reality, succumbs to a potentially destructive *will to power*. This is an uncontroversial conclusion, given that we now live in a world in which various atomic and technology-driven apocalypses are considered almost inevitable. A civilisation that integrates its parts, like an integrated individual, is wiser.

It should be stressed that neither Jung nor Pauli were in any sense 'against' rationality or science. What they objected to was scientific tunnel vision and an incomplete view of reality. In his commentary on *The Secret of the Golden Flower*, Jung wrote: 'Science is the best tool of the Western mind and with it more doors can be opened than with bare hands. Thus it is part and parcel of our understanding and only clouds our insight when it lays claim to being the one and only way of comprehending.'

Jung's thoughts on individuation, integration and personal

growth have implications for how we address problems like depression and anxiety, especially in the second half of life, where they tend to manifest in particularly pernicious forms – for example, disappointment, regret, loss of purpose, and existential terror. He wrote – somewhat surprisingly for a psychotherapist – that the most significant problems of life are 'fundamentally insoluble'. However, there is still a way forward. If we cannot solve our most significant problems, then our only real option is to outgrow them. The inner journey of individuation, the integration of the person, can promote new, transformative perspectives. Reflecting on his clinical practice, Jung described how some patients did not resolve their psychological problems, but rather were lifted above them by raised consciousness. 'Some higher or wider interest arose on the person's horizon, and through this widening of his view, the insoluble problem lost its urgency. It was not solved logically on its own terms, but faded out in contrast to a new and stronger life-tendency.'

We have become accustomed to the idea that with the aid of psychotherapy or drugs unhappiness can be eradicated. And of course, where psychological symptoms *can* be successfully removed, they *should* be. But where distress is related to an aspect of existence that cannot be changed – the approach of death being the standard example – then Jung's alternative has obvious appeal. He offers us an encouraging image: 'This does not mean that the thunderstorm is robbed of its reality; it means that, instead of being in it, one is now above it.'

Jung's account of the individuation process is quite refined, and some might conclude that it is too refined (or abstract) to be truly practicable. So, to what extent can an interested and sufficiently motivated person follow Jung's prescriptions with the goal of becoming whole?

The British composer Sir Michael Tippett couldn't afford Jungian analysis in his thirties – Jung's notional turning point – so he decided he would undertake his own analysis. He reflected on his dreams, identified his inner divisions, and engaged in a profitable dialogue with his unconscious. Tippett subsequently flourished as a composer, and as he got older he managed to retain a youthful outlook and youthful qualities. Indeed, youthfulness was perhaps his defining characteristic. He was engaged with the politics and cultural issues of his time, and he claimed to be much more interested in the future than the past, even when he was in his nineties. His last great accomplishment was the opera *New Year*, a vital, energetic work that was cutting-edge thirty years ago and still feels very contemporary. It features a child psychologist, a Rastafarian, a dystopian town, a spaceship, time travel and a 'computer wizard'.

Self-analysis – as a practical means of achieving psychological adjustment in later life – was central to the work of Marion Milner, a gifted psychoanalyst who has regrettably become something of a historical footnote. Although it is true that many of her 'techniques' are much the same as those espoused by Jung, the fact that she gives special emphasis to self-exploration distinguishes her from her contemporaries. Psychoanalysis was (and still is), for most people, not only unaffordable but also geographically inaccessible. Milner became interested in devising what the psychosocial historian Emilia Halton-Hernandez has called an 'autobiographical cure'. That is, a form of do-it-yourself psychotherapy that anyone can attempt.

Milner was loosely connected with the Bloomsbury group and her first book, *A Life of One's Own* (originally published under the pen name Joanna Field), clearly alludes to Virginia Woolf's *A Room of One's Own*. She was once analysed by Donald Winnicott, who found her 'lovely' and 'tantalisingly unfathomable'. In 1943 he wrote to her and said: 'as I cannot eat you I shall probably want to choose from among the possibilities which leave life manageable as a going concern'. His reference to 'eating' is rather unexpected and sexual. Milner was also attracted to Winnicott, but this, of course, does not excuse him from what by today's standards would be considered unprofessional conduct.

Although Milner became a distinguished psychoanalyst, she always retained a degree of scepticism. Indeed, she could be accused, perhaps, of subverting psychoanalysis to serve her individualism. Consistent with Jungian theory, Milner started publishing her inward-looking self-help books when she was in her thirties. Her principal aim was to achieve greater ontological security – a more satisfactory sense of continuous selfhood.

Collectively, Milner's self-help strategies have in common with Jung's the objective of liberating unconscious material. She recommends keeping 'free associative' diaries (daily writing without censorship); self-dialogues; 'free associative' painting and drawing (which might involve, for example, allowing a realistic landscape to acquire fantastic elements); and noting recurrent themes and powerful emotions in dreams. For Milner, the recording of dreams offers a secondary opportunity for interpretation, because she was also interested in the spontaneous thoughts and feelings that enter consciousness when dreams are recalled. Milner believed that art – both creating art and reflecting on art – can open profitable channels of self-enquiry. She urges her readers to ask questions such as: What are the images that 'stick' in your mind and what might their persistence mean? Milner employs a compelling analogy to describe how her free associative writing could be used to trawl her own unconscious. It was, she said, like a net of words that entangled the shadowy and elusive aspects of her deeper self.

Milner found that the regular practice of her techniques resulted in 'answering activity', first described in her 1937 book *An Experiment in Leisure*: 'Just in so far as I held myself still and watched the flickering movements of the mind, trying to give them expression in words or drawings, just so far would I become aware of some answering activity, an activity that I can only describe as a knowing, yet a knowing that was nothing to do with me ... It seemed like something I could trust, something that knew better than I did where I was going.' This 'answering' can be understood as a close relative of Jung's sage-like visitor Philemon: the voice of hitherto unconscious wisdom.

It is of considerable interest that Milner identified two forms of attention: 'wide focus' and 'narrow focus' – the former giving her access to what she described as 'back-of-the-mind thoughts'. 'Wide focus' is perhaps a harbinger of the awakened awareness described by Lisa Miller (see chapter 3). The idea of integration also appears (albeit obliquely) in Milner's work, when she discusses 'bead memories' – memories of great personal significance. She talks of stringing such memories together. Her 'memorial necklace' functions as a metaphor for inner unity and wholeness.

Today, few people outside the psychoanalytic community have heard of Marion Milner, but she has exerted a subtle influence on modern reading habits. Many late twentieth-century and early twenty-first-century personal development titles – especially those written by women, for women – owe a debt to Milner. She is the grande dame of sophisticated self-help. The British Psychoanalytical Society houses a Marion Milner archive, and it contains many fan letters, correspondence from ordinary people who found her work inspiring.

The psychoanalyst and historian of psychoanalysis Brett Kahr became acquainted with Milner when he was a young postgraduate student. Even though she was in her mid-eighties at the time, Kahr discovered that Milner was still seeing patients, still interested in new developments in psychoanalysis, eager to continue publishing, and excellent company. She spoke in a 'soft but musical voice' and was so charming, so delightful, that after only brief acquaintance he had 'evidently fallen in love' with her.

Jung wasn't the only 'analyst' to consider psychological adjustment in later life. Erik Erikson was also interested in this area, although his approach was more closely aligned with the mainstream clinical thinking of his day. There are no archetypal figures or metaphysical dimensions to Erikson's psychology. Like Jung, Erikson believed that personal development proceeded throughout life, and he identified eight phases. His students dubbed this serial progression 'From womb to tomb'. Each of these phases is dominated by a dichotomous issue which can be resolved successfully – or not. For example, the first phase is about developing a basic sense of trust (or failing to do so and becoming mistrustful). Success strengthens the ego, whereas failure creates vulnerabilities. Moreover, the successful resolution of each stage results in the acquisition of what Erikson described as a virtue. The virtue that arises from successful negotiation of the first phase is 'hope'. For present purposes, we will consider only the eighth and final phase of Erikson's scheme in detail.

According to Erikson, the final phase of the life cycle is characterised by a polarity that he described as *integrity versus despair*, and the virtue associated with successful resolution of this polarity is wisdom. Erikson's notion of integrity has in common with Jung the ideas of cohesion, unity and inner harmony.

The final stage of life should, ideally, involve a kind of mental stocktaking: the individual should acknowledge personal accomplishments and failures, and accept the deficiencies of those with whom the individual has been closely associated (for example, parents and loved ones). Forgiveness is a form of self-healing. Memories are exhumed, blocked feelings are ventilated, and the tensions created by inner conflicts are released.

If an individual fails to achieve integration, they will

experience despair. The despairing individual, conscious of the proximity of death, is overwhelmed by regret – a sense of unfulfilled promise and disappointment because of unrealised goals. The accumulated bitterness and resentment of a lifetime will poison the 'soul'. Erikson's warning is blunt. Only 'integrity can balance the despair of the knowledge that a limited life is coming to a conscious conclusion, only such wholeness can transcend the petty disgust of feeling finished and passed by, and the despair of facing the period of relative helplessness which marks the end as it marked the beginning'.

Erikson's harsh dichotomy feels somewhat uncompromising; yet, the point he is making, however unpalatable, merits serious consideration because there doesn't seem to be much middle ground with respect to mental health in old age. Despair in later life tends towards extremity. When I saw distressed older patients for psychotherapy, the fact that they were *still* struggling with anxiety and depression – after a lifetime – always evoked a sharp pang of sympathy. Ageing is challenging enough without psychiatric complications. They were pitifully similar, heads bowed by a weight of regret. I should have done *this* – I should have done *that*. Why did I do *this* – why didn't I do *that*? Profound sadness, sudden eruptions of anger followed by tears, embarrassment after the expression of ineffectual rage. Erikson stresses that mental anguish is intensified by states of helplessness reminiscent of infancy. I have vivid recollections of my older patients having difficulty standing up at the end of sessions. Pained expressions as they pressed their palms on the arms of the chair to raise themselves – the sheer frustration of inhabiting a weak body that won't respond to instruction. 'What am I to do?' It was a desperate, rhetorical appeal, tacitly expressed when my eyes met theirs.

The idea that there is an essential task underlying psychological adjustment in later life is appealing because it is a singular objective. It obviates the need to pursue multiple objectives, because, by pursuing this single, fundamental objective, multiple and lesser objectives are effortlessly accomplished. There is no need to combat depression; its alleviation will be one of many incidental benefits or by-products of realising the single, fundamental objective. This is what Jung meant by 'outgrowing' problems. As a result of personal growth, Stoic truths – the traditional recourse of those faced with existential anxiety – will cease to be merely intellectual exercises and become owned, felt truths.

For Jung, the essential task in later life is individuation leading to wholeness. Erikson also believed that becoming an integrated whole was necessary in the very final stage of life, and that failure to accomplish this would result in despair. Before Jung and Erikson, William James came to a similar conclusion; unity is associated with resilience and wisdom. These great thinkers were all building on the most basic finding of psychotherapy. Divisions within the self tend to be associated with distress, inner conflict and confusion, and unity is associated with mental health. Traumas fragment the self; therapy reassembles the pieces into a whole. The general notion of integration is so fundamental to psychology that it has appeared repeatedly and in different forms in the work of many major psychologists and psychotherapists. Sometimes an integrative concept appears in very unlikely places. For example, the highly influential French psychiatrist and psychoanalyst Jacques Lacan, whose extremely abstract revisions of Freudian theory ultimately reject notions of authentic selfhood, still found it necessary to introduce an integrative concept into his system of thought. He described three modes of experiencing the world – Imaginary, Real and Symbolic – that are tied together in the form of (what he described as) a 'Borromean knot' (three interlinked hoops). Severing one hoop will cause the other two hoops to separate.

The Imaginary, Real and Symbolic operate together – in other words, they are integrated – and if one of these orders of experience becomes 'separated' from the others, the knot 'unravels'. This was how Lacan explained psychosis.

Jung's individuation process is psychological and the whole that emerges is a hypothetical construct. It cannot be seen or weighed. For those raised in the western materialist tradition, hypothetical constructs are often perceived as suspect entities, because they are not 'real'. From a philosophical point of view, this is a very questionable assertion. Opinions vary concerning what should or shouldn't be considered real. Nevertheless, it is understandable that a materialist might be sceptical, and that such a sceptic might be reassured if correspondences can be found that link psychological ideas and the brain. After all, the phrase we use to imply that something is unreal is 'all in the mind'. The mind is strongly associated with the illusory, and materialism demands fixed anchor points. In Jung's time, it was impossible to connect his psychology with the brain. Not enough was known. Today, however, major advances in technology and brain science have made it possible to generate plausible hypotheses concerning the biological substrates of otherwise quite abstract ideas – such as integration – which hitherto suffered from being somewhat vague and untethered from material reality. How concepts such as integration and wholeness can be mapped on to the brain will be the subject of the next chapter.

6

Circuits in Conversation: The Integrated Brain

Integrate your brain

I have a very distinct memory of undertaking my first neuropsychological assessment. It was almost forty years ago. I was a clinical psychology student and exceedingly keen. I can remember sitting in a rather dilapidated hospital consulting room with grubby paintwork and dirty windows. A desk was positioned against one of the walls and its wood-laminate surface was covered in scratches. The atmosphere was rather gloomy. Outside, the sky was typical of London in autumn: low, grey, and shedding the kind of paradoxical luminescence that seems to make everything look darker rather than lighter. I set out my test materials and waited for my patient.

There was a knock on the door and a nurse appeared accompanied by a gangly man with thinning hair and a stubbly chin. He wore glasses with heavy frames and thick lenses and his loose dressing gown flapped open revealing plain white pyjamas. The nurse introduced me to Ralph, who shook my hand, before making a slow, awkward descent into the chair next to mine. He was probably in his early to mid-seventies. As I was considerably younger at that time, he seemed ancient to me – teetering on the edge of the void. The nurse retreated from the room, closing the door softly behind her, and Ralph and I sat together, facing each other, chatting.

Ralph was from a working-class background, and he had left school without qualifications. He appeared relaxed, and although his speech was effortful, his manner was friendly. When I smiled to encourage him, he smiled too, and sometimes he produced hearty gusts of laughter. It occurred to me that he was, perhaps, a little too relaxed – an impression that was reinforced by the frequency with which his hand squeezed his genitals through the cotton of his pyjamas. Ralph had been visited a few times by one of my female colleagues, and when I mentioned her, something very strange happened. Ralph's face crumpled into an expression that suggested agony, total despair, and he cried out: 'I love Miriam, I love her – I *love* her!' His eyes welled up and tears began to stream down his cheeks. I tried to comfort him with some anodyne words, and I offered him a sympathetic smile. Almost immediately, his face began to brighten, and when I intensified my smile, his smile widened and a few seconds later he was laughing again.

I administered several neuropsychological tests and Ralph's general performance was quite good given his age and education; however, he performed very badly on a test designed to assess mental flexibility. Once he had chosen a particular problem-solving strategy, he couldn't generate alternatives. Telling him that his strategy was no longer working had absolutely no effect on his behaviour.

Ralph was suffering from frontal lobe dementia and during our short time together he displayed many of the key symptoms:

inappropriate social behaviour, loss of inhibition, hesitant speech, stiff movements, extreme emotional volatility and difficulty shifting mental set. There are many more symptoms associated with frontal lobe dementia, and I am simply describing those that Ralph exhibited over a period of approximately two hours.

The brain is not an amorphous lump of gelatinous matter in the skull. It is a collection of structures and neural circuits that support specific or more usually multiple functions. It is a finely coordinated whole. Patients who suffer from neurodegenerative diseases, brain injuries, or both, are extreme examples of what happens when the brain ceases to function as an integrated whole; however, undamaged brains must also show varying degrees of neural integration along a normative spectrum.

The brain is integrated vertically and horizontally. Vertical integration refers to the interrelationship between the cortex (the outer layer of the brain) and the subcortex (the structures within the brain). Horizontal integration refers to the quantity and quality of information that is exchanged between the left and right hemispheres of the brain. There is also a third axis – front to back – but this polarity has generated less speculation among theorists interested in integration.

Ralph was a good example of what happens when the brain 'dis-integrates' and becomes 'unbalanced'. The cortex mediates 'higher' mental functions (like self-control and thinking) and subcortical structures are associated with 'lower' aspects of mental life (for example, sexual impulses and emotion). This is an over-simplification, but it is serviceable and broadly accurate. Ralph's atrophied frontal lobes were unable to regulate his emotions, which is why he oscillated between crying and laughing. He was evidently 'unstable'; however, his lack of mental equilibrium was caused directly by a problem with his brain. Ideas such as integration, holistic functioning and 'balance' are not abstractions. They are underwritten by material reality.

In a sense, the goal of Freudian psychoanalysis is improved vertical integration. The higher and lower divisions of the mind are brought into optimal relationship. Fundamental desires are managed more effectively, thus dispensing with the need for excessive repression, and the ego is then able to engage more directly with reality (and particularly with social reality). Ordinarily, impulses and images arising from the unconscious are beneficial. For example, they motivate the formation of intimate relationships and inspire creativity. However, the unfettered release of instinctual 'energies' could lead to inappropriate behaviour, and too much unconscious material invading consciousness might cause confusion. Freud supposed that something like a censor must operate in the brain, to keep the lower division in check and maintain 'balance'.

The most striking division in the brain, the division that almost anyone will notice if they are shown a photograph or a model of the brain, is the longitudinal fissure – a groove, from front to back, that appears to split the brain into two symmetrical halves. It is an obvious potential fault-line along which a mind might break apart. The two hemispheres are in fact connected in several places, but the principal connection is a wide tract of nerves called the corpus callosum. All brains, even those belonging to very basic creatures, are divided, which suggests that from an evolutionary point of view a divided brain must possess adaptive properties. There is now a vast body of research showing that the hemispheres of the brain are specialised, and it is accepted that the nature of this specialisation has evolutionary significance. Animals are more likely to survive if they possess two forms of attention: focused attention, which can be trained on food, and a much wider form of attention, which can be used to detect predators. These two forms of attention are supported by the left and right hemispheres respectively. In humans, this fundamental difference has served as a catalyst for an ongoing process of much more complex bilateral differentiation.

During the 1970s and 1980s, hemispheric specialisation became a pet topic of 'pop psychologists' who classified individuals as 'left brain' or 'right brain' according to whether they were scientific and language-based thinkers or artistic and image-based thinkers. Although this distinction is based on very respectable research findings, it is crude and misrepresents a much more fascinating and complicated reality. It would be impossible to do justice to these complexities without embarking on a lengthy diversion; however, a few key differences are listed here to give the reader a flavour of the range and scope of bilateral specialisation. The left hemisphere, in addition to supporting focal attention, supports language, analytic thinking (breaking things down into parts) and representing what is already known or fixed, and its operations are broadly conscious. The right hemisphere, in addition to supporting wide, vigilant attention, supports imagery, holistic thinking (that is, seeing how things are related and contextualised), the representation of what is new or fluid (for example, events occurring over time), narrative, metaphor, humour, irony, empathy, the total body image, melancholy, and all the elements of music (with the exception of rhythm). The right hemisphere is also strongly associated with the unconscious and unconscious processes (for example, intuition). If one had to reduce these complexities to a simple dichotomy that improves on those favoured by pop psychologists, it would be to suggest that the primary function of the left hemisphere is to manipulate the world, whereas the primary function of the right hemisphere is to understand the world and invest it with meaning.

The brain is 'wired' to the body contralaterally. Therefore, the left hemisphere controls the right hand, and the right hemisphere controls the left hand. Around 90 per cent of people in the West are right-handed, and almost all of them have their language centres located in the left hemisphere. The remaining 10 per cent, or thereabouts, are left-handed and have either reversed hemispheres or some idiosyncratic rearrangement of functions across both hemispheres. Approximately three quarters of left-handed people still have their language centres located in the left hemisphere. Even though brain-wiring varies in the general population, there is clearly a standard pattern or organisation common to the vast majority.

Hemispheres communicate continuously, although it should be noted that the corpus callosum *inhibits* the exchange of information between the hemispheres more than it facilitates the exchange of information. Presumably, this is because hemispheric 'separation' must be protected for specialisation to be optimally adaptive. All functions performed by one hemisphere can be performed by the contralateral hemisphere – although perhaps not as well if the contralateral hemisphere is non-dominant. For example, right-handed people can write with their left hand, but with considerable difficulty and not very well. When a specialised area is activated in one hemisphere the corresponding area in the contralateral hemisphere is briefly 'excited' and subsequently inhibited. Although both hemispheres are involved in almost everything we do, there are processing asymmetries, which means that at any single point in time, it is reasonable to suggest that either the left or right hemisphere is biasing how we are experiencing and engaging with the world. We can also assume that biases within the processing system will influence which hemisphere determines the nature of experience over more extended periods of time. This is perhaps the kernel of truth around which popular psychology elaborated notions of left and right brain personality types. But once again, it should be stressed, a simple and absolute division between the hemispheres is not consistent with current knowledge concerning how the brain works.

In the 1960s, studies of patients who had had their corpus callosum surgically severed or removed to treat severe epilepsy demonstrated that the two hemispheres of the brain can function independently. What we think of as consciousness is really a form of 'double consciousness'. The surgeon who undertook these operations, Roger Sperry, received the Nobel Prize for his contributions to physiological medicine in 1981, and Sperry's collaborator, the cognitive neuroscientist Michael Gazzaniga (who undertook much of the laboratory research on 'split-brain' patients), became a figure of considerable renown.

If an image of an object is displayed in the left visual field of a split-brain patient, and relayed to the non-speaking right hemisphere only, he or she will not be able to name the object; however, he or she will be capable of identifying the concealed object by feeling it with the left hand – which is controlled by the right hemisphere. This paradigm has been used to explore the phenomenon of simultaneously knowing and not knowing (see chapter 3). For example, something frightening can be shown to the mute right hemisphere and the experimental subject might deny that they have seen anything. Yet, at the same time, he or she might then report feeling uneasy and attribute these feelings to other causes (such as a feature of the room or the experimenter). Some split-brain patients develop so-called 'alien hand' or 'Dr Strangelove syndrome', although it can also develop in patients who have naturally occurring lesions in the corpus callosum (and other specific brain areas). In Stanley Kubrick's film, *Dr Strangelove*, the protagonist is constantly stopping his right hand from performing a Nazi salute with his left hand. This comic device dramatises the defining feature of alien hand syndrome: involuntary but *purposive* hand movements. The alien hand has its own agenda. One patient reported that as soon as her right hand selected one TV channel, her rebellious left hand would choose another. Patients often chastise their wayward hand and address it like a separate personality.

Split-brain research has profound implications. It proves that selves can be divided and that these divisions have a neurobiological basis. As such, the split-brain literature represents a powerful refutation of those critics who have argued against the divisibility of the person, a notion that they allege serves merely as a metaphor and has no physical reality (see Preface).

After an initial wave of excitement, interest in hemispheric asymmetry plateaued and then slowly dwindled. This was partly due to the accumulation of new evidence that seemed inconsistent with existing knowledge about which hemisphere performed what functions. Unfortunately, the discovery of an increasingly nuanced relationship between the hemispheres led to a degree of frustration and some concluded that perhaps the basic notion of hemispheric specialisation wasn't as robust as early findings had suggested. However, over the last decade or so there has been a revival of interest in hemispheric specialisation (across disciplines and among general readers), largely due to Iain McGilchrist, a psychiatrist with experience in neuroimaging research whose academic book *The Master and His Emissary* became a surprise best-seller. McGilchrist has argued that hemispheric specialisation is not only fundamental to our understanding of what it means to be human, it is also a determinant of cultural trends and social evolution. His arguments were subsequently developed in the epic two-volume work *The Matter With Things*, which was published in 2021. If human beings have specialised hemispheres that bias attention and shape the quality of experience, clearly this will be hugely consequential. Yet, curiously, prior to the publication of *The Master and His Emissary* it seems that the ramifications of hemispheric asymmetry, not only for the individual but also society and culture, were given scant consideration.

The contrasting perspectives of the left and right hemispheres are reflected in the writings of numerous philosophers, who identify two modes of being or engagement, characterised as either analytic or holistic. For example, Nietzsche identified two artistic drives, which he called the Apollonian and Dionysian; the first tends towards order and clarity, the second towards intuition and wholeness. None of these 'dichotomies' (and there are many) map precisely on to the processing characteristics of the hemispheres, but they do indicate that a relatively large number of significant thinkers have identified a core psychological 'duality' that manifests across a range of human activities.

McGilchrist has argued that the two hemispheres cooperate in the following way. We see the world as a totality (predominantly with the right hemisphere). Specific features are subsequently analysed (by the left hemisphere). Then, the left hemisphere passes information back to the right hemisphere where it is contextualised. The degree to which the two hemispheres cooperate successfully will vary from person to person; however, the more the two hemispheres cooperate, the more likely it is that the person will be functioning at an optimal level. When information exchange is obstructed or halted, which happens dramatically when individuals suffer from brain disease or brain damage, the consequences (emotional, intellectual, perceptual) can be profoundly debilitating.

It should be noted that the two hemispheres are not equal partners. The right hemisphere possesses a much larger spread of competencies; however, optimal functioning is only possible if the right and left hemispheres cooperate in a way that is comparable to the relationship between a master (the right hemisphere) and a loyal emissary (the left hemisphere). McGilchrist offers a cautionary fable to illustrate the cost of disturbing this optimal power relationship. There was once a selfless spiritual master who ruled a small but prosperous domain. As the domain expanded it became increasingly necessary for the master to dispatch his emissaries to remote locations to ensure the safety of citizens. The master could not be personally present everywhere, and besides, it was neither requisite nor desirable for him to become 'involved' with local concerns. Naturally, the success of the domain was predicated on trust. In due course, the most intelligent and ambitious emissary began plotting to overthrow the master; he construed the master's wise forbearance as weakness, he connived to accumulate wealth, and he cultivated influence. Eventually, the master was usurped, and the emissary ruled as a tyrant – until the domain could no longer prosper under his restrictive autocracy and it collapsed in ruins.

When the proper relationship between right and left hemispheres is disturbed, the most likely outcome is a distorted and incomplete world view, dominated by a left hemisphere that has ceased to recognise its primary purpose and limitations. The circuitry of the left hemisphere is more 'self-contained' than the right hemisphere. This suggests that the left hemisphere is more 'self-referential' than the right hemisphere, more inclined towards 'creating' its own world – a focused and orderly world, but one that is also inflexible and somewhat lifeless. Michael Gazzaniga described the left hemisphere as the 'interpreter'. It explains the world using words. However, the more we rely on this interpretation, the more 'unspoken' aspects of experience – the intuitive, the mystical – are dismissed. Expressed differently, increasing reliance on the left hemisphere creates a division (and blind spots) in the totality of selfhood.

A good example of self-referential, left hemispheric thinking is post-structuralism. Philosophers such as Jacques Derrida deconstructed texts to the extent that meaning becomes elusive and vaporous. The American writer Jonathan Rosen has amusingly described the impact of Derrida's ideas on the intellectual life of American universities and the prevalence of voguish student discussions in the 1960s and 1970s concerning the properties of language and the impossibility of knowing. Rosen writes: 'As a result of this central semiotic problem, of which I had been unaware, there would always be an unbridgeable distance between the word "glass," for example, and the transparent receptacle for liquid in your hand arbitrarily *called* a glass. This seemed like the sort of problem that could be overcome just by asking for a glass of water, but I had never studied philosophy.' Rosen's wry observation underscores the fact that unrestrained analysis, divorced from the felt and the intuitive, can lead to nonsensical accounts of the world that seem to have little bearing on how we experience it. It is interesting that in instances where deconstructionism has influenced psychoanalytic writing, somewhat inevitably, authors typically conclude that selves do not exist. Which begs the question: who was it then that reached this conclusion?

McGilchrist's account of hemispheric cooperation complements psychological frameworks that stress the importance of integration for well-being. Indeed, the idea that the intuitive mind (associated with the right hemisphere) should be in close conversation with the analytic mind (the left hemisphere) resonates with Jung's writings on the individuation process. The left hemisphere, which supports language and focused attention, is associated with consciousness; however, the right hemisphere, which supports many aspects of pre-conscious processing (for example, the processing of social information, emotionally salient information, and the detection of peripheral stimuli), is associated with the unconscious. Brain scans and electroencephalographic recordings show that dreaming, one of Jung's cardinal forms of unconscious communication, is a predominantly right hemispheric phenomenon. The right hemisphere supports 'metaphor', which explains, perhaps, why dreams favour symbolic representations over literal representations. Jung also emphasised the importance of integrating opposites in personal development. Again, although one cannot map aspects of Jungian psychology precisely on to the processing characteristics of the two hemispheres, the general idea of a creative reconciliation of 'opposites' is common to both Jung's analytical psychology and McGilchrist's account of optimal hemispheric cooperation.

McGilchrist's concise summary of the individuation process emphasises correspondences between Jungian theory and his own hemispheric hypothesis: 'For him [Jung], the self is the product of psychic integration over time and unites conscious and unconscious processes, while the ego is that part of the self identified with the conscious will, and which, though necessary in the early stages of development in order to anchor the growing individual in the world, comes to be transcended in the process of spiritual growth. In being transcended it is not abolished, but changes its nature by being taken up into a new whole where its role is altered.' Essentially, the 'ego' becomes a good servant.

The right hemisphere is associated with emotions in general; however, McGilchrist has pointed out that it has a particular 'tendency to melancholy'. It is more 'in touch' (than the left hemisphere) with the social universe, and the natural sympathy arising from this strong connection will inevitably engender a certain amount of sadness. William James asserted that melancholy 'constitutes an essential moment in every complete religious evolution'. Moreover, it will be recalled that Abraham Maslow's 'transcenders' – individuals who have reached the summit of personal development – reported a comparable 'tendency to melancholy' that can be understood as an aspect of spirituality rather than a symptom of psychopathology.

McGilchrist has suggested that the way we attend to the world, which is influenced by differing levels of hemispheric involvement, will determine the kind of world that we bring into being. Cultural trends will reflect the degree to which the world is being attended to by one or other of the hemispheres. It should be stressed that the cultural effects of hemispheric asymmetry – for example, the shift from Romanticism (predominantly right hemisphere) to modernism (predominantly left hemisphere) – are not caused by changes in the brain, but rather a change in how the brain is being 'used'. McGilchrist offers the analogy of tuning a radio to clarify this point: 'to begin with you try different channels, but after a while you begin to tune into only one. The other channels are still there – it's just that you are no longer listening to them.' McGilchrist asserts that we currently live in a world in which the emissary has unseated the master: 'An increasingly mechanistic, fragmented, decontextualised world, marked by unwarranted optimism mixed with paranoia and a feeling of emptiness . . . reflecting, I believe, the unopposed action of a dysfunctional left hemisphere.' We have *manipulated* the world, creating ideal conditions for extinction, while somehow maintaining a hollow, defensive confidence which is comprehensively betrayed by a pervasive sense of meaninglessness.

McGilchrist's analysis has much in common with that of Jung and Pauli (chapter 5). The reader is reminded of Pauli's conviction that science and mysticism are complementary opposites, and that neglect of one, at the expense of the other, represents a threat to civilisation. He wasn't the only great scientist to recognise the value of this kind of holism. When Einstein was asked if he had any regrets, he replied: 'I wish I had read more of the mystics earlier in my life.' The analytic faculty is extremely powerful – indispensable, in fact – but it can easily become detached, autonomous, prepotent, and if unchecked, self-destructive.

Perhaps the most comprehensive account of neural integration and its relationship to well-being has evolved from an ongoing programme of research conducted by Daniel Siegel, a clinical professor of psychiatry at the UCLA School of Medicine. In addition to horizontal and vertical integration, Siegel also acknowledges the importance of integrating other aspects of the person that have a neural basis, such as memory. Although, for Siegel, the concept of integration is relevant to almost every dimension of being and selfhood. For example, when the mind and body are integrated, the mind can make better use of information supplied by the body. We benefit when we attend to what our bodies are trying to tell us. One is reminded of Nietzsche's observation that 'bodies' are often wiser than 'people' (see chapter 3). Our sense of self is strengthened by integrated narratives (the stories we tell ourselves about ourselves) and social integration has incalculable benefits for a social animal.

The brain is 'differentiated' and possesses specialised functions; however, Siegel suggests that 'when we focus our attention in specific ways, we create neural firing patterns that permit previously separated areas to become linked and integrated'. In effect, we have the power to rewire our brains.

Siegel finds support for his integrative neuroscience in the mathematics of non-linear complex systems. Integrated complex systems are flexible, adaptive, coherent, energised and stable. These characteristics can be regarded as mathematical analogues of human attributes. For example, coherence – according to Siegel – corresponds with narrative coherence. An integrated complex system is harmonious; however, when a complex system is not harmonious, the two most likely outcomes are either chaos or rigidity. Siegel has argued that almost all psychiatric diagnoses can be understood as an example of chaos, rigidity, or a combination of the two. Erikson proposed that in later life a failure to integrate will result in despair. It is noteworthy that despair in old age commonly manifests as existential panic, an emotionally *chaotic* state, or alternatively, various forms of paralysis – fixed habits, stasis, emptiness – emotionally frozen or *rigid* states.

As successful integration across multiple domains progresses, a 'new dimension' of interconnection – 'transpiration' (or 'breathing across') – begins to emerge. This is associated with a growing awareness of being 'part of a much larger whole'. Once again, there are obvious parallels with Maslow and the emergence of 'transcendence'.

Siegel suggests that the key to achieving integration is the cultivation and deployment of a form of attention – 'mindsight' – that is open and objective. 'Openness' is a state of non-prejudicial receptivity, and 'objectivity' is an attitude of 'detachment'. This class of meta-awareness clearly overlaps with the Buddhist meditation practice of mindfulness. Siegel writes that with 'reflection we can observe ourselves with openness and objectivity. We can sense the flood of out-of-control emotions as a mere part of the story of who we are. We gain the crucial capacity to deal with an intense emotion without becoming lost in it.' Siegel adds clarity to the standard 'guidelines' for practising mindfulness by identifying four domains of attentional deployment. We can become aware of what we experience through our senses, the inward sense of our body, our minds (our thoughts, feelings, memories) and our connections (especially our social relationships). In practical terms, the outcome of deploying open and objective attention in these domains is inner calm and 'presence'. We inhabit the moment more fully.

Although Siegel's approach is rooted in mathematical formulations and neuroscience, the reader will surely recognise what by now has become a familiar and recurring idea. Attention must be directed inwards to heal divisions within the self, and integration yields benefits such as connectedness and, ultimately, wisdom. We have not strayed too far from Dante's dark wood or Campbell's monomyth. And perhaps it is not too fanciful to suggest that embarking on Jungian explorations of inner space might, over time, 'rewire' the brain. Siegel asserts that 'experience creates the repeated neural firing that can lead to gene expression, protein production, and changes in both the genetic regulation of neurons and the structural connections in the brain. By harnessing the power of awareness to strategically stimulate the brain's firing, mindsight enables us to voluntarily change a firing pattern that was laid down involuntarily.'

Psychopharmacological research has also revealed a close relationship between well-being and neural integration. In chapter 4, reference was made to clinical outcome studies showing that psychedelic drugs can produce swift improvements in existential anxiety and a range of psychiatric conditions. One of the ways that psychedelics alter consciousness is by disrupting the default mode network – the biological substrate of the everyday self; however, psychedelics also increase neural connectivity. Magnetoencephalography can be employed to produce 'maps' of electrical activity in the brain, and when maps of the normal waking brain are compared with maps of the brain under the influence of psilocybin, a critical difference is self-evident. In normal waking consciousness, the various networks of the brain are relatively self-contained; however, the picture that emerges under the influence of psychedelics is one of massively increased interconnectivity. More circuits and more *varied* circuits are exchanging information. Clearly, there must be a limit beyond which integration is no longer helpful. If every circuit were to communicate with every other circuit in the brain the outcome would be undifferentiated sensory and semantic 'noise'. Similarly, if the contents of the unconscious mind were to flood the conscious mind, the experience would be much the same as a psychotic episode. Even Jung acknowledged that his hallucinatory encounters with archetypal figures were uncomfortably redolent of psychosis. Nevertheless, magnetoencephalographic evidence strongly suggests that in addition to ongoing, optimal neural integration, bursts of intense and temporary neural integration can produce lasting psychological and 'spiritual' benefits.

We can 'attend' to our inner world – 'listen' to our bodies – and 'register' liminal communications from the unconscious. This will increase connectivity in the brain, which will then make further attending, listening and registering increasingly automatic. The result will be 'raised consciousness', or at least intermittent episodes of raised consciousness, which will engender feelings of connectedness, purpose and meaning. Once established, a virtuous circle of mutual influence between mind and body will continue indefinitely, enriching experience and endowing the individual with the mental outlook that we associate with wisdom.

Not so long ago, this account of personal development would have been considered nonsensical. Brains were thought to have a finite number of cells located in circuits that could only perform specific functions. There were always dissenters, of course. For example, in the 1950s, the psychologist Karl Lashley suggested that if one part of the brain is damaged, another part can take over. It is now accepted that the brain *can* reorganise – a characteristic known as 'neuroplasticity'. The brain can even grow new nerve cells – 'neurogenesis'. Although it is true that neuroplasticity decreases with age, the brain always retains some 'equipotentiality'.

An extraordinary discovery was made in the 1980s: individuals who, having shown no signs of cognitive decline in old age, were found (at autopsy) to have biological markers associated with advanced dementia. Such individuals should have been severely impaired in their final years, but in fact they functioned normally. This was (and still is) extremely puzzling. After these results were first published, neuroscientists began referring to the concept of 'cognitive reserve' – a theoretical reserve of functionality that can be created (and protected) when brains 'improvise' and recruit alternative circuits and pathways to compensate for those that have been damaged.

Dementia can be viewed as a condition characterised by deep divisions in the person – divisions that are so deep, the 'whole' cannot hold together and consequently 'falls apart'. This process of 'dis-integration' can be so extreme that in the end all that remains of the person are some residual long-established habits, some isolated memories and an attenuated consciousness. Perhaps a well-integrated brain – a brain in which a broad range of circuits are in constant conversation – is also a more flexible brain, a brain more likely to be rich in 'cognitive reserve', a brain that will 'hold together', even as the cortex shrinks, and abnormal proteins begin to cluster between nerve cells. I am not suggesting that integrative psychological practices are a cure for dementia. However, most respected medical authorities *do* recommend 'protective' activities, and 'intellectual stimulation' always features among them. It is conceivable that the open and objective deployment of attention or the frequent practice of 'active imagination' could be examples of a special class of stimulation – a class that is potentially more effective as a means of preserving a fully functioning totality of self than the current gold-standard recommendations of learning a language or a musical instrument.

When Jung started conversing with archetypal figures, perhaps he was doing a great deal more than just daydreaming. Perhaps he was stitching the conscious and unconscious divisions of his mind together; binding the left and right hemispheres; interlacing his cortex with subcortical structures. Perhaps he was simultaneously ensuring not only the integrity of his mind but the integrity and flexibility of his brain. And perhaps this is the reason why he was eventually able to declare, with decisive optimism, that the greatest potential for growth and self-realisation exists in the second half of life.

He makes ageing and getting old sound like something everyone should look forward to. A call to adventure.

7

Shadowlands: Negotiating Obstacles

Know your shadow

In so-called primitive cultures, there is an appreciation that wisdom comes at a cost. The inner journey is perilous. Encounters with ancestors and animal spirits can end in delirium and madness. An unlucky voyager might never come back.

Shamans commune with the numinous and are afforded insights into the deeper nature of reality. However, they also have another role: they often act as guides; they initiate, they oversee and protect aspirants who are participating in rites of passage. Modern psychedelic therapists have adopted the same model because it is self-evidently a good idea. Patients who are given LSD or psilocybin are not left alone in a room while their default mode networks shut down and the products of pre-conscious processing rise into awareness. They embark on their 'journey' with a psychotherapist present, someone who can help them if they veer off course and find themselves stumbling through the nightmare landscape of a 'bad trip'.

The mythopoetic trope of a journey accompanied by a guide

is common to many cultures. The poetic zenith of this tradition in western literature is, of course, Dante's *Inferno*. Dante needed Virgil by his side because hell is a dangerous place. And so is the unconscious.

In Joseph Campbell's monomyth, after the 'hero' – that is, me or you – responds to 'the call' and crosses the 'threshold', he or she is tested by a series of trials. Campbell points out that this section of any mythological narrative is usually the most exciting. Characters must cross abysses, find their way out of labyrinths, and escape confinements. They must outwit witches and creep past sleeping dragons. Campbell says: 'There can be no question: the psychological dangers through which earlier generations were guided by the symbols and spiritual exercises of their mythological and religious inheritance, we today (in so far as we are unbelievers, or, if believers, in so far as our inherited beliefs fail to represent the real problems of contemporary life) must face alone, or, at best, with only tentative, impromptu, and not often very effective guidance.'

In most modern accounts of personal development, there is a strong emphasis on the positive. Various routes to happiness – or even enlightenment – are signposted, and there is hardly any consideration of pitfalls, perils or unintended consequences. Campbell's studies of comparative mythology suggest that many cultures acknowledge that the route to happiness often passes through treacherous territory. Jung's experience as a psychotherapist aligned his thinking closely with 'ancient wisdom'. Although the individuation process can heal inner division, integrate the person and engender well-being, it can also be hazardous. The darker aspects of human nature, slumbering in the unconscious, can become empowered and seize control. What we have then is an outcome that resembles demonic possession.

Jung's summary term for the dark side of human nature is the 'shadow': 'the "negative" side of the personality, the sum of all those unpleasant qualities we like to hide, together with the insufficiently developed functions and the contents of the personal unconscious'. This negative aspect of the person can be organised by an archetype and personified. For example, in the dreams of Europeans, the shadow often takes the form of beings who are alien or 'primitive'. Jung claimed that identifying the shadow – or at least, the repressed, negative content of the personal unconscious – is one of the first tasks of psychotherapy. And naturally, the shadow is also encountered when people embark on their inner journeys.

According to Jung, we should not view the shadow as a 'medical' problem. There is no 'cure'. The shadow is part of who we are; it isn't something that we can simply eliminate or exorcise using psychotherapy. We all have a dark side, because we are human, and we must work with it, or around it. This is eminently practical advice because there really is no alternative. Even saints admit to possessing undesirable characteristics. Most of the stains on our souls are indelible.

Jung's account of the shadow is complicated by an additional qualification. The shadow isn't *wholly* bad. We can also think of it more neutrally as 'inferior' and more forgivingly as 'awkward'. We can even think of it as possessing childish qualities that can be enriching. An old person with a mischievous twinkle in the eye is not usually reprimanded for being immature. 'Loveable rogues' have become a staple in world literature because their bad behaviour has redeeming qualities; they amuse us in the same way that cheeky children can sometimes amuse us.

Knowledge of the shadow is essential self-knowledge; however, our natural tendency is to deny or repress our negative attributes, which makes acquiring self-knowledge of this kind extremely difficult. If our 'badness' is separated from our totality by denial and repression, our refusal to recognise our own flaws may create our most substantial inner division. Typically, we project on to others those things we resist acknowledging about ourselves. If you abhor arrogance, your shadow will be self-important; if you hate liars, your shadow will be duplicitous. Our dislike of others signals where work is required, where we must be brutally honest and make challenging accommodations.

Jung applied this principle to global politics. In *The Undiscovered Self*, published in 1957, he saw parallels between the iron curtain, which then divided the world, and a 'boundary line' of 'barbed wire' running through 'the psyche of modern man'. East and West project their worst attributes on to each other: 'the normal individual, like the neurotic, sees his shadow in his neighbour or in the man beyond the great divide. It has even become a political and social duty to apostrophize the capitalism of the one and the communism of the other as the very devil, so as to fascinate the outward eye and prevent it from looking within.' Global politics hasn't changed very much since the 1950s: accusations, counter accusations and hypocrisy are still commonplace. Today, the general atmosphere of suspicion and paranoia is even more pervasive because of social media. Countless digital lines of metaphorical barbed wire have been laid across cyberspace, allowing millions to take up increasingly hostile, extreme and largely hypocritical positions. It is telling that those who defend their own rights and freedoms most aggressively are usually the same people who are keen to 'cancel' or silence others who express different views.

Projection is an unconscious defence, but it can be justified with post-hoc rationalisations: I am the victim of your offensive world view, victims are good, therefore I am good, you are bad, and it is reasonable for me to insult you and deny your right to free speech. Social media posts, particularly encouraged by an inciting herd, reveal even darker motivations. Calls for humiliation, retribution – punishment. Hypocrisy is a convenient haven for sadists.

Self-knowledge leads to self-acceptance, and self-acceptance obviates the need to style others 'evil'. This does not mean that there is no such thing as objectively 'bad' behaviour, and that morality is always relative. The Taliban's decision to ban women from speaking in public is incontrovertibly wrong. When we accuse those with whom we disagree of being like the Taliban, in all probability we are trying to deny the existence of our very own inner Taliban. Our extremity suggests that when, in solitude and silence, we are obliged to lock eyes with ourselves in a mirror, we will feel discomfited. We might even prefer to look away.

Accepting one's dark side might seem incidental to the grand, overarching project of individuation, but Jung asserted that the task of accommodating the shadow was among the most significant psychological problems to engage his attention. If the object of individuation is the creation of a harmonious totality, then achieving some form of rapprochement between 'good' and 'bad' will be self-evidently challenging because they are such strong (indeed, almost repulsive) opposites.

Coming to terms with one's shadow is highly relevant to psychological adjustment in later life, because – as William James observed – one has had more time to accumulate failures, blunders and misdeeds. There is more to look back on with regret. Guilt and shame are not uncommon in old age. We can repress, or deny, but such defences are difficult to maintain, and we will very likely be discomfited by intermittent and unwanted reminiscences. Guilt can be defined as a feeling of discomfort that arises when we reflect on past acts (or failures to act) after we have broken a subjective rule of conduct. Shame, on the other hand, can be defined as a more diffuse negative evaluation of the self. Sometimes, such feelings can be ameliorated by reparative behaviour – apologies, gifts, reunions. But this isn't always possible. Decisions made decades ago can't always be reversed, and injured parties may no longer be alive. Research findings show that an important factor associated with insomnia in old age is worry; however, in clinical settings, discussing worry with elderly patients frequently reveals that worrying overlaps considerably with ruminative depression. The elderly worry about the future, or what remains of the future, but they also tend to 'orbit' significant memories. Actions or failures to act are replayed as if they are on a continuous loop. Recollections associated with guilt and shame can be repressed, but when defences weaken (lying in bed and in darkness) they often rise into awareness and cause considerable distress. The idea of positive and enlightening personal growth is so much more appealing than exhuming painful memories, but accommodating painful memories is a part of personal growth. According to Jung, it is a necessary first step.

The very desire for personal development – to find deeper truths, to make 'spiritual' progress – can be subverted by narcissism. Truth seekers are prone to what Jung called 'inflation', an unhealthy expansion of the ego. He believed that this happens when the ego is super-charged with archetypal energies. These energies flow from two gender-specific archetypes: the 'old wise man' and the 'great mother'. Scripture, myth and literature frequently feature 'types' of this kind, for example Sophia the goddess of wisdom, and they continue to appear in new guises, such as the Jedi master Yoda from *Star Wars*. A more straightforward way of understanding the phenomenon of inflation is to view it as a form of over-identification. Cultural instantiations of archetypes have a particular appeal for certain individuals, and they are subsequently 'copied'.

Many gurus, particularly celebrity gurus, exemplify inflation. Whatever they may have done formerly to achieve fame – comedy, radio, TV, drama – and however 'unenlightened' their past behaviour, they suddenly feel empowered to reinvent themselves as 'spiritual' authorities. Some acquire a messianic appearance. The eminent psychiatrist Anthony Storr once observed that the point at which otherwise ordinary mortals decide that they are endowed with the qualities necessary for spiritual leadership is very often a midlife crisis. Which suggests that the midpoint of life can be 'spiritually' dangerous as well as transformative.

Most voguish gurus – celebrity or otherwise – enjoy a period of influence, after which their shallowness becomes all too apparent when they become embroiled in financial or sexual scandals. Drug addiction also seems to be relatively common among gurus. They fall from grace with remarkable reliability. Tumbling reputations are not surprising, perhaps, when the gurus concerned were previously comedians or TV personalities; however, even gurus with more refined pedigrees seem vulnerable to the very same weaknesses. The Buddhist lama Sogyal Rinpoche, author of the highly praised *Tibetan Book of Living and Dying*, and one of the most respected spiritual teachers of modern times, ended his ministry in disgrace after allegations of sexual abuse and embezzlement. Bhagwan Shree Rajneesh, who once commanded such a large following in the West that his orange-clad devotees were literally unavoidable, became addicted to Valium and nitrous oxide. Even the Dalai Lama displayed remarkably poor judgement when he was filmed asking a child to suck his tongue.

Celebrity gurus dramatise something that Jung suggested we should all take pains to avoid: the derailment of personal development by our darker potentialities. Translated into everyday terms, the principal danger of embarking on an inward journey of self-discovery is grandiosity and entrapment in the prison of our own self-absorption. We become caricatures, contemplating how good we will look sitting in a perfect lotus position or hugging trees. Successful individuation results in the exact opposite outcome. The whole, complete, integrated individual that emerges from the process feels more connected to nature, the world and other people. Research has shown that the wise, although reflective, are remarkably outgoing and engaged. A very good indicator of mental health in old age is transpersonal interest – for example, concern about global warming, even though the person will very likely be dead before the worst happens.

When I was in my late teens, lured by the promise of enlightenment, I became the devotee of a guru. This admission is rather embarrassing; however, in my defence, it was the 1970s and pursuing enlightenment and following gurus seemed much more sociably acceptable back then. I was 'seduced' by a convert who captured my interest with a sales pitch that played on my anxieties, flattered my ego, and offered as an incentive the promise of an experience of indescribable transcendent bliss. I knew nothing then about meditation or eastern mysticism, so this sounded very exciting. Soon after, I started attending spiritual discourses at ashrams, where I was encouraged to loosen my ties with family and friends and devote myself to the only thing that really mattered, the pursuit of ultimate truth. This didn't strike me as unreasonable. If there was such a thing as ultimate truth, then pursuing it *should* be a priority. Moreover, I was assured that once I had experienced truth directly – in meditation – any residual doubts and reservations would simply evaporate. There was a proviso, however: I would only experience ultimate truth with the help of a guru. Metaphors, presumably honed over millennia, were employed to win my compliance. 'If you are thirsty and you want to fill a glass, you must hold the glass beneath the tap – or it will not fill.' And so on. I was then informed that I would have to spend even more time listening to spiritual discourses in ashrams by way of preparation. I was being brainwashed.

In due course, I was asked to demonstrate my commitment

to the pursuit of truth by travelling across Europe to hear the guru speak, doing jobs at ashrams without pay, and donating money. The guru had a lavish lifestyle to support. Most of his followers were poor, or had taken vows of chastity, poverty and obedience, yet the guru was married, flew a personal jet, owned a fleet of cars, several mansions, and seemed exceedingly fond of luxury goods. There were also stories circulating concerning some very questionable behaviour. One of them involved violence. When I floated the idea that the guru's immense wealth might be put to better uses – medical research, foreign aid, and education, for example – I was told that I was stuck in my own preconceptions: 'You're in your head, man . . .' It was even suggested that the guru's extraordinary wealth was in some way ironic. He was teaching us that the acquisition of material possessions was ultimately meaningless.

I had invested so much time and energy in my spiritual development I felt unable to walk away and I continued attending meetings until I was deemed ready to commune with the eternal. I was taught some meditation techniques in the basement of an ashram and informed that the experience of transcendent bliss I had been promised was in fact entirely contingent upon the grace of the guru – who it seemed I was now expected to believe was omniscient and omnipotent.

I experienced nothing.

I dutifully meditated every day – and still experienced nothing.

It was suggested to me that the answer to my spiritual paralysis might be 'darshan' – to prostrate before the guru. Consequently, I travelled to a spiritual festival, lined up for hours, and eventually passed through a room where the guru sat enthroned, garlanded with flowers, while his devotees kissed his feet. The experience was so bizarre, I felt that I had entered an alternative universe.

That evening, there was a massed gathering of followers. The guru appeared, delivered some spiritual teachings, and afterwards I found myself swaying in a crowd of thousands, while loud music played and the guru beamed at us from a distance. To my surprise, I *did* experience an altered state of consciousness. I felt deliriously happy and suddenly quite certain that my decision to embark on a spiritual odyssey was beyond any form of criticism. Indeed, I felt that I was approaching a moment of supreme revelation. Given what I know now, I would say that what I experienced was not raised consciousness, but rather the kind of disturbed consciousness associated with mass hysteria. When I returned to my tent, confident that the guru would now grant me an encounter with the divine, I sat cross-legged on the ground and began to meditate.

Again, I experienced nothing.

I continued meditating for over a year, but eventually I had to accept the painful truth. Clearly, the guru was not divine, my naivety had been exploited and the meditation techniques I had been taught were not 'secret' keys to sacred knowledge but well-known yogic practices I could have discovered myself if only I'd taken the trouble to visit a library.

Of course, this is an entirely personal account. Many devotees I spoke to claimed to have been granted an inexpressibly wondrous experience of 'bliss'. I'm sure they had; however, I doubt very much that whatever they experienced was a gift, carried to them on a river of grace, the source of which was the guru.

The guru continued to attract many followers until, perhaps sensing a change in the cultural climate, he reinvented himself as a 'peace educator'. After the 1970s, without the impetus provided by the Beatles and the eagerly anticipated Aquarian dawn, the pursuit of spiritual enlightenment became less popular among the young. It was much more difficult to sell eastern mysticism to punks and new romantics than hippies. Materialism was in the ascendant, and by the 1990s, the idea of following a guru had become quaint and rather passé. Somewhat predictably, many gurus liquidated their missions in the same way that businessmen close failing enterprises. And some – like mine – continued to operate after major rebranding.

My guru had used some quite sophisticated psychological techniques to recruit and indoctrinate the unsuspecting young and naive; however, it would be unfair of me to blame him entirely for manipulating my expectations, because I was a willing accomplice. I wasn't the victim only of salesmanship, I was also the victim of my own narcissism. Had I been chosen? Why accept an *ordinary* life? I must in some way have felt entitled to – or at least eligible for – admission into a higher plane of being. And I can see now that I was extraordinarily compliant. Sophistry can *never* legitimise a spiritual master who exhibits an inordinate fondness for Rolex watches or vintage automobiles. Even though I was never persuaded that self-indulgence on this scale could ever be compatible with spiritual leadership, I was blinded by the prospect of transcendence, and foolishly discounted my gravest concerns. My father, who was a barely literate barber, who had never read a book in his life and whose interests were limited to placing bets and football, told me I was being a fool (perhaps more colourfully than I am recording here) – and he was indubitably right. I find some solace in a sentiment that was expressed first in the classical world, and then by George Orwell, that some ideas are so absurd that only an intellectual would believe them. The pursuit of enlightenment, justified by lofty arguments, offers many opportunities for quite spectacular displays of stupidity.

Euripides wrote: 'The wisest men follow their own direction and listen to no prophets guiding them.' It is a recommendation for the inner journey. We can be our own gurus. However, as Jung warned us, the inner journey has risks. We must accommodate our dark side without succumbing to its influence, we must process unpleasant memories, and most of all, we must resist inflation. Personal development is easily subverted, and then we become versions of the countless gurus who, ordinarily, we rightly suspect of being inauthentic.

There is a contradiction here that merits clarification. On the one hand, indigenous cultures and religions provide individuals with social structures, rituals and guidance that promote psychological adjustment. Some of these traditions represent thousands of years of thought and experience. They are an immensely valuable resource and without them, as Joseph Campbell suggested in the quotation cited at the beginning of this chapter, we face 'dangers' alone. On the other hand, rejecting knowledge accumulated over thousands of years is what seems to happen when people adopt a 'do-it yourself' approach and embark on an inner journey.

This contradiction isn't quite so stark as it first appears.

The perspective being presented in this book is essentially Jamesian: pragmatic, and focused on outcomes. There are clear correspondences between indigenous practices, religion and – for example – Jungian formulations. Psychologically, these 'journeys' arrive at similar destinations. The desired goals are the acquisition of qualities such as acceptance and connectedness. For many people, traditional religious practices are entirely appropriate to their spiritual needs and world view; however, as has been stressed previously, the majority of 'westerners' do not find it easy to follow a faith. There is clearly a demand for an alternative. If you are in any doubt of this, spend a few minutes browsing online or leafing through some glossy magazines. It is a demand that is being increasingly met, sadly, by celebrity gurus and legions of messianic life-coaches. The inner journey (a reflective form of psychological development that integrates the self in a way that makes neurological sense) obviates the need for subjugation of will. Naturally, there are costs and benefits associated with any approach. But a clear advantage of Jamesian pragmatism is independence of thought and freedom from false prophets.

8

Meaning: Existence and Purpose

Live meaningfully

Existentialism is strongly associated with mid-twentieth-century Paris and a particular cultural ambience. Intense intellectuals sitting in smoky Left Bank cafés discussing freedom and the meaning of life; jazz clubs and open relationships; the men wearing black turtleneck jumpers and the women, with their long straight hair, in jackets with rolled-up sleeves. No other school of philosophy has produced its own 'look'.

Parisian existentialism coalesced around Jean-Paul Sartre and Simone de Beauvoir, who produced influential twentieth-century masterpieces such as *Being and Nothingness* and *The Second Sex*. Their work explored everything from phenomenology to revolutionary politics; however, fundamentally, they were interested in answering the big questions. Does life have a purpose? How can we live meaningfully in a meaningless universe?

They were weighty intellectuals, but probably less intense in person than we usually imagine. Sartre gave impromptu renditions of 'Old Man River' and impersonated Donald Duck. Beauvoir was a reckless hillwalker (she survived falling off a precipice) and liked wearing turbans. French existentialism, with its penchant for chic accessories and its promise of sex, has always attracted young enthusiasts (especially so in the 1960s and 1970s). Moreover, the stock protagonist of existential fiction, the outsider, remains a seductive role model for those in need of a stabilising identification to help them through the turbulent transitional years of adolescence and early adulthood. We are all outsiders before we find our place in the world.

Be that as it may, existentialism (and certainly existentialism beyond associated wardrobe choices and strong coffee) is a universally applicable philosophy and it may, in fact, have *even more* to offer the old than the young. Existentialism concerns itself with those things that become more pressing as the years accumulate – the consequences of embodiment, authenticity and the inevitability of death, for example. Existential prescriptions for achieving good mental health in later life are becoming increasingly relevant in a world of superficial distractions in which we frequently hear the refrain 'Life is pointless'. Under these conditions, how *can* we find meaning and live meaningfully?

The terms 'poly-crisis' and 'meta-crisis' are now used to describe the unprecedented combination of existential threats that humanity is currently facing: climate change, increased risk of nuclear war, an unstable global economy, displaced populations, loss of social cohesion, the uncontrolled ceding of power to artificial intelligences, international cyber crime, antibiotic-resistant superbugs and the depletion of essential natural resources. After a period of relative post-war stability and prosperity, generations raised to be optimistic about the future are now baffled by a world that seems to be edging closer and closer to a variety of plausible extinction scenarios. A pervasive atmosphere of uncertainty has generated an insatiable appetite for commentary. We want to be told what things mean, largely because it is becoming extremely difficult to extract meaning from our environment. The environment is glutted with information and much of it is 'faked'. We don't even know if what we read or see is the work of a human being any more. Almost half of internet traffic is produced by bots.

Our sense of purpose is undermined further by over-exposure to 'bullshit'. In the 1980s the philosopher Harry Frankfurt alerted his readers to the potentially disruptive effects of an ostensibly unremarkable human foible. Bullshit is a more nuanced idea than the colloquial bluntness of the term suggests. It is more pernicious than fakery or lying because the bullshitter is only concerned with the power of his claim. Thus, the 'bullshitting' of politicians, influencers and various vested interests functions beyond falsity and truth. A liar (although morally transgressive) is still responding to truth by misrepresenting it. The same cannot be said for the bullshitter. Truth doesn't signify. Without falsity and truth as helpful orientation points, it is extremely difficult to determine what is and what isn't meaningful.

One of the subheadings lodged beneath the rubric of the meta-crisis is the 'meaning crisis', a term associated with John Vervaeke (a professor of psychology, cognitive science and Buddhist psychology at the University of Toronto, Canada). Around a quarter of people living in western democracies believe that life has no meaning. According to Vervaeke, our sense of purpose is in decline, and we have lost the essential qualities that 'animated' earlier societies, particularly those qualities that helped human beings to make sense of being alive in a universe of seemingly infinite complexity.

Vervaeke has identified several large-scale responses to the meaning crisis: consumption of books about Stoicism, renewed interest in psychedelics, and the ubiquity of mindfulness meditation. People seem to be trying to find a philosophy, drug or practice that will 'treat' states of unease and emptiness that could also be understood as symptoms of an 'existential sickness'. For Vervaeke, the search for meaning is comparable to a question, to which the answer is the acquisition of wisdom.

Meaninglessness contributes significantly to anxiety and depression in the second half of life. A previously vague sense of encroaching demise acquires a palpability that, if honed by disappointments, can become sharp enough to penetrate our defences. Then we are prompted to ask, 'What has it all been for?' And all too often, a defeated inner voice is disposed to reply, 'Nothing.'

The French writer and philosopher Albert Camus (who some, but not all, count as an existentialist) saw parallels between a life without meaning and perhaps the cruellest punishment meted out by the gods in Greek mythology. Sisyphus is condemned to roll a rock to the top of a mountain, whereupon the rock rolls back down again – and he must repeat this hopeless labour in perpetuity. Sisyphus's labour is futile and emblematic of the absurdity of many of life's effortful but ultimately pointless repetitions. Camus applauds Sisyphus, somewhat ironically, as a 'hero' of the absurd. Sartre and Beauvoir enjoyed spending time with Camus. They got on well together. But even the dynamic duo of French existentialism baulked at his moribund world view. As far as they were concerned, life *could* be meaningful. They did not believe in a single overarching purpose – the meaning *of* life – but they did believe that it was possible to find meaning *in* life.

Although existentialism is a broad church that accommodates a plurality of opinions, most existentialists can agree that life makes us anxious. Existential unease is ever-present – an undercurrent, flowing like a submerged stream beneath our day-to-day activities. Typically, it rises to the surface and fills temporal lacunae – extended silences – moments of stasis. Suddenly there is grief, panic, terror.

I can remember seeing an elderly woman for psychotherapy during one bitterly cold December. She had led an extremely privileged life. Outside, the sun was floating above a row of raked roofs and chimney stacks. An unforgiving white light poured through the window, illuminating every wrinkle and crevice on her face. Time seemed curiously suspended. She covered her eyes with an arthritic hand and said in a brittle, aristocratic accent: 'Oh, God! I can't stand a low winter sun.' Her tone was despairing. She wasn't really talking about the sun. She was talking about reality. The bright, blinding light was the hard edge of existence, and she could no longer cope with it. She was like a vampire countess, about to crumble into dust. Her fragility was disturbing.

Sartre explored what it is like to be overwhelmed by reality in his novel *Nausea*. His anti-hero, the writer Antoine Roquentin, declares, 'Something has happened to me: I can't doubt that any more. It came as an illness does, not like an ordinary certainty, not like anything obvious.' For Roquentin, everyday activities like opening a door or shaking someone's hand have started to feel distinctly odd. Even a beer glass – with a handle and a little coat of arms – has the potential to trigger an episode of alienation: 'I can no longer explain what I see . . . I am gently slipping into the water's depths, towards fear.'

When we stop taking things for granted and look at them – that is, *really* look at them – their contingency (the fact that they are there when they might not be) and their appearance (sometimes strange when studied closely) can make us feel profoundly uneasy. The 'thing' that we normally call a cat is suddenly revealed to be an unlikely combination of fur, eyes, sharp pieces of keratin, blood and wiry extrusions. We might observe this curious life form stretching in a trapezium of light, the photons of which started their journey a hundred thousand years ago in the core of a nuclear inferno that we usually refer to, with casual indifference, as the sun. We can mute reality by converting it into words and allowing ourselves to be carried along by everyday routines. But occasionally reality breaks through with disconcerting force and, like Roquentin, we sink towards fear. The reality of a beer glass is the same reality that will eventually kill us.

If, as we get older, we feel existential threats more keenly, then it should come as no surprise that existential psychotherapy, as a body of knowledge, has much to say that is relevant. Existential psychotherapy, as the name suggests, is a treatment approach closely linked to existential philosophy. It draws on the work of many philosophers and writers – even the novels of Dostoevsky – but its beginnings were greatly influenced by Martin Heidegger. Heidegger was born in the late nineteenth century, began his academic career as a theology student, but later turned to philosophy. He became an associate of Edmund Husserl and his key work, *Being and Time*, was published in 1927. It has been described as one of the hardest books ever written. Heidegger had intended to enlarge the work, but the new sections he planned were never added.

Heidegger's paramount concern was the nature of being. He used the German word *Dasein* to describe both the individual and the quality of 'being' that individuals possess. The literal translation of *Dasein* is to be here – or there. A person cannot exist independently of his or her environment, so 'being' has an inescapable worldly aspect. Embodiment is important to Heidegger because the body is attuned to the world and its truths. The body apprehends truth with a degree of immediacy that suggests some overlap with the idea of 'gut feeling', which was discussed in chapter 3. We should respect our bodily feelings and they should not be considered inferior to thought. Embodiment also demonstrates that freedom has natural limits. We cannot choose to be born or to live for ever, for example.

Heidegger conceptualised birth as the person being cast or thrown into the world; however, while respecting natural limitations, the individual can still shape his or her life. A flexible 'potentiality' precedes actuality. The German words *existieren* and *Existenz* are derived, like the comparable English verb and noun, from 'to stand forth' or 'standing forth' in Latin. *Dasein* stands forth, creating its own way of being in the world. The choices we make can be either authentic or inauthentic. Authentic choices reflect the needs and core values of the person, whereas inauthentic choices are influenced by factors such as social expectations and conventionality. Naturally, authentic choices are more meaningful than inauthentic choices. If we fail to make authentic choices, we become divided selves, the falsity of our existence disconnected from who we really are. We find ourselves participating in a life, but it isn't really our life. Therefore, authenticity can be understood as another means of achieving unity. A common outcome of inauthenticity is anxiety. The individual is unable to 'stand forth', to stand upright in the headwinds of existence, and instead he or she will seek refuge in deadening routines and docile acquiescence. Ultimately, such a life can only ever be anaesthetic and meaningless.

Death is inextricably connected with being, because being moves forward in time towards it. We are aware that we must die, and we are also aware that death can occur at any moment. A ruptured vessel in the brain could effectively kill me (or you) before either of us reach the end of this sentence. Yet awareness of death (or as Heidegger called it, 'being-towards-death') can make us wiser. The philosopher A. C. Grayling has written that 'being-towards-death' is 'the fundamental key to authenticity: when Dasein accepts its own finitude in the inevitability of death, it opens up – discloses – Dasein's own Being to itself, and completes it by making sense of it as a whole'. Judicious awareness of death will influence how we choose to live; it makes us more appreciative of every second, because every second is booby-trapped with our own potential demise. It discourages procrastination and encourages engagement.

Heidegger has been enormously influential, but for many, his stature as a twentieth-century sage is negated by his advocacy of National Socialism. Although it is true that he was critical of some aspects of Hitler's regime, since the publication in 2014 of the *Black Notebooks* (collected writings from 1930 to 1970), apologists have found it difficult to defend him. To suggest that Heidegger was a great man whose naivety led him to make an innocent error of judgement is no longer tenable. He believed, for example, that Jews were a threat to the destiny of the German people, and he reportedly attended a book-burning in Freiburg. Before the Second World War, he was romantically involved with the young Hannah Arendt, the Jewish political philosopher who would eventually report on the Eichmann trial in Jerusalem in 1961 and whose potent phrase 'the banality of evil' has since become convenient rhetorical shorthand. Bizarrely, Arendt continued to support Heidegger after the war, and they maintained a relationship of sorts until her death in 1975. Heidegger died the following year. Sartre was also remarkably forgiving: 'Don't you know that sometimes a man does not come up to the level of his works?'

What we now call existential psychotherapy began to evolve when ideas such as those generated by Heidegger penetrated the pre-existing framework of psychoanalysis. It is difficult to identify a precise starting point because among German-speaking intellectuals, interdisciplinary boundaries were extremely porous; however, it is reasonable to suggest that the first significant clinician to be influenced by existential philosophy was the Swiss psychiatrist Ludwig Binswanger, who developed a form of treatment in the 1920s and 1930s that eventually became known as 'Daseinsanalysis'. Binswanger was a great admirer of Freud (in fact, he knew him very well) but he found psychoanalysis too mechanistic; he was much more interested in exploring how people consciously experience 'being in the world' rather than trawling the unconscious for repressed memories. Suffering, he supposed, cannot be understood by peering into 'world-less' interiors.

One of Binswanger's acolytes, Medard Boss, superseded Binswanger as the most important existential practitioner. He aligned clinical practice even more closely with Heidegger's philosophy and established the first Daseinsanalytic Institute in Zurich. Boss believed that because human beings exist in the world, and the body is attuned to reality, psychological adjustment is best served by cultivating 'openness' to experience. Conversely, psychological problems are caused when individuals 'close off' experience. This closing off – which is comparable, perhaps, to the deployment of defences – attenuates the immediacy of being and ultimately stymies potential. Indeed, within Boss's framework, mental illness is almost synonymous with strangulated potential, the reduction of ways an individual might be in the world. An agoraphobic, for example, can only be in the world in one way. That is, in the home. He or she is not 'open' to the many ways of being in the world that are available just beyond his or her front door.

Existential psychotherapy has evolved continuously from Boss's time to the present, and it now exists in a variety of forms; however, there are some common features. Existential psychotherapists focus on 'lived experience'. What is happening in your life? How do you feel about it? What are you going to do? Existential psychotherapists are much more interested in a person's unique experience of being in the world than trying to plumb the depths of the unconscious. Choice and responsibility are viewed as critically important. It is by being 'authentic' and 'owning' the consequences of our decisions that we make progress towards the goal of a meaningful life. In addition to coming to terms with mortality, we must also come to terms with our aloneness – an equally potent source of anxiety. No matter how much we are loved, no matter how intimate we are with others, we remain islands of consciousness. Subjectivity cannot, by definition, be shared. This does not mean that existential psychotherapists ignore relationships. Much of what is meaningful in life has a social aspect. Even so, ultimately, we stand alone.

Existential psychotherapy reaffirms the Stoic virtue of acceptance. We should strive to accept reality, embodiment, responsibility, aloneness – and death. If we deny reality, we are also denying ourselves. The world is all we have, and if we are not fully in the world, then where are we? What sort of a life is that? We are haunting the world rather than living in it.

Although Boss is credited with having initiated what has since become a thriving therapeutic modality, he is largely forgotten today. Indeed, both Boss *and* Binswanger have been eclipsed by Viktor Frankl, who is the only existential psychotherapist to have gained (and retained) a large and international non-academic readership. *Man's Search for Meaning* (originally titled *A Psychologist Experiences the Concentration Camp* and published in 1946) is an autobiographical work treasured by millions which documents Frankl's incarceration in several Nazi concentration camps, including Auschwitz, and his subsequent development of logotherapy (a new form of existential analysis). *Logos* is the Greek word for meaning. In fact, Frankl had worked out the tenets of logotherapy before he was a prisoner, and the concentration camps were not really where he devised his theories, but rather where he *tested* them.

For Frankl, meaning is the deepest human motivation, and it makes almost any level of adversity bearable. He had observed that those prisoners who survived or lived longest in concentration camps were also those who had managed to preserve a sense of meaning. Meaning, according to Frankl, is not an absolute. We are not obliged to find *the* meaning of life. If we can choose a way of being in the world that is personally meaningful, this will be sufficient to improve psychological health. His position is reminiscent of William James's pragmatism.

All meaning-based therapies are ultimately founded on the same assumption. Because the human animal is motivated to find meaning, absence of meaning will cause distress. It is an assumption supported by neuroscience. One of the principal functions of the frontal lobes of the brain is to set goals. When we achieve our goals the neurotransmitter dopamine is released, and we experience pleasure (or perhaps more accurately, increased motivation to seek pleasure). Although the right hemisphere of the brain is associated with a multiplicity of functions, according to Iain McGilchrist, its ultimate objective is to understand the world and invest it with meaning. We can assume that purpose and meaning are fundamental, simply because much of the brain is dedicated to establishing purposes and finding meanings.

For some, the absence of meaning is experienced as an *existential vacuum*. Many feel hollow, adrift – restless. Frankl suggested that we often try to fill this inner emptiness with substitute gratifications, for example cigarettes, booze, drugs or junk food. Thus, the absence of meaning is the seedbed of addiction. We might even invent *substitute purposes* – diverting schemes, time-filling projects – but what we really want, and need, is *authentic purposes*.

Frankl was raised in a devout Jewish family and some of his writings are clearly influenced by the Talmud. He acknowledges 'callings' and endorses the idea that suffering can be beneficially transformative. He supposed that human beings have three dimensions of being: physical (relating to bodily functions), psychical (relating to drives and emotions) and spiritual. Again, it should be stressed that Frankl's use of the word 'spiritual' does not equate with religiosity. He uses spiritual to designate the noetic – the deeply personal. It is noteworthy that for Frankl, existentialism – material, worldly and Godless – must be extended 'metaphysically' to fulfil its therapeutic promise. Human beings have spiritual needs, and one way or another these needs must be met. The alternative is to ignore them – a course of action that comes with attendant risks. Realism becomes nihilism, and nihilism encourages us to see everything as absurd. There is nothing more chilling than a severely depressed patient smiling and saying, 'Life's a joke, isn't it?' When nothing makes sense any more, why go on living?

Frankl's thesis, that meaning is essential for mental health, is relatively well known because of the enormous popularity of his best-selling book. Even if you have never read it, you will probably be familiar with the general idea. *Man's Search for Meaning* is ranked among the top ten most influential books in the USA. However, the development of logotherapy did not come to a halt in 1946. Frankl continued writing until his death in 1997 and meaning-centred existential psychotherapy continued to evolve. Unfortunately, few readers of *Man's Search for Meaning* ever learn about subsequent discoveries. This is consequential, because neglect of these discoveries can limit an individual's capacity to make use of Frankl's original formulations.

Alfried Längle, a psychiatrist and clinical psychologist who was once Frankl's close associate, has been widening the scope of logotherapy since the 1980s. He has proposed that Frankl's motivation for meaning is in fact preceded by three other motivations. Firstly, we are motivated by the fundamental question of existence. We must be able to affirm that we exist and that we possess the wherewithal to exist. If the foundations of being are insecure, we are likely to experience anxiety. Secondly, we are motivated by the fundamental question of life. We must be able to affirm that we are alive – have access to our emotions – and feel that life is good. If we do not feel that life is good, we are likely to experience depression. Thirdly, we are motivated by the fundamental question of self. We must be able to affirm our personhood, the sense of being 'myself'. If we do not have a sense of who we are, we will have an increased likelihood of developing personality disorders. And, finally, we are motivated by Frankl's question of meaning. We must be able to affirm that we are alive *for a purpose*. If we do not feel that we have a reason to live, we will be vulnerable to suicidal thoughts, addictions and dependencies. Affirming that we exist, that life is good, that we are unique individuals and that life has meaning constitute the 'inner consent' necessary to achieve existential fulfilment. One can think of this inner consent as a complex achievement that involves the bringing together of various layers of existence. The end point of this process is a sturdy affirmative: 'Yes', to life.

Längle's framework is interesting because it suggests that one can't just decide, apropos of nothing, to have a meaningful life. Meaningfulness has developmental preconditions. This is consistent with the idea expressed earlier in this book, that you can't simply decide to be a Stoic. A certain amount of personal development must take place – namely, integration – before Stoic truths can be translated from intellectual abstractions into owned, felt truths. Meaning is more like an emergent property than a choice. It is something that we discover, after accomplishing preparatory existential goals.

Although Längle precedes 'motivation for meaning' with three other motivations, we shouldn't suppose that personal development follows a strict stepwise progression, in which one stage is 'completed' before the person moves on to the next. Realistically, personal development is an ongoing, flexible process – a general but logical trend. We continue to develop throughout life and respond accordingly to our changing circumstances.

Längle points out that as we age, physical limitation, loss of competence and increasing awareness of mortality prompt us to ask new questions concerning the nature of our being in the world: What have I lived for? Have I lived a good life? What do I still live for? And so on. Ultimately, this class of reflective thinking, which often involves looking back and surveying one's history, inevitably leads to questions of meaning: Does my life have meaning? Will my death have meaning? Does life have a transcendent purpose? We could, of course, simply ignore these questions, but Längle advises against this, because the endorsement of a 'position' – an existential stance – benefits psychological health. One must 'stand forth', rather than get 'carried along'. If we fail to adopt such a position, we will feel uneasy, or as Längle says, 'a seed of unrest will remain' – a seed that might ultimately produce the sickly flowering of mood disturbance. Like Frankl, Längle asserts that meaning is not an absolute. It does not matter whether the pursuit of meaning leads to faith in God or atheism. The important thing is to find *personal* meaning.

'It is the task of the person,' Längle writes, 'as well as of the integrating "I", to deal with every part of himself that is aging and has to do with the self.' The notion of existential integration is somewhat different from Jamesian, Jungian or neurological integration. Within an existential framework, wholeness is achieved not so much by integrating hypothetical parts of the self – the shadow, for example – but by integrating aspects of experience. This includes the residua of experience (our store of memories) and our ongoing (age-transformed) experiences. One must accept responsibility for one's past actions and consequences – and one must accept the person (me, myself, I) created by those choices. One cannot disown aspects of 'having been in the world' just because they produce discomfort.

Längle concludes his thoughts on old age in the following way: 'Whoever has done what he wanted, whoever has lived for what he wanted to live for, can let go and say farewell more easily than one who secretly is still waiting.' Typically, much of life is waiting. Which explains, perhaps, why Samuel Beckett's *Waiting for Godot* is performed so regularly. We recognise its truth. It is a play in which two characters famously wait for nothing to happen. Many of us postpone important decisions because we are waiting for an unspecified event that we imagine will transform us. We continue waiting, sometimes for decades, and if the event doesn't happen, we feel disappointed. Obviously, it is better to seize the day sooner rather than later. However, Längle offers encouragement, even to those who realise only late in life that they have been 'secretly' waiting for nothing to happen. We can still make choices. Even in old age. 'Whoever is able to newly find himself in old age and be with himself, has brought final maturity to his life, like the last sweetness given to a fruit by the autumn sun.'

The language of existential philosophy can be alienating because it often sounds pretentious and overblown. But the patient reader can expect to be rewarded with many useful insights. Moreover, existentialism attempts to grapple with big questions – those most likely to trouble people in the second half of their lives. When existential philosophy is translated into psychotherapy it is possible to evaluate its effects by conducting clinical outcome studies, and recently there has been considerable growth in this area of research. Summarising results in 2017, the British existential psychotherapist Mick Cooper concluded: 'there is compelling evidence to suggest that helping clients to find meaning and direction in their lives – through relatively structured and directive methods – can be of considerable value, and this finding is consistent with the well-established link between the presence of meaning in life and wellbeing'.

Psychologist and philosopher Joel Vos has identified several categories of meaning. There are *material types* (for example, career, wealth); *hedonistic types* (for example, physical excitement, pleasure); *self-oriented types* (for example, creativity, autonomy); *social types* (for example, belonging, altruism); *larger types* (for example, religion, spirituality); and *existential-philosophical types* (for example, freedom, gratitude). Implicit in this typology is the notion of ascending value. A significant majority would probably agree that finding meaning through helping others is more elevated than finding meaning through making money. Which begs the question: do altruism and the accumulation of wealth (as meaningful pursuits) have differential effects on mental health?

Theoretically, one can find meaning anywhere and in anything. An individual who finds collecting coins meaningful, for example, will have an 'additional' motivation in their lives. Even if they are getting old and infirm, they might still be motivated to look for more coins. They will do things that otherwise they might not. They will have a reason for being in the world: another day, another coin. But clearly, there are levels of meaning. One can search for 'meanings' that enrich existence far more than those offered by numismatics. One can search for meanings connected with love, nature or truth, for example. These are much more likely to have a greater impact on the totality of the person. Depth of meaning is correlated with depth of existential fulfilment. Lives expand to accommodate larger questions and a truly meaningful life will have broad horizons and lofty peaks. Meaning enhances vision, and another name for that vision is wisdom.

9

The Subjective Hourglass: Time and the Perception of Time

Work with time – not against it

When I was a teenager, I can remember my English teacher giving out blank exercise books – one for every pupil in the class – and then telling us that we should fill them with poems that we had enjoyed reading. I knew instantly that I'd never complete the task. Filling an exercise book with poems would be arduous. Besides, I didn't read poetry. The first 'poem' I chose wasn't a poem, but the lyrics of the song 'Time' from Pink Floyd's latest album, *The Dark Side of the Moon*. A few lines had struck me as being quite poignant. They concerned the experience of being young and then suddenly realising that ten years had slipped by, bringing death that much closer. From my schoolboy's perspective, a decade – ten whole years – felt like an age. Which is understandable, given that I'd only been 'self-conscious' for a little over ten years. A decade for me was the literal equivalent of a lifetime. But still, time passes. And the lyrics made me think.

Eventually, I too would be in the same position as the singer. The following week I found a 'real' poem to copy into my exercise book: 'Days', by Philip Larkin. It expressed a similar sentiment to 'Time'. 'What are days for?' the poet asked. And where else can we live? It's a mystery that 'Brings the priest and the doctor in their long coats running over the fields.'

'Days' is a poem of less than fifty words, yet it still manages to imply (regardless of its brevity) that life is essentially a series of futile repetitions that lead inexorably to death. It distils truths that are so powerful and discomfiting that they can provoke philosophical reflection even in an indifferent schoolboy. Incidentally, this reminiscence serves to demonstrate the incalculable value of heroic teachers who encourage children from working-class families in 'bad' schools to read poetry. 'Days' has been a part of my intellectual armamentarium for over half a century – and I have never forgotten it.

Since discovering 'Days', my days have been steadily accumulating and I've collected another eighteen thousand or so. These are the days that have made up (and will now always make up) the bulk of my life. Realistically, if I'm lucky, I've probably got another seven thousand or so days left.

'Days' is a poem about the passage of time and how we are, to an extent, prisoners in time. You are free to move in space, through three dimensions, but you are confined to a single point in time – the present moment. The present moment is experienced as moving forward, from dawn to sunset, thus, you are obliged to live in *your* days. Larkin's economy and conversational lightness are at odds with the magnitude of his subject matter. Time is *everything* because everything exists in time. We are temporal beings and human psychology is intimately related to the passage of time. Which makes it truly remarkable that academic psychologists and neuroscientists have shown such little interest in time and time perception.

Perhaps 'time perception' has been under-researched because time itself is elusive and difficult to define. St Augustine was fully aware of this problem well over a thousand years ago. 'What then is time?' he asked. 'If no one asks me, I know what it is. If I wish to explain it to him who asks, I do not know.' We 'feel' time passing, but when we try to say what time is, our definitions tend to be circular. For example, we might say that 'time is duration' – which is effectively saying nothing more than 'time is time'.

Physicists have tried to understand the nature of time, but there is no consensus. Some believe that the present moment only is real and that the past and the future do not exist. Once something has happened, it is gone, and what is yet to come is not there. Others believe that the past and the future are 'fixed' aspects of reality and that the present moment is just an arbitrary reference point. This model is usually referred to as the 'block universe'. Our experience of the passage of time is an illusion and all moments in time are equally 'real'. Thus, consciousness 'travels' through time like a spotlight sweeping across a landscape, revealing what is already there. Still other physicists believe that the past exists – but not the future. Once something has happened, it is locked into reality. The present is continuously solidifying and becoming the past. If you had a time machine, you couldn't go forward in time because there is nowhere to go.

The first account of time given above – only the present is real – is consistent with everyday experience. We feel that the present moment advances, constantly converting an uncertain future into a fixed (but thereafter inaccessible and vaporous) past. We don't have any sense of the past and future co-existing in a 'block universe'. Moreover, our experience of time suggests that the pace of its steady progress never varies. Wherever you go, time appears to be passing at the same speed. In the early years of the twentieth century, Einstein's theory of relativity revealed that our subjective impression of time is inaccurate and misleading. Time isn't universal, but flexible and relative. In fact, time is so elastic, it passes more slowly at the level of your feet than your head. Moreover, apparent temporal absolutes, such as simultaneous occurrences or the order in which events occur, are equally relative and qualified by factors such as the speed at which observers are travelling. Some physicists have proposed that reality is essentially granular, and that there is a theoretical minimum limit of temporal measurement beyond which time cannot meaningfully be said to pass. If you look closely enough at time, it vanishes altogether.

Reviewing recent advances in contemporary physics, Carlo Rovelli writes: 'At the most fundamental level that we currently know ... there is little that resembles time as we experience it.' He continues: 'Physics helps us to penetrate layers of the mystery. It shows us how the temporal structure of the world is different from our perception of it. It gives us the hope of being able to study the nature of time free from the fog caused by our emotions.' Physics is infinitely more precise than human perception. But the fog of emotions is where we live. As *Dasein* – as beings in the world – our relationship with time is defined by our limitations. Even a physicist with a detailed understanding of how time works will experience time passing in much the same way as a shelf-stacker in a supermarket.

It appears that we can only think about time indirectly by employing 'spatial' metaphors. We talk about having been away for a 'long' time, or having been so busy that we are 'short' of time. The past is 'behind' us and the future lies 'ahead'. Neuroscientists believe that as human beings evolved, pre-existing 'spatial' circuits in the brain were appropriated to enable thinking about time. Although the precise way in which time is spatialised differs across languages, almost all languages use spatial metaphors. Similarly, we sometimes think of time as a physical quantity. Time mounts up. We consult clocks that don't measure time, but simply accumulate discretionary units that we call seconds, minutes, hours and days. Be that as it may, even if our subjective sense of time is inaccurate, indirect and divorced from reality, it is an immensely significant aspect of being 'in the world'.

Naturally, we become more sensitive to the passage of time as we get older. Our bodies remind us that we are not immortal with increasing frequency, and we tend to make more and more unfavourable comparisons with how we felt when we were younger, fitter, and our senses were sharper. Old photographs of ourselves start to look like other people; certainly nothing like who we see in the bathroom mirror every morning. We also have more history to reflect on, more memories of holidays, friends, romances – special occasions – and this temporal 'baggage' inevitably creates an amount of emotional drag: nostalgia, regret, yearning. We pull the weight of our past behind us, and its heft reminds us once again that Larkin's 'priest' and 'doctor' will soon be running in our direction.

Melanie Klein suggested that in old age, preoccupation with the past allows us to avoid the frustrations of the present: 'Some idealization of the past is bound to enter into these memories and is put into the service of defence. In young people, idealization of the future serves a similar purpose.'

The word nostalgia is derived from the Greek *nostos* (a homecoming) and *algos* (pain). It appeared for the first time in a seventeenth-century medical treatise, and it was introduced to describe a pernicious form of homesickness affecting soldiers. Typically, melancholy and lethargy were followed by loss of appetite and death. It became a significant diagnosis in the nineteenth century and the last person to officially die of nostalgia did so in 1918. There is nothing inherently unhealthy about reflecting on the past. Indeed, making sense of one's past is essential for good psychological adjustment. But, to paraphrase L. P. Hartley, if the past is another country, then, unlike the motherlands of homesick soldiers, it is a country that we can never find our way back to. Constant yearning for the landscapes of memory will engender feelings of loss and melancholy – a 'malady' for which there is no cure – because we can only ever live as permanent exiles in the present.

There are two questions that people ask as they become increasingly time-sensitive with age. The first is: How can I make the most of the time I have left? And the second is: How can I make time pass more slowly?

We possess only a finite (and dwindling) quantity of time. Therefore, the way we manage time is important; however, the idea of 'time management' – perhaps because it is strongly associated with the business world – carries assumptions concerning productivity and gain. Employees who manage their time well will increase company profits. Similarly, it is assumed that a life in which time is well managed will also be, in some sense, correspondingly profitable. Of course, what is and what isn't profitable will depend entirely on the individual and their wants and needs. The question of how best to manage one's time can only be answered by those who have achieved a critical level of self-understanding. It is *impossible* to make decisions about the optimal use of time without having first established what is personally important and why. Those who are psychologically equipped to use time most 'profitably' have usually attained the kind of 'inner consent' described by existential psychotherapists such as Alfried Längle (see chapter 8). They are ontologically secure and live purposefully. This proposition might seem so blindingly obvious it is hardly worth stating. Clearly, if you don't know what you want, then you won't be able to establish priorities. Yet, it is remarkable how often one encounters individuals in psychotherapy who have made rash decisions in the throes of an existential panic. *Oh my God, time is running out!* In such cases, it is necessary to review their hastily put-together bucket lists and slipshod plans for a 'new life' and work in a more measured way towards some kind of meaningful realignment of objectives and the person. As has already been suggested, sometimes, optimal use of time can involve doing less rather than more. And although some activities – for example, gazing across a still lake at twilight – are ostensibly 'unprofitable' in some ways, they can be extremely profitable in others. Attempting to follow time-management advice in the absence of insight is like following directions without reference to compass points. Yes, you are undoubtedly on the move, but whether you are moving in the right direction is far from certain. When you know how to use your time wisely, you'll probably discover that you have more time than you thought. As Goethe observed: 'We always have time enough, if we will but use it aright.'

Our sense of the speed at which time passes changes according to circumstance. For example, time 'flies' when we are sitting in a cinema enjoying a great film but it 'crawls' when we are waiting for a job interview. The nineteenth-century Swiss geologist Albert Heim was perhaps the first person to study the effect of context on time perception. He collected accounts of climbers who had experienced potentially fatal falls and almost all of them reported that 'time became greatly expanded'. Some of these climbers recalled having enough time to 'review' their entire lives. Time slows when we are in danger, but it also seems to lag when we get bored or impatient. A closely observed kettle can take an eternity to boil. Under one, very specific condition, time appears to stop. Most people have had the experience of glancing at a wall-clock only to discover that the second hand is stationary. After what seems like a curiously extended period of temporal stasis the second hand suddenly jerks forward and our sense of time passing is restored to normality. This illusion (caused by a discrepancy between actuality and prediction) offers us a fleeting but compelling experience of arrested temporal flow. Perhaps the most dramatic time dilation effects are achieved by ingesting drugs. Cannabis and opium can make minutes feel like months. Because we experience time passing at different speeds, many have wondered if it is possible to manipulate time perception to make life feel longer.

'In general,' William James observed in 1890, 'a time filled with varied and interesting experiences seems short in passing, but long as we look back. On the other hand, a tract of time empty of experiences seems long in passing, but in retrospect short. A week of travel and sight-seeing may subtend an angle more like three weeks in memory; and a month of sickness hardly yields more memories than a day.' Here, James is suggesting that the sense of having lived 'more' is attributable to eventfulness and memory. He is undoubtedly correct. Anyone who has spent a weekend lazing at home doing nothing followed by a weekend of sight-seeing in a foreign city will have a strong sense of the latter having been 'longer' than the former.

This well-attested effect suggests that we can add subjective 'length' to our lives by travelling or filling our diaries with activities. Indeed, one can imagine a life so exhaustingly rich in events and sensation that the prospect of rest and repose – perhaps even eternal repose – might start to seem appealing. However, one of the principal reasons that travel creates vivid memories (and the subjective impression of retrospective time dilation) is novelty. Novelty also explains why we remember the summers of childhood as sweltering epochs. Back then, everything was fresh and new. The problem with travel as a means of manipulating our sense of having lived longer is that, like everything else, the more you do it, the less novel it becomes. I have seen fabulously wealthy patients in psychotherapy who have spent decades circling the globe, flying from one glamorous location to the next, who felt, not that life was being lengthened by eventfulness, but shortened. They felt as if they were hurtling at breakneck speed towards death. Without contrast, novelty quickly wears off. This suggests that an optimal strategy must involve a combination of routine and novel experiences. The precise ratio of one to the other will of course vary according to the person's individual characteristics. Given that it *is* possible to influence our sense of having lived more, then striving to achieve an optimal balance of the familiar and unfamiliar should be considered a legitimate and pragmatic objective. It is important, however, to be clear about what this objective is. We are discussing conditions for creating a particular sense of satisfaction – the sense of having had a long and full life. This is self-evidently better than feeling that life has been short and empty. Even so, we should not lose sight of the fact that achieving the desired balance between routine and novelty is merely a modest manipulation of memory to create a retrospective illusion. It does not, in any real way, 'stretch' time.

One of the most fascinating aspects of time perception is how we perceive the present moment. Larkin asked, 'Where can we live but days?' But it is even more pertinent to ask, 'Where can we live but the present?' The present is fixed (because we can't live anywhere else) but it is also disconcertingly fluid. William James wrote: 'Let any one try, I will not say to arrest, but to notice or attend to, the present moment of time. One of the most baffling experiences occurs. Where is it, this present? It has melted in our grasp, fled ere we could touch it, gone in the instant of becoming.'

In philosophical and spiritual writings, the present moment has acquired special status. It is frequently presented as a key to deeper understanding and better living. We are exhorted to inhabit the present moment. 'When your mind wanders,' we are advised, 'gently bring it back to the present.' One of the most influential books to be published after the spiritual renaissance of the 1960s was *Be Here Now* by Baba Ram Dass (formerly the academic psychologist Richard Alpert). The cover of my 1971 edition shows a circular arrangement of the words 'Be Here Now' with the word 'Remember' repeated at the four compass points. Just reading the cover becomes a spiritual exercise. The eye is invited to follow the circle – which has no exit point – while the multiple injunctions to 'remember' focus and refocus the mind with each revolution. This is the desired state: *Remember . . . be here now. Remember . . . be here now.*

The idea of 'being here now' also appears in the writings of many significant psychotherapists – Carl Rogers and Erich Fromm, for example. For those who spend too much time worrying about the future, or regretting the past, trying to be more 'present' can be helpful. Making efforts to focus on the 'here and now' can strengthen an otherwise weak connection with ongoing reality. Whether the circumstances that constitute reality are 'good' or 'bad', benign or challenging, it is a precept of psychotherapy that full engagement with reality is almost always beneficial (sooner or later). Detachment from reality carries implications of solipsism, social isolation, inaccurate thinking, and even delusion.

Being fully present is synonymous with paying attention, which creates more memories, and a rich store of memories contributes to the feeling of having lived longer. When we are not inhabiting the present moment, when our attention is unfocused or dispersed – when we are, in effect, inattentive – we are less 'in the world' and therefore less likely to remember it. Much has been written recently on the deleterious effects of smart phones on the attentional capacity of children and adolescents, but older people are probably just as vulnerable. The modern world offers many opportunities for distraction. Indeed, for the first time ever it is possible to be *so* distracted that you are in danger of missing your own life.

Fully inhabiting the present moment is also associated with altered states of consciousness – for example, the peak experiences described by Abraham Maslow (see chapter 4). Such episodes of 'full presence' are sometimes associated with 'loss of self'. Paradoxically, individuals who have had peak experiences frequently recall having been both *more* and *less* present at the same time. This isn't necessarily a contradiction. The 'loss of self' reported by those who have had peak experiences is probably best understood as ego transcendence: a separation of consciousness from the quotidian – aches and pains, paying bills, making shopping lists. The person is fully conscious of 'being', rather than the drudgery of 'being'. Narcissistic preoccupations are also transcended – concerns about appearance, status and recognition. What is lost during a peak experience, perhaps, is not the self, as such, but those aspects of the self that ordinarily interfere with a more direct and uplifting engagement with reality.

Aldous Huxley's essay on the effects of mescalin, *The Doors of Perception*, published in 1954, remains a genre classic and one of the most closely observed accounts of self-transcendence. It is germane to the present discussion, because it was Huxley's view that his total occupancy of the present moment was facilitated by the dissolution of the mundane, anxiety-prone self: 'that interfering neurotic who, in waking hours, tries to run the show was blessedly out of the way'. Mescalin 'delivered' him 'from the world of selves, of time, of moral judgements and utilitarian considerations, the world ... of self-assertion, of cocksureness, of overvalued words and idolatrously worshipped notions'. In this elevated state, Huxley was able to see the world undimmed by the 'fog' of complacency. Even ordinary objects were transformed: 'That chair – shall I ever forget it? Where the shadows fell on the canvas upholstery, stripes of deep but glowing indigo alternated with stripes of incandescence so intensely bright that it was hard to believe that they could be made of anything but blue fire.' Time slowed down. 'For what seemed an immensely long time I gazed without knowing, even without wishing to know, what it was that confronted me . . . the percept had swallowed up the concept. I was so completely absorbed in looking, so thunderstruck by what I actually saw, that I could not be aware of anything else.'

Attempting to explain the neurobiology underlying his altered perceptions, Huxley presents us with a fascinating hypothesis: 'These effects of mescalin are the sort of effects you could expect to follow the administration of a drug having the power to impair the efficiency of the cerebral reducing valve.' Huxley is suggesting that ordinarily the brain attenuates reality to make it more manageable; however, when we ingest psychedelics they open the 'reducing valve', and consequently we have a more direct and authentic experience of 'being in the world'. A controversial corollary of this hypothesis is that traditional neuroscience has misunderstood the fundamental relationship between the brain and consciousness. We think of the brain as generating consciousness, but perhaps the brain's primary function is to limit consciousness.

Huxley's hypothesis is consistent with the intriguing phenomenon of terminal lucidity. As death approaches, many individuals who have suffered (sometimes for decades) from neurological conditions characterised by dulled consciousness experience an inexplicable return of clarity. It is as though illness (for example Alzheimer's disease) has had the effect of increasing the efficiency of the 'reducing valve', and as the brain dies, the valve's efficiency is compromised, and consciousness expands. Terminal lucidity has been reported in the medical literature for 250 years. Estimates vary considerably, but some surveys suggest that terminal lucidity occurs in up to 40 per cent of cases.

There are very good reasons why the wise have always urged others to attempt to live in the present. It is advice that makes a great deal of sense. However, like travelling to make life feel longer, attempting to inhabit the present moment might yield diminishing returns if taken to an extreme.

Obeying the command of sages to 'be here now' – to live *completely* in the here and now – is impractical and potentially quite problematic. Human beings might be physically trapped in the present moment, but they are not psychologically trapped, and psychological health necessitates a great deal of mental time travel. We reflect on the past, learn lessons, and predict the future. We come to terms with traumatic memories. Our sense of who we are is rooted in a personal, historical narrative. Plans must be formulated and executed. Focusing on the present moment all the time might be a reasonable objective for a Siddhar in a cave, but it is simply not a realistic option for someone living and working in a western democracy. Of course, 'being here now' can be interpreted as a state of mind that is as relevant to reflection and planning as it is to pursuing enlightenment. For example, one can be fully focused on one's thoughts and feelings. But this would be a wilful misreading of what mystics mean when they urge us to be here now. 'Present moment' practices like mindfulness meditation often involve self-observation and the imposition of 'distance' between thoughts and feelings. Moreover, the kind of 'presence' associated with raised consciousness typically involves 'hyper-real' sensory experiences combined with feelings of universal connection. This is all quite different from paying close attention to thoughts, feelings and memories, to inform life decisions or process emotions. Clearly, there are times and circumstances when it is more appropriate and beneficial to inhabit the present moment than others. Even ancient wisdom must be applied judiciously.

Neuroscientists have been unable to identify a particular structure in the brain that 'tells the time'. Even so, the brain possesses the neural equivalent of many timekeeping mechanisms and each of these can track or estimate the passage of time on different scales. The psychologist and neurobiologist Dean Buonomano has called this the 'multi-clock principle'. The body is also full of 'clocks' (of varying sizes) that function independently of the brain. For example, there are liver cells that 'know' the time of day. In fact, a certain amount of timekeeping takes place in almost every organ in the body. This is because we have evolved on a planet that revolves as it orbits its star, creating days and nights, and the chemical processes that keep us healthy and alive are synchronised with these diurnal repetitions. Certain biological events, for example the release of enzymes and hormones, *must* happen at certain times. Without internal timekeeping, the sequential release of vital chemicals would break down.

The coordination of circadian biochemistry is managed by only fifty thousand neurons located in a region of the brain known as the 'suprachiasmatic nuclei'. This local 'group' could be described as a master clock, although every one of these neurons functions independently. Studies have shown that individual cells removed from the suprachiasmatic nuclei of rats continue to keep time (as indicated by electrical activity) at different rates.

Sleep problems are very common in the second half of life, but they are difficult to disentangle from instances of more generalised dysregulation of biological timekeeping. This is why 'sleep and circadian rhythm disruption' (or SCRD) is now sometimes used as a convenient catch-all term. It was introduced by the molecular neuroscientist Russell Foster (now based at the University of Oxford) and his team. The effects of SCRD are profound. It has been linked with poor mental health and a broad range of physical conditions such as colitis, irritable bowel syndrome, ulcers, atherosclerosis, dementia and cancer. Indeed, SCRD is relevant to almost every health concern.

Although there are some features of SCRD that are attributable to ageing – for example, natural deterioration of the mid-frontal region of the brain is associated with poor 'deep' sleep – circadian disruption is frequently exacerbated by the way we live in the modern world. Our days are not 'natural' days. We no longer get up when the sun rises and prepare for bed after sunset. We extend the day with artificial lighting and noisy entertainments. We eat large evening meals at times when our ancestors would have been asleep. Sometimes, we work all night. All of which is enormously consequential.

Our circadian clocks are not entirely accurate. They can run a little fast or a little slow. Which means that they must be corrected daily. Without daily correction, they will become increasingly misaligned with the astronomical day. The technical term for this correction is 'entrainment', and we are entrained mostly by the sun. Light, especially at sunrise and sunset, realigns the biological day with the astronomical day. Blind people frequently become 'time blind' because their internal clocks are never reset. They can easily drift 'out of time' – sleeping through the day and rising at midnight.

In the past, when societies were largely agrarian, it was almost impossible for the biological day to become misaligned with the astronomical day. Everyone was obliged to expose themselves to increasing levels of light at dawn and retire due to decreasing levels of light at dusk. Thus, the inner day and the outer day were locked together.

If we want to remain psychologically and physically healthy then we should be mindful of our circadian neurobiology.

Neolithic and ancient civilisations did not suffer from our time blindness. Nor do indigenous peoples. It is only since the industrial revolution that the citizens of western nations have become increasingly indifferent to sunrises and sunsets – solstices and equinoxes. We have become detached from the astronomical day which is a cycle embedded in a system of much larger cycles. Our body clocks connect us to a massive cosmic clock made from planets, stars and galaxies. This is not an unmerited New Age observation, because our relationship with the heavens is far more intimate than we commonly suppose. The moon (the phases of which give us our months) stabilises the earth's axial inclination (which gives us our seasons). Without the moon, it is possible that the earth would not have been stable enough to support life. The moon, time and human biology are profoundly interconnected. Perhaps, instead of trying to make the most of time, or manage time, or slow time down, we should stop attempting to control it – and allow *it* to control us. There are few things a human being can do to improve physical and psychological health better than the harmonisation of each day with the workings of the cosmos.

The philosopher Henri Bergson made a distinction between 'clock time' and 'duration'. The first is measured time, whereas the second is immersion in the flow of time. We need both. It would be difficult to cope with life in the modern world without making appointments; however, there can be little doubt that clock time dominates our day-to-day existence. In *Life Lessons from Bergson*, the writer Michael Foley observes: 'The last few years have seen the birth and dramatic growth of an evangelical movement known as the Quantified Self, which promotes, as the key to well-being, a self constantly measured and monitored in as many ways as possible. This movement, which began in the USA in 2007, now has organisations in fifty cities worldwide, including London, and spreads its message via meetings, films, literature and a website. The overt message is that quantification provides control over one's life, and the covert message is that this control will nullify time and enable the Quantified Self to live forever.' We have returned to the first chapter of this book: time as the enemy, time as something that must be defeated with the aid of immortality projects.

For decades, it has been assumed that evolution has 'no time' for middle-aged and elderly animals. Post-reproductive lifespans are uncommon in the natural world. Once we have reproduced, and our genes have been transferred to the next generation, we are surplus to requirements. The eminent biologist Peter Medawar famously asserted that ageing animals enter the 'shadow of natural selection'. Once you have passed the 'midpoint', evolution wants you dead as soon as possible. You have become, to put it bluntly, a wasteful drain on resources.

Jung claimed that the individuation process is an innate, natural tendency; however, if we are 'genetically programmed' to simply reproduce and die, why do human beings have the capacity to individuate? And why would evolution select transpersonal (or spiritual) instincts? Once we enter the shadow of natural selection, surely it doesn't matter whether we are happy or sad, well adjusted or despairing. How do old people who are disposed to look up at the stars, and wonder, benefit the species? Life is 'nasty, brutish and short'. Why would it be any other way?

There is, however, an alternative possibility, a legitimate evolutionary justification for energetic engagement and continuous psychological development in later life. This is now known as the 'active grandparent hypothesis'.

In the ancestral environment, a typical hunter-gatherer mother could collect around two thousand calories a day. This wouldn't have been enough to sustain herself and several offspring. Therefore, she would have needed help – help that was probably supplied by middle-aged and elderly relatives. Anthropologists have shown that older individuals in foraging populations remain active, gather more calories than they consume, and provide surplus calories for children, grandchildren, nieces and nephews. Summarising this new wave of evolutionary and anthropological research, Harvard physiologist Daniel Lieberman writes: 'our unique system of intergenerational cooperation, especially food sharing, postpones Medawar's grim shadow. Instead of becoming obsolete, middle-aged and elderly hunter-gatherers bolster their reproductive success by provisioning children and grandchildren, doing child care, processing food, passing on expertise, and otherwise helping younger generations ... Over time, humans were evidently selected to live longer to be generous, useful grandparents.'

Evolutionary pressures have extended the human lifespan, and nature, as Jung claimed, has a vested interest in human beings making healthy psychological adjustments in middle age and old age. In this sense, time is on our side.

10

Conclusion: How it Works

There is a difference between knowing and doing

We began with Dante, halfway through his life, feeling lost, entering a deep, dark wood – embarking on a metaphorical inner journey. Dante's wood is emblematic of many journeys that appear in myth and literature, all of which, according to Joseph Campbell, are distillations of essential learning. The human condition is uniquely challenging, and the key to meeting those challenges is to undertake an inner journey that, if successfully completed, bestows wisdom.

Although wisdom is a desirable attribute, as a subject of study it hasn't attracted very much interest from social scientists. Consequently, there is no real consensus concerning definitions and measurement. Even so, in recent years, various research projects have identified several characteristics that the wise share. The wise are reflective and have usually achieved above average levels of self-understanding; they are emotionally stable and tend to experience more positive than negative mood states; they value relativism over absolutism; they are 'open' to new experiences; and they possess a conspicuously good sense of humour. The wise are pro-social; they are empathetic, compassionate and altruistic. They are also decisive (particularly in situations that require social judgements), although when they decide not to act, they are comfortable with uncertainty. Finally, the wise are 'spiritual' (albeit predominantly in the Jamesian sense rather than the religious sense).

There is some variation concerning what is judged to be emblematic of wisdom across cultures; however, two features are remarkably stable. Data collected from Slovakia, Morocco, Canada, Ecuador, Peru, America, Japan, South Korea, India, South Africa and China – from subjects with very different backgrounds – show that 'reflectiveness' and 'socio-emotional awareness' are *reliably* associated with perceptions of wisdom.

Becoming wise, or at least wiser, can be viewed as an aspect of personal development that equips the individual to meet the very substantial difficulties associated with the second half of life. Much has been written about ageing, longevity and well-being. Indeed, there has been a great deal of excellent scientific research published about these subjects and the results have been widely dispersed through magazine articles, social media, radio broadcasts and television features. Even those who don't pay much attention to public information platforms will know what is and what isn't good for them. We now know that regular exercise, good diet, plenty of sleep, avoiding toxins, managing stress, a primary loving relationship, seeing friends and intellectual stimulation are *all* beneficial. Achieving physical and psychological well-being in the second half of life is ostensibly straightforward. Just follow these recommendations. But of course, it is *never* that easy.

Knowledge is an unreliable predictor of behaviour, and intention is almost always modulated by contextual variables. One can't just decide to have a good night's sleep. It is necessary to be physically comfortable and to be in the right state of mind. A smoker can look at an image of blackened lungs on the side of a cigarette packet and still reach for his or her lighter. Almost everyone knows that eating moderate amounts of unprocessed food will result in weight loss, but a significant number of people are still obese.

I once worked in HIV and AIDS, at a time when infection with HIV meant certain death. I saw patients who were fully aware that having unprotected sex in particular environments would very likely result in infection. Yet, they chose to take that risk and were subsequently infected. They had effectively exchanged a potential half century of life for, in some cases, a pitifully brief ten minutes of sexual excitement. Knowing that this might be the outcome did not stop them from making a staggeringly *unwise* decision.

The standard recommendations for well-being in later life presuppose that a person's situation is relatively benign and that he or she is motivated to change. In a sense, what is being assumed is that the person is already wise. He or she has made optimal choices in the past, enjoys satisfactory circumstances, and is free to make optimal choices in the future. He or she can use knowledge 'profitably'. Clearly, this is not the case for many people.

Knowledge or philosophical insight *can* catalyse change. But *only* if the person is in a state of readiness. This understanding has been shared in religious communities for thousands of years. It is an insight consistent with an observation made by many twentieth-century psychologists that a certain amount of personal development must occur before an individual can make good life decisions. Philosophical truths must be 'absorbed', felt or 'owned' if they are to become enabling truths. A particular form of personal development, consisting of reflective self-exploration (and which lends itself to metaphorical representation as an inner journey), has been proposed as a method for 'readying' the individual. Moreover, there is evidence (both psychotherapeutic and neurological) to suggest that this readiness arises when the parts of the self are optimally integrated.

According to this theory, an optimally integrated person should be able to follow the standard well-being recommendations with minimal effort. Indeed, it may be that for such a person, adhering to the standard recommendations requires little or no self-discipline because desirable behaviours are emergent. They are not choices, as such, but consequences. For example, the health benefits of friendships will manifest because integrated individuals are pro-social. They do not have to decide to make friends. They will form friendships by simply following their pro-social inclinations. If you are a volunteer, for example, you will meet other volunteers who are likely to become friends.

Many of the topics covered in previous chapters (for example, openness to unconscious communication and universal connection) are quite abstract. For those eager to translate theory into practice, this level of abstraction might be frustrating. *What should I do, exactly? How does this work?* In the present chapter, an attempt will be made to explain how the goal of integration – or wholeness – can be practically accomplished. However, from the outset, it should be stressed that the inner journey, the process of individuation that leads to integration, is, by definition, deeply personal. The provision of definitive prescriptions is contrary to the spirit of the enterprise. We are all different, and what works for one person might not work for another. This approach to psychological adjustment was anticipated by several philosophers, most notably Friedrich Nietzsche, who counselled: 'No one can build you the bridge on which you, and only you, must cross the river of life. There may be countless trails and bridges and demigods who would gladly carry you across; but only at the price of pawning and forgoing yourself. There is one path in the world that none can walk but you. Where does it lead? . . . thus to dig into oneself, to climb down roughly and directly into the tunnels of one's being.' We can make use of the wisdom accrued by previous generations (myths, traditions and libraries of inspirational poetry and prose) without having to accept dogmatic assertions or submit to the will of 'demigods' (or their modern 'celebrity' equivalents).

In the manner of a Jamesian pragmatist, it is possible to follow general principles, experiment with different strategies, and select those strategies that prove to be most effective. Ranked highly among desired outcomes will be reduced existential anxiety, greater self-understanding and 'spiritual' enrichment. For those who are still troubled by the word 'spiritual' on account of its religious connotations, it might be helpful to think of spirituality as 'elevation'. Clearly, activities and experiences can be plotted on a continuum that ascends from abasement or degradation at one end to elevation at the other. When we feel spiritually enriched, we are usually feeling that in some sense we have been 'raised'. Our perspective has altered in a way that has expanded our purview.

A frequently paraphrased declaration of the French philosopher Blaise Pascal is that every human heart has a 'God-shaped hole'. For 'believers', this hole can be filled with God. But the 'Godless' also seem to be aware of an inner emptiness (comparable to Pascal's God-shaped hole) that requires 'filling'. Atheists tend to fill it with awe and wonder engendered by the natural world. Freud, who was a militant atheist, felt obliged to use the word 'soul' to describe the essence of a person's being, because no other word would do. Any account of the human animal that fails to acknowledge the ineffable is incomplete. Spiritual experiences are associated with specific patterns of brain activity and there is some evidence to suggest that spiritual sensitivities are genetically determined. Spirituality is a protective factor, associated with improved physical and psychological health. Therefore, cultivation of spirituality, even if it is construed more neutrally as 'elevation', qualifies as a pragmatic, Jamesian goal.

As religion has declined, and with it opportunities for worship, people in the West have found a range of ready substitutes: money, royalty, luxury goods, rock stars, Hollywood. When the spiritual urge is frustrated, it seems that we still need to worship something. If the psychic economy demands that we exchange God for a substitute, it would be wise to review one's investment choices. Why make idols and totems of celebrities and designer handbags when by simply tilting one's head back on a cloudless night one can behold the majesty of the universe? Of course, one could 'worship' a celebrity. But the associative network of concepts and meanings that a celebrity might activate would be relatively impoverished compared to the profoundly rich networks of association that will very probably be activated by the spectacle of a bejewelled infinity. For most people, the latter will be far, far more likely to inspire transformative reflection.

Approaching truth is still valuable, even if we never fully apprehend truth. Unfortunately, we tend to think in black and white terms. Those who do not achieve enlightenment are deemed unenlightened. This kind of thinking is discouraging. It devalues anything less than pinnacles and perfection. But small gains make a difference. One or two tentative steps in the right direction are preferable to paralysis. A little insight is always better than none.

Jung believed that healthy adjustment in the second half of life is divisible into two phases. The first involves a general loosening up of old patterns of thought and behaviour, and the second, the creation of opportunities for self-discovery to occur. The first phase, which can also be understood as a task, when successfully accomplished, serves as a setting condition for further development.

There is a performative aspect to social functioning. We enter the social arena in character (mother, sister, daughter) and conform to traditional expectations (good mother, supportive sister, dutiful daughter). Jung supposed that if we over-identify with the 'character' we present to the world, we are also limiting opportunities for growth. He called this outward-facing 'personality' the *persona* – the term used to describe the mask worn by actors in Greek drama. We must weaken our attachment to the constraining persona to allow individuation to proceed.

In practical terms, this means being less rigid, less constrained by habit, and trying out new things. A person who has been cerebral might try doing something physical (yoga, t'ai chi, table tennis, tango classes), and vice versa. It doesn't really matter what these new things are, providing they help us to question the 'calcified' sense of who we are. What is being suggested here is *not* that the person should escape into an entirely new identity – that would be more typical of a midlife crisis – but that he or she should 'relax' the sense of self (particularly the socially constructed self) to be more psychologically flexible, more able to accommodate growth, and more receptive to a broader range of experiences.

Jung's first phase recalls the dissolution of self, reported by patients 'transformed' by psychedelic medication. Indeed, a degree of dissolution – which usually precedes reconstruction – is a feature of both psychedelic and conventional psychotherapies. When people 'break down' during a psychotherapy session, an astute therapist will recognise an opportunity to help his or her patient to discover new ways of being. Reconstitution, which can also be understood as a kind of rebirth, is easier when the psyche becomes more plastic.

In this context, Jung's concept of synchronicity can be understood as a catalyst of change, because instances of synchronicity are spontaneous and surprising. The occurrence of a meaningful and arresting 'coincidence' provides an opportunity to think beyond habitual entrenchments. When we notice acausal connections, we will very probably find ourselves thinking about something that we wouldn't otherwise have thought about. We are escaping the limitations of the calcified self, which for many is also a false self – a *persona* rather than a person. It isn't necessary to embrace Jung's metaphysics. One can simply use instances of synchronicity to redirect thinking in less predictable directions. In this way, we are more likely to make adventitious discoveries about ourselves.

Perhaps certain divinatory methods have survived for thousands of years because they promote personal growth by similar means. Chinese cleromancy, for example, involves casting yarrow stalks into patterns (hexagrams) which direct the enquirer to cryptic entries in the *I Ching*, or *Book of Changes*. The element of randomness and the ambiguity of the text forces the individual to think laterally – to discern patterns of personal relevance that are ordinarily too oblique to be appreciated.

Psychological defences can be viewed as an aspect of general rigidity. When defences are functioning optimally they have a valuable role to play in emotional regulation, but in the second half of life they tend to be employed excessively to combat existential anxiety. Defensiveness can take many forms, but immortality projects and 'fuzzy mathematics' (calculations that serve to misrepresent how little time we have left) can be particularly pernicious.

A desire to live a long and healthy life is perfectly understandable, but this same desire can easily seed delusion and self-deceit. 'To make God laugh,' a Yiddish proverb advises, 'tell him your plans.' A heavily defended individual is detached from reality, complacent and unprepared. When death can no longer be denied, the defensive architecture collapses, and he or she is vulnerable to episodes of existential terror and despair.

As the Stoics suggested, regular meditations on death are probably a helpful corrective. This is not a morbid practice. On the contrary, the purpose of these meditations is to obviate the problems that result from denial, and to encourage a full appreciation of being alive. Some people find it helpful to reflect on mortality in 'sacred' places – irrespective of religious conviction. A place of worship, the very fabric of which might be hundreds or even thousands of years old, will almost certainly heighten one's sense of transience. Sometimes, we need palpable manifestations of the passage of time to stress our defences, to weaken them beyond what can be achieved with philosophical reflection alone.

Freud argued that none of us believe in our own death. Yet, in a sense, being alive presents a far greater challenge to our powers of comprehension. We live in a universe of finely tuned mathematical values. If the cosmological constant (which is thought to drive universal expansion) was even slightly larger, there would have been no stars, no planets and no life. The fact of our existence – each one of us formed by repeatedly recombining DNA over a period of several billion years – is fantastically improbable. We can afford, perhaps, to lower our defences when reflections on death guide us towards gratitude. Meditations on death may not bring us to the point when we are ready to die. But if we do not deny death, if we do not deny reality, we are surely less likely to experience the imminence of death as a surprise.

For Jungians, the second half of life begins somewhere in the fourth decade; however, the critical transition from the first half of life to the second half of life is not determined by a number, but by psychology. The half point is notional and associated with a person's mental state rather than how many years they have been alive. Even so, usually around the age of thirty-five many people living in western democracies begin to feel a form of 'spiritual' dissatisfaction. Having been to school and perhaps university, having found a job and perhaps been promoted, and having found a partner and perhaps started a family, it may seem that all of this 'doing', this effort, has been successful in one way, but not in another. More 'doing' of this kind doesn't seem to move the person forward any more; it is unable to satisfy a growing and deeper need that is typically difficult to articulate. The discontent arising from this 'crisis' is associated with questions such as 'Is this all there is?' or 'There must be something more?' The Jungian psychotherapist James Hollis has described this juncture as a 'calling' to the inner life: 'In the end we will only be transformed when we can recognize and accept the fact that there is a will within each of us, quite outside the range of conscious control, a will which knows what is right for us, which is repeatedly reporting to us via our bodies, emotions, and dreams, and is incessantly encouraging our healing and wholeness. We are called to keep this appointment with the inner life, and many of us never do. Fortunately, this insistent invitation comes to us again and again.'

In recent years there have been a plethora of popular self-help publications that espouse what has come to be called 'slow living'. For example, books on meditation, *ikigai*, pets, pastoral pleasures, gardening, crafts and feng shui. As life gets faster (think of the astonishing speed at which people flick through social media feeds), slowing down has become a more widely recognised imperative. From a psychological perspective, this slowing down is helpful, because when we slow down we are more likely to notice the 'insistent invitation' to keep our 'appointment' with the inner life. It is not necessary to abandon twenty-first-century urban living to be receptive. Nor is it necessary to retreat from the world and lead a monastic existence. All that is required is a certain amount of stillness – some time set aside in which to be 'open' – and a willingness to consider the kind of thoughts, images, memories and impressions that we typically ignore or dismiss as psychological flotsam.

The process that underlies becoming 'whole' is integration. Divisions in the mind are associated with poor mental health, and, conversely, unity underlies inner coherence and promotes wisdom. For over a hundred years, clinical practice has confirmed this general view. However, integrative psychology is also consistent with contemporary neuroscience. The brain can be divided along horizontal and vertical axes, and when such divisions widen (because of damaged neural pathways), cognitive, affective and social functioning can be profoundly impaired. The cognitive neuroscientist Daniel Levitin has suggested that 'The wisdom we attribute to older adults may well be neurobiologically based, born out of changes to the brain that allow the two hemispheres to communicate more freely, to combine the logical with the intuitive, the quantitative with the qualitative, the fact-based thinking with the artistic. Greater wisdom is also marked by freer connection between the frontal lobes and the much older limbic system, and by age-related changes in neurochemistry.' It is possible that the 'inner journey' influences connectivity in the brain, which in turn creates a neurobiological state that favours the emergence of wisdom.

Minds have many facets and functions, but for most 'integrative' psychologists (from William James onwards) the unity of conscious and unconscious divisions of the mind has always been given special emphasis. The paramount importance of this unity is readily supported by a simple thought experiment. Imagine what would happen if an unbridgeable chasm suddenly opened between your conscious and unconscious. Your sense of self would shrink to whatever it is you are currently thinking about and from that moment onwards you would not be able to access any of your memories. You would have no depth or intimations of your inner vastness. Without complementary conscious and unconscious divisions of mind, you would be little more than a meniscus – a membrane of awareness receiving perceptual information that could no longer be contextualised. I am describing an extreme mental state to make a point; however, there must – in the real world – exist a broad range of individuals who have varying capacities for successful information exchange between conscious and unconscious divisions of mind. Therefore, it is reasonable to assume that some of them have less access to their totality than others. According to most integrative psychologists, this lack of 'transparency' can be corrected.

Jung was a vociferous advocate of marrying the conscious and unconscious divisions of the mind – especially in the second half of life – and this marriage, he believed, was sanctified largely in dreams. If we record and think about our dreams, we are actively engaged in completing ourselves.

There are different ways of interpreting dreams. Freud suggested that each individual element can be isolated and used to prompt associations, which can then be given further consideration. Dreams are also stories. Even if a dream isn't coherent, it will often have a narrative quality: 'I was looking for something' – 'I was trying to get away'. The type of story a dream is 'telling' can be illuminating. The unconscious is prepared to say things about your life that you are reluctant to acknowledge. The unconscious might offer you the unadulterated true story rather than your preferred fiction. *But I'm happy – I don't want to run away!* Really? The emotional tone of a dream can also be revealing, irrespective of its unfolding narrative. 'I was walking on a path through a beautiful rose garden, but I felt frightened'. *Where does that fear come from?* And perhaps most importantly, dreams sometimes contain symbols or symbolic imagery. 'A figure holding up a sword was blocking my way'. Symbols (and archetypal personifications) frequently encode complex meanings, and when they appear, they usually deserve careful deconstruction.

The important thing to remember about your dreams is that they are *yours*. They arise in your head and dream content is determined entirely by your life experiences. At some level, dreams must be saying *something* about you. And what they have to say arises from the depths of your being. This is why Jung (and Freud) judged dreams to be extremely important.

From ancient times, dreams have been associated with the occult, and for much of the twentieth century – outside of the psychoanalytic community – dreams were regarded as a relatively trivial phenomenon caused by random brain activity. Brain scanning studies have since shown that the physiological activity subserving dreams is far from random, and modern sleep scientists believe that dreams are essential for psychological health. Dreaming has been linked to processing emotions, coming to terms with trauma, memory consolidation, problem-solving and creativity. Other benefits have been posited, but those cited above are the most well supported by research.

In addition to paying attention to dreams, Jung also recommended 'active imagination' – that is, allowing fantasies to evolve (with minimal conscious interference) as a means of 'catching' unconscious communications. He approved of his patients entering 'dreamy' states, because 'dreaminess' blurs the boundary between conscious and unconscious mental activity.

Daydreaming is probably more important to healthy ageing than is generally appreciated. We tend to think of daydreaming as the brain 'idling' rather than a beneficial mental state. Freud wrote an interesting article on creativity and daydreaming in 1907, in which he suggested that great works of literature might originate in childhood fantasies; however, the subject of daydreaming was not given serious consideration again for another half century. In the 1960s, a clinical psychologist, Jerome Singer, identified a particular type of daydreaming that he described as 'positive-constructive'. This could be contrasted with less beneficial forms of mind wandering that were related to either an attentional deficit or a tendency to get caught up in anguished, guilt-laden fantasies. Positive-constructive daydreaming is associated (as Freud suggested) with creativity, but it is also linked to problem-solving, memory consolidation and therapeutic self-reflection. Daydreamers have thicker cerebral cortices. This is relevant to ageing because thinning of the cortex is associated with age-related cognitive decline.

The resting brain state is described by neuroscientists as the 'default mode'. When the brain is resting, with the mind wandering, the 'default mode network' is active. Consequently, the default mode is sometimes also referred to as the daydreaming mode. Default mode network activation is also related to ego awareness; thus, daydreaming and personhood are mediated by the same neurobiological complex. The default mode network is less active in people who suffer from Alzheimer's disease and frontotemporal dementia (both of whom possess only a weak or residual sense of identity). There is insufficient evidence to suggest that daydreaming (and the increased connectivity associated with daydreaming) can prevent cognitive decline. But the general picture is intriguing and tantalisingly consistent with Jung's supposition that 'active imagination' can be used to 'strengthen' the totality of the self. Conscious and unconscious divisions of the mind achieve greater unity and ego-integrity is preserved.

There is an obvious area of potential overlap here with slow living. Islands of stillness, in which the mind is allowed to wander, provide opportunities for self-discovery. When sitting on a park bench, perhaps it would be wise to leave your smart phone in your pocket. Facebook, Instagram or X will, in all probability, offer you fewer potentially life-changing insights than your own unconscious (an internal 'internet' of almost unimaginable complexity).

From the nineteenth century onwards, it has been widely acknowledged that creativity is rooted in unconscious mental activity. This is largely because the process of creation is frequently initiated by an idea or concept appearing, without prior development, in the stream of consciousness. Under conditions where inspiration is sustained, creative artists often say that they feel as if they are merely conduits. Many famous pieces of music were 'dreamed' – Paul McCartney's immensely popular song 'Yesterday', for example. Creativity 'bridges' the conscious and unconscious. Thus, when we are being creative, we are widening a channel of communication between the principal divisions of the mind.

Creativity can be employed as a means of accelerating integration, even if the person doing the creating isn't particularly talented. In *A Study of the Process of Individuation*, Jung described a patient whose artistic deficiencies facilitated unconscious communication. Her 'boulders' looked more like 'eggs' than rocks and this was interpretable: 'the unconscious made use of the patient's inability to draw in order to insinuate its own suggestions. I had not overlooked the fact that the boulders had surreptitiously transformed themselves into *eggs*. The egg is a germ of life with a lofty symbolical significance.' Jung believed that these 'eggs' meant that his patient was ready for *rebirth* – ready to embark on the inner journey. Psychoanalysts value errors. Mistakes of all kinds – slips of the tongue, slips of the pen, misreadings, dropping things, trips, blunders – all deserve reflection because they can also be understood as 'insinuations' from the unconscious.

Jung was very adept at finding ways of accessing his own unconscious through creativity. He painted a great deal, but he also discovered more personal, idiosyncratic methods. For example, he built miniature villages with stones and sand on the shore of a lake – like a child, playing.

Another window on the unconscious is our conduct in the context of intimate relationships. Naturally, we treat our life partners differently than anyone else. However, unique declarations of love are often complemented by exceptional levels of criticism. Intimacy promotes disinhibition; we are less judicious, less guarded, more likely to be rude, spiteful – even cruel. Reflecting on what you said when your self-control slipped during an argument will help you to become better acquainted with your shadow. Most people are reluctant to make their shadow's acquaintance – it is, after all, a summation of what we repress – but we should recognise that when we hurt the person we profess to love, we are also discovering a potential programme for self-improvement.

A significant feature of Jung's later writings, and one shared by many transpersonal psychologists, is a non-medical view of psychological distress. A crisis can be a 'sign' rather than a symptom, and depression (or dissatisfaction) should prompt reflection rather than immediate reparative action. This may feel uncomfortable for the average westerner; we have been raised in a culture where dynamism is applauded, and everyone wants a 'quick fix'.

The medical model of mental illness has been questioned since the middle of the nineteenth century, although it wasn't until the 1960s that a comprehensive and philosophically coherent critique entered the popular mainstream. Figures like Thomas Szasz and R. D. Laing argued that mental illness exists only as a metaphor, and that minds cannot 'sicken' in the same way that bodies 'sicken'. In its extreme form, anti-psychiatry rejects biological causation and accuses medicine of mistaking the human condition for a brain disease. More recently, evolutionary psychiatrists have also criticised the medical model and advocated an alternative framework that, at least in some respects, leads to formulations consistent with Jungian and transpersonal psychology. Distress can be functional, motivational – essential for survival. This shift of perspective has major implications for how we respond to mood disturbance in later life.

Depression can be viewed as a form of awakening – an invitation to shift focus and rediscover deeper aspects of being. It can be understood as something that spurs growth rather than shrinkage. When we become depressed, our first response shouldn't be 'How can I get rid of this feeling?' Instead, we should ask: 'What does this feeling mean?' I am not dismissing biological psychiatry. Depression can be the end point of many different pathways, and there are some people who suffer from forms of depression that appear to be strongly associated with biological factors (for example, postpartum or menopausal depression); however, historically, the dominance of the medical model has stifled appreciation of alternatives, of which Jungian and transpersonal accounts are good examples.

Related to this topic is the idea that certain forms of psychological distress are not only functional but enlightening. This view was encouraged by anthropological studies of shamanism. In the 1960s, particularly due to the popularity of R. D. Laing's works, it became fashionable to suggest that individuals suffering from schizophrenia are comparable to tribal wise men and women; that their hallucinations are 'visionary' and that during altered states of consciousness they gain access to deeper truths. Schizophrenia is still a controversial diagnosis, but if we accept its legitimacy, we must also accept that its consequences are usually painful, problematic, and sometimes catastrophic for the affected individual. Although shamans may exhibit schizotypal features, tribal societies do not treat individuals with symptoms that resemble 'full-blown' schizophrenia as 'holy'. Just like us, they recognise that some behaviours are detrimental to the affected person and the tribe, and they do not confuse a distressing mental condition with spiritual elevation. It should be noted that Jung was completely cognisant of this distinction. When the great Irish writer James Joyce took his 'schizophrenic' daughter to see Jung, Joyce made the following observation: 'Doctor Jung, have you noticed that my daughter seems to be submerged in the same waters as me?' It is said that Jung answered: 'Yes, but where you swim, she drowns.'

The unconscious is associated with depth and profundity, but it is also associated with madness and chaos. So why should we listen to it? To some extent, this question is addressed by Jung's assertion that human beings have an innate tendency to evolve towards personhood. Individuation melds conscious and unconscious parts of the mind into an *optimal* relationship. Ordinarily, we can trust it to do its work.

Jung wasn't the only psychologist to posit an innate tendency to evolve towards 'personhood'. Indeed, many representatives of the humanistic and existential schools of psychotherapy arrived at the same conclusion. The organismic theorist Kurt Goldstein introduced the idea of 'self-actualization' – a drive that maximises potential – and this was subsequently endorsed by Abraham Maslow. Carl Rogers believed that human beings have an 'actualising' tendency. Rollo May wrote that the drive to become a person is the primary purpose of human existence. The psychoanalyst Erich Fromm also believed in an innate developmental impetus that culminates in self-discovery. In *The Sane Society*, he wrote: 'The whole life of the individual is nothing but the process of giving birth to himself; indeed, we should be fully born when we die – although it is the tragic fate of most individuals to die before they are born.' Again and again, the same idea has surfaced in the psychotherapy literature: if an individual is not excessively defended or self-alienated, it is assumed that he or she will evolve naturally towards wholeness.

He or she will become the integrated individual that Carl Rogers called the 'fully functioning person'.

Individuals who become integrated and whole tend to live meaningfully. This is consequential beyond mental health considerations. It is customary to link happiness with longevity, and several studies have now confirmed what was once just medical folklore. Happiness is a protective factor, independent of variations in negative affect. However, the relationship between meaning and longevity is stronger. In 2024, Frank Martela and colleagues published the first large-scale study comparing the predictive power of 'purpose' and 'satisfaction', and it was purpose that proved to be the better predictor of longevity. Those who lead meaningful lives can be more confident that they will live longer than those who live happy lives. Martela, a philosopher who specialises in the study of meaning, has proposed a pragmatic answer to the question 'What is the meaning of life?' It is to achieve internal connectivity (which equates with self-knowledge) and social connectivity (so that our 'selves' become meaningful to others). Martela's admirably concise answer to philosophy's most vexed question does not, perhaps, reflect the amount of personal development that usually precedes 'meaningfulness'. As Alfried Längle has argued, meaning is more likely to manifest after the accomplishment of more fundamental existential goals. Rather than pursuing meaning (or happiness, for that matter) directly, it is probably more effective to focus on personal development and allow 'meaningfulness' to emerge as a natural consequence of optimal integration.

As we get older, time becomes more precious, and naturally we want to make the most of what time we have left; however, focusing narrowly on time, like focusing narrowly on happiness, is problematic. Decisions concerning the best use of time are only meaningful to the extent that they are congruent with objectives. If you don't know yourself, the likelihood is that you won't know how to use your time beneficially. A curious feature of modern living is a constant, generalised pressure to 'save' time – and those who are swept along by the headlong rush often have no clear idea of what uses the time they have saved will serve.

Our sense of time can be manipulated, albeit modestly. For example, novel experiences can produce retrospective time dilation. A weekend can be subjectively 'stretched' if it is filled with stimulating activities and events; however, if there is too much novelty in life, novelty will lose its novelty, and the retrospective time dilation effect will disappear. Inhabiting the present moment is associated with many psychological benefits, including retrospective time dilation (because reality is experienced more directly, memories are more vivid, and consequently we remember more of life). Unfortunately, present-moment living has been traditionally 'over-sold' as a universal panacea. We cannot inhabit the 'here and now' continuously, because a certain amount of mental time travel is necessary if we are to prepare for the future, and mental time travel is also essential for the maintenance of psychological health.

Heraclitus famously declared that it is impossible to step into the same river twice. The universe is constantly changing and there is nothing we can do about it. Attempts to manipulate time perception reflect our desire to control the uncontrollable. Time cannot be slowed down or stopped. Even when we have transcendent experiences that seem to take us 'out of time', clocks continue to 'tick' and Heraclitus's river keeps flowing. Efforts to manipulate time perception are really another form of immortality project. Instead of trying to resist the passage of time, we should surrender to its forward momentum. We should fall into step with time, because when we do so we are also falling into step with the cosmos – the natural order of things. A pragmatic way of accomplishing this is by acknowledging our circadian nature. Our sleep–wake cycle connects us to the sun, the solar system, and the greater universe beyond. The more we respect biological timekeeping, the more likely it is that we will be healthy and live longer. Current research suggests that if we abandon attempts to squeeze more life into every artificially extended day, we are rewarded, not with a few extra hours, but many more years of physical and psychological health.

The topic of raised consciousness is central to the study of wisdom. From the shamanistic practices of the earliest cave dwellers, through the meditation and ritual practices of the great religions – by way of twentieth-century transpersonal psychology – up to the current 'psychedelic renaissance', wisdom and altered states of consciousness have always been inextricably linked, and the nature of this relationship seems to be circular. The wise tend to have more spontaneous experiences of raised consciousness, and episodes of raised consciousness have the effect of deepening wisdom. Logically, the more a person places him or herself in situations likely to provoke 'peak experiences', the more likely it is that they will also experience accelerated personal development.

The transition from ordinary to elevated consciousness seems to be facilitated by a shift of emotional state, and the emotion that most frequently initiates this process is awe. Awe is strongly associated with the majesty of nature – an association consolidated in the West by the artists and poets of the Romantic movement. A recurring motif in Romantic art is the solitary wanderer, journeying through a dramatic landscape and occasionally stopping to commune with the 'world soul' (the ultimate reality behind appearances).

Awe is experienced when we encounter aspects of reality that do not fit easily into our existing conceptual frameworks and models. We feel that we are in the presence of something that transcends understanding. Awe is pleasurable, but it also carries registers of fear. Be that as it may, awe-related fear – unlike, for example, fear of being harmed – tends to have lasting, beneficial consequences. The narcissistic carapace that ordinarily restricts personal growth crumbles when humans are faced with a humbling vastness, and reduced ego entrenchment often facilitates the expression of pro-social behaviour. Indeed, increased pro-social behaviour is perhaps the most visible consequence of having had an experience of awe.

Dacher Keltner, a professor of psychology at the University of California, Berkeley, has identified the circumstantial determinants of awe. In addition to immersion in nature, he found that awe is frequently provoked by life and death experiences, epiphanies and mystical experiences. To these he has added some comparatively modest triggers: observing the inspirational behaviour of others, participating in groups, and enjoying works of art. Keltner has called awe engendered by these ostensibly commonplace activities 'everyday awe' – a concept reminiscent of the day-to-day episodes of reflective spirituality that Maslow dubbed 'plateau experiences'. 'Everyday awe' also resonates sympathetically with the Buddhist dictum that even domestic drudgery can connect us with the 'sacred' if we are sufficiently open to that possibility. There is also some overlap here with something the TikTok generation have noticed: the mental health benefits of 'glimmers' – micro-moments of joy such as seeing a rainbow, suddenly becoming aware of bird song, or feeling an unexpected swell of affection.

Well-being is linked to individuation and becoming whole. *We find ourselves.* But at the same time, personal development leads to greater connectedness, which must (it seems reasonable to suppose) blur the edges of the self and reduce self-definition. There is *loss of self.* This feels like a contradiction. However, what happens when people 'connect' is perhaps more accurately described as self-expansion. The parts of the self are integrated as a person individuates, then the integrated self, through connectivity, is integrated into the greater whole of the social and material universe. This would recast peak experiences and awe as forms of higher-order integration. The self is not being lost, as such, but massively enlarged. And how does that feel? Raised consciousness tends to be described using superlatives like rapture, ecstasy and bliss. What is being experienced can no longer be represented by language. It can only be 'felt'. Understanding individuation as a continuous process that extends to the transpersonal reduces the tension created by polarising self-discovery and self-loss. In fact, what we call self-loss might be, paradoxically, the pinnacle of self-discovery. The spokes of connectivity extend the self beyond the customary wheel rim of subjectivity. Expansion necessarily attenuates the ego, but when consciousness subsequently contracts, the experience always proves to have been enriching.

For some, the notion of connectivity is nothing more than a New Age banality. That everything is connected is a tired and frankly obvious observation. But we shouldn't forget that clichés are truths that have lost their power to affect us because of overexposure. A truth that has been repeated ad nauseam is still true. If we mistake concept-fatigue for sophistication, we run the risk of depriving ourselves of opportunities for growth.

The feeling of 'loss of self' during episodes of awe is associated with *reduced* default mode network activation. This is the opposite of what happens when people daydream. It was suggested above that daydreaming – a close relative of Jung's active imagination – can facilitate integration, and that this is consistent with brain scanning evidence that shows an *increase* in default mode network activation during daydreaming. Again, we have an apparent contradiction. Both awe and daydreaming promote personal development, but they pull in different directions biologically. What should we want? More default mode network activation, or less? A tightly unified self, or a diffusing self? The answer is both. Daydreaming is *primarily* integrative. It opens channels of communication between conscious and unconscious divisions of mind. Whereas awe is instructive. An experience of raised consciousness leads to realisations and motivates behaviour change. Almost all wisdom traditions combine a body of knowledge (for example, scripture) with practices intended to raise consciousness (for example, meditation). This suggests that wisdom is acquired through repeated cycles of reflection and dissolution. The self is periodically strengthened, and then temporarily weakened, to accomplish progressive and optimal forms of recrudescence.

One of Dacher Keltner's sources of 'everyday awe' is music, perhaps the most mysterious of all art forms due to its essential ineffability. In *The Birth of Tragedy*, Nietzsche wrote: 'Language ... can never by any means disclose the innermost heart of music; language, in its attempts to imitate it, can only be in superficial contact with music; while all the eloquence of lyric poetry cannot bring the deeper significance of the latter one step nearer.' Music stirs memories and feelings, it awakens parts of the self, directly, without words. It is an effective means of opening alternative channels of communication within the self.

The controversial film director Ken Russell experienced a kind of Jamesian 'conversion' while listening to music: 'I was recuperating from a mini-breakdown at the end of the war and leading a vegetable existence at home, recovering. The radio was on all the time and for several months I sat in a chair not paying much attention when suddenly some music came on that made me sit up and take notice. The announcer gave the title of the piece and I dashed outside, pumped up the tyres of my bicycle and cycled to the nearest record shop where I asked for Tchaikovsky's B flat minor Piano Concerto played by Solomon and the Hallé.' Russell later claimed that hearing Tchaikovsky's first piano concerto had cured his mental illness.

I cannot recall any of my patients reporting such a dramatic transformation, but many of them *did* describe pivotal moments in which music played an important role. Usually late at night or in the early hours of the morning, listening to music had helped them recover courage, resolve or hope; a part of themselves that they had somehow lost had been found again. Melodies leave trails, pathways that can guide listeners to important inner locations, zones of discovery. Blocked emotions can be released when we hear a poignant chord change. Even subtle shifts of feeling that occur while listening to music merit at least some reflection.

The Austrian musicologist Viktor Zuckerkandl observed, 'Words divide, tones unite.' Listening to music engages almost every area of the brain: the auditory cortex, the frontal lobes, the mesolimbic system (especially the nucleus accumbens which is associated with reward), some language areas, the basal ganglia and the cerebellum. Complete immersion in music creates a brain state that is perhaps comparable to psychedelic connectivity. Music recalibrates the mind and the body. Our brains 'light up' and we tap our feet. The rate at which we are breathing changes, as does blood pressure, heart rate and body temperature. We shiver, get goosebumps, our hair stands on end, and sometimes, we cry. For many, music is more than art, more than a provocation of 'everyday awe', and something closer to a portal through which we can catch glimpses of the numinous.

Today, people are living longer than ever before. Indeed, so much longer that researchers have found it necessary to introduce a new codification – 'old-old age' – to reflect this trend. The fastest-growing age group in the world is composed of centenarians.

Long lives are more desirable if they are also happy and meaningful. The prospect of entering a ninth or even tenth decade in a state of despair is, for most people, quite disturbing. Our preferred cultural representations of advanced old age tend to be of smiling sages, comfortably ensconced in a favourite armchair, surrounded by grandchildren, or even great-grandchildren. We are unnerved by alternative scenarios: emptiness, regret, stupor, loneliness – grief.

Compared to middle age, old age is (at least superficially) a time of relative contentment. There are ostensibly fewer pressures to deal with, especially those associated with the demands of work. But old age – and old-old age – are undoubtedly testing, and episodes of happiness usually become less frequent as the years accumulate. Around a third of people over sixty-five suffer from depression, anxiety, or both. For these individuals, depression and anxiety have not prompted personal growth. Instead, they have become locked into states of unhappiness and fear.

By contrast, there is a sub-group of the old and very old who exhibit exceptionally good psychological adjustment. When studied, their well-being appears to be strongly associated with pragmatic, transpersonal attitudes, and engagement in reflective practices that appear to have resulted in superior levels of horizontal and vertical integration.

The term 'gerotranscendence' was invented by the Swedish sociologist Lars Tornstam, who in the 1980s, after some preliminary investigative work, began to question the somewhat pessimistic view (expressed by many contemporary gerontologists) that good psychological outcomes are rarely observed among the elderly. Tornstam was acquainted with the works of Jung and Erikson, which explains why, when he was conducting his initial qualitative research, he was alert to the signs of successful individuation and integration. He soon noted a mismatch between the dispiriting orthodox consensus and what appeared to be a more encouraging reality. Tornstam became particularly interested in old people who were reflective, psychologically well adjusted and content – a sub-group he identified as 'gerotranscendent'.

Tornstam chose the suffix 'transcendence' because the informants he interviewed had in common 'going beyond' or 'rising above' the limitations that had circumscribed their earlier lives; however, as his work progressed, 'gerotranscendence' acquired more 'spiritual' connotations.

Summarising his early investigations, Tornstam said of his informants: 'A transpersonal sense of affinity with others and with earlier generations had developed, as well as a sense of being part of a whole. Informants also talked about a kind of redefinition of time, space, life and death, and an increased need for positive contemplative solitude.' These aspects of personal development were associated with relatively high levels of satisfaction and acceptance. Tornstam's informants were not raging against the 'dying of the light'. Quite the contrary. They were prepared to go gently into 'that good night' whenever fate decreed.

According to Tornstam, gerotranscendence has three dimensions that reflect attitudes and qualities pertinent to spirituality, selfhood and social relationships.

The first of these, the 'cosmic dimension', is characterised principally by changes in time perception. Respondents tended to treat the past and present as 'equal'. They did not feel like 'isolates' and were acutely aware of being links in a generational chain. A strong sense of affinity connected them, not only to the dead but also to the unborn. Their 'sense of time' had become increasingly correspondent with the 'block universe' (see chapter 9). They embraced mystery, accepted intellectual limitations, and no longer had the need to find absolute answers. Episodes of spiritual elevation comparable to 'everyday awe' were experienced with some frequency and, interestingly, music had become especially important to them.

The second dimension of gerotranscendence reflects aspects

of personal development and self-understanding. Critical self-examination (comparable to Jung's coming to terms with the shadow) was important for Tornstam's respondents. In addition, memories were reviewed in a reconciliatory manner and life decisions were consciously 'owned'. A marked reduction in self-centredness was complemented by an increase in altruism. Respondents were also health conscious, but not obsessively so.

The third dimension of gerotranscendence concerns social and personal relationships. Received opinion suggests that socialising is so beneficial in old age, one can never get enough of it; however, Tornstam's research qualifies this assertion. His respondents described shying away from shallow socialising and becoming increasingly selective in their choice of company. They had abandoned their 'personas' and expressed a clear preference for more meaningful and authentic communication, usually with a single person (at any one time). Tornstam also noted a characteristic that he called, somewhat opaquely, 'emancipated innocence', the essence of which is not worrying about looking stupid and being less hidebound by social conventions. Perhaps what we ordinarily disparage as eccentricity in some elderly people is simply the discarding of the straitjacket of self-consciousness. Respondents rejected dichotomous 'right–wrong' thinking, exhibited tolerant attitudes, and were generally broad-minded. Finally, they reported that they felt happier unencumbered by possessions. This is included as a feature of Tornstam's social dimension because gerotranscendent individuals often start giving things away, especially to their children and grandchildren.

Tornstam's inventory of *all* the characteristics associated with gerotranscendence is more exhaustive than the above summary; however, if the *core* elements of gerotranscendence are present, this will usually be enough to meet our cultural expectations of wisdom – and the wise are psychologically well adjusted.

For Tornstam, gerotranscendence is an imperative. Reflecting on probable alternative outcomes, he wrote that it is 'a tragedy that many of us live our entire lives with the erroneous idea that it is only during the first half of life that we develop and mature. Practising such a way of life ends up in our dying as only half-matured individuals. Then, according to Jung, we develop psychiatric symptoms including depression, anxiety, fear of death, disgust and a feeling that life has been stolen from us. For some, suicide becomes the final escape from this.'

Tornstam (who died in 2016) has been criticised for displaying New Age naivety. Many think that his work is too positive, too optimistic, a misguided attempt to 're-enchant' old age – and he has been accused of promoting a 'weak' theory. However, his account of the gerotranscendent individual has much in common with the approach to personal development that has 'emerged' from the ideas that have been brought together in this book: Jamesian spirituality, Stoicism, scrutinising one's shadow, existential courage, connectivity, altered time perception, integration of the parts of self, raised consciousness and a reflective 'inner journey'. This degree of overlap could be interpreted as convergence – an indication of underlying conceptual 'solidity'.

The active grandparent hypothesis suggests that evolutionary pressures have extended the human lifespan. Human females are unique among primates because they live well beyond the menopause. We are meant to grow old. That is how we have been 'designed'. Perhaps what psychologists have dubbed self-actualising tendencies have been selected – along with life-preserving and reproductive instincts – to ensure that we fulfil our evolutionary destiny. Providing we are not excessively defended, we will tend towards wholeness, balance, stability and inner cohesion. We will progress towards a state that is, in all its essential parts, gerotranscendent.

There are countless books and theories that offer advice on

how to live longer. We are embodied, so maintaining physical health is of paramount importance; however, this excessive emphasis on the physical has resulted in a neglect of the psychological. Historically, mental health has always been seen as a secondary concern. Yet, psychological health has an enormous impact on longevity. Even one's attitude to getting older makes a difference. Individuals who have more positive self-perceptions of ageing live seven and a half years longer than those with less positive self-perceptions. It is an effect that seems to be partially mediated by 'the will to live'. And of course, as Viktor Frankl tells us, the will to live is far stronger in individuals whose lives are meaningful.

Once, I saw an ageing psychiatrist for psychotherapy who was suffering from depression. He held a senior position at a London teaching hospital, and he had also published many academic papers. He was a skilled clinician, and it was a little daunting, seeing a man like him for psychotherapy. After all, he knew as much as I did about the discipline – probably more, in fact. What could I offer him that he didn't know already? After some inconsequential introductory remarks, I asked my first question. I'd hoped that it would be penetrating, but all I could think of was the standard question that anybody who had read a basic textbook on the therapeutic modality I was employing would have asked. At first, the psychiatrist didn't answer. I imagined that he was disappointed by my lack of imagination. Then I noticed his eyes glittering, and a tear trickled down his cheek. He took a deep breath, and said: 'It's not the same when you're in the other seat, is it?' Knowing about psychotherapy and being a patient in psychotherapy are quite different things. I think both of us had underestimated the power of experiencing something compared to just knowing something.

Psychological adjustment in later life is achieved not by acquiring knowledge, but by applying it. This might seem elementary, but human beings frequently fail to apply what they know.

One of the most powerful images of old age in western art is *St Jerome Writing* by the baroque master Caravaggio. Caravaggio painted a second version a few years after completing the first, but the original shows a more obviously 'aged' saint: he is almost completely bald, except for some tufts of thin hair, and he has a long white beard. Jerome was an early Christian confessor, translator and historian, and his image is frequently paired with that of an owl to signal his wisdom and scholarship. Yet, he is reputed to have been a sensual and sexually active youth. Somewhere along the path of life, he changed direction. And his vigour was transferred from the loins to the soul.

Caravaggio's Jerome sits at a simple wooden table and he is working on a Latin translation of the Bible, surrounded by darkness. It isn't just any darkness, it is Caravaggio's signature darkness, an impenetrable black void. Caravaggio was aware (more than most, perhaps) that the void is never far away. It is the backdrop of life, the hem of the grim reaper's habit. Caravaggio's darkness serves two purposes: it reminds us of our mortality, but it also throws life into sharp relief. His exquisitely illuminated figures are extraordinarily vital. They appear so real, so full of life, that one wouldn't be surprised if they suddenly started moving. If Caravaggio had bathed Jerome in sunlight, his presence would be less intense. The darkness gives him definition.

Mortality is underscored by the staple prop of a *memento mori*, a human skull, which reiterates the reflective dome of the saint's bald head. The visible skull directs us straight to the 'implied' skull beneath the flesh. You *will* die and all your immortality projects will fail. Yet, despite the undeniable morbidity of this portrait, Caravaggio's depiction of Jerome is curiously uplifting.

Here is a man of substance, a thoughtful, compassionate man. The 'closed' space in which he sits is suggestive of introspection, interiority – the successful accomplishment of inner journeys. His eyes are dark-adapted and he sees things in the shadows that would otherwise be invisible, lost in the glare. Moreover, Jerome doesn't look like a feeble old man. He is thin and sinewy, but his extended arm is well muscled. He is swathed in red cloth – a vibrant, sanguine red – that gives him a dignified, martial appearance. He resembles a Roman commander – Marcus Aurelius, perhaps, on campaign, composing his meditations outside Vienna. The battle of life goes on, and however old you are, you are always, in a sense, on the front line, always in the present moment, always part of the advance guard.

The most distinctive feature of Caravaggio's portrait of Jerome is that the saint is depicted with a quill in his hand, writing. He might be alone in his cell, but he is performing an act that will connect him with other people in perpetuity. It is a transpersonal act. He is a unique link in a chain of being, and his existence completes the universe.

The thematic essences of Caravaggio's *St Jerome Writing* find complementary expression in a lyrical and inspirational passage composed – in reflective mood – by the philosopher Bertrand Russell in an essay titled 'How to Grow Old'. It is wisdom distilled, the pith and marrow of meaningful insight, and it provides us with a fitting final cadence:

> Some old people are oppressed by the fear of death. In the young there is a justification for this feeling. Young men who have reason to fear that they will be killed in battle may justifiably feel bitter in the thought that they have been cheated of the best things that life has to offer. But in an old man who has known human joys and sorrows, and has achieved whatever work it was in him to do, the fear of death is somewhat abject and ignoble. The best way to overcome it – so at least it seems to me – is to make your interests gradually wider and more impersonal, until bit by bit the walls of the ego recede, and your life becomes increasingly merged in the universal life. An individual human existence should be like a river – small at first, narrowly contained within its banks, and rushing passionately past boulders and over waterfalls. Gradually the river grows wider, the banks recede, the waters flow more quietly, and in the end, without any visible break, they become merged in the sea, and painlessly lose their individual being. The man who, in old age, can see his life in this way, will not suffer from the fear of death, since the things he cares for will continue. And if, with the decay of vitality, weariness increases, the thought of rest will be not unwelcome. I should wish to die while still at work, knowing that others will carry on what I can no longer do, and content in the thought that what was possible has been done.

References

Preface

'At one point, midway on our path in life . . . blurred and lost' I have borrowed from several translations: *The Lost – Dante's Inferno Canto I, lines 1–3*, translated by Chrissy Williams (https://modernpoetryintranslation.com/poem/the-lost-dantes-inferno-canto-i-lines-1-3/); Dante (2013), *The Divine Comedy: A New Verse Translation by Clive James*, Picador: London; Dante (1949/1977), *The Divine Comedy: I Hell*, translated and with an introduction by Dorothy L. Sayers, Penguin Books: Harmondsworth; *Dante's Divine Comedy* (2009), translated by Henry Wadsworth Longfellow, edited and with introductory text by Anna Amari-Parker, Arcturus: Bermondsey Street, London.

Nevertheless, a recent working paper . . . individuals from 'rich nations' Giuntella, O., McManus, S., Mujcic, R., Oswald, A., Powdthavee, N. & Tohamy, A. (2022), 'The Midlife Crisis', National Bureau of Economic Research, WP 30442.

For example, in the sixteenth-century Jewish mystical tradition Kabbalah . . . Iain McGilchrist (2021/2023), *The Matter With Things: Our Brains, Our Delusions, and the Unmaking of the World*, Volume II, Perspectiva Press: London, 825–6.

Brain scanning studies . . . the default mode network James J. Gattuso, Daniel Perkins, Simon Ruffell et al (2022), 'Default Mode Network Modulation by Psychedelics: A Systematic Review', *International Journal of Neuropharmacology*, Oct 22; 26(3): 155–88 (https://www.ncbi.nlm.nih.gov/pmc/articles/PMC10032309/).

Chapter 1 – Denial: The Quest for Immortality

'He Who Saw the Deep' The Epic of Gilgamesh (1999/2003), translated with an introduction by Andrew George, Penguin: London, xv–xvi.

'I am afraid of death' Ibid, 70.

Terror management theory . . . knowledge of death Greenberg, J., Pyszczynski, T. & Solomon, S. (1986), 'The causes and consequences of a need for self-esteem: a terror management theory', in R. F. Baumeister (ed.), *Public Self and Private Self*, Springer-Verlag: New York, 189–212.

'*the skull will grin in at the banquet*' William James (1902/1985), *The Varieties of Religious Experience*, edited and introduced by Martin E. Marty, Penguin Classics: London, 141.

'Oh, why isn't man immortal? . . .' Anton Chekhov (1971), 'Ward No. 6', in *Lady with Lapdog and Other Stories*, Penguin: Harmondsworth, 150.

'*Good gracious me . . .*' Ibid.

'Consciousness of death *is the primary repression, not sexuality*' Ernest Becker (1973/2020), *The Denial of Death*, Souvenir Press: London, 96.

Some transhumanists . . . first immortals have already been born Mark O'Connell (2017), *To Be a Machine*, Granta: London, 29.

'*A key capability in the 2030s . . . millions-fold by 2045*' Ray Kurzweil (2024), *The Singularity is Nearer: When We Merge with AI* (Chapter 1: 'Where Are We in the Six Stages?'), Vintage: London.

'*Babel of views*' Ernest Becker (1973/2020), *The Denial of Death*, Souvenir Press: London, xviii.

'*One of the reasons . . . no throbbing, vital centre*' Ibid.

'*I think that taking life seriously . . . it is false*' Ibid, 283–4.

'*In my early seventies did I really care . . . an oral surgeon*' Daniel Klein (2012/2018), *Travels with Epicurus*, Oneworld Publications: London, 5.

Another tech billionaire, Bryan Johnson . . . hoping to be revitalised Peter Salmon (2024), 'New Life in the Veins', *New Humanist* (Winter), 37.

In advanced old age, brain tissue mass . . . a seven-year-old child Dilip Jeste and Scott Lafee (2020), *Wiser: The Scientific Roots of Wisdom, Compassion, and What Makes Us Good*, Sounds True: Boulder, Colorado, 51.

'*I had blithely assumed . . . the rising tide of the sea*' Henry Marsh (2022), *And Finally: Matters of Life and Death* (Part One, Denial), Vintage: London.

'*As I looked at the images . . . helplessness and despair*' Ibid.

'*I believe that those who speculate . . . quite literally right*' Ernest Becker (1973/2020), *The Denial of Death*, Souvenir Press: London, 27.

'*taken for dead for two good hours*' Michel de Montaigne (1991), *The Complete Essays*, translated by M. A. Screech, Penguin Classics: Harmondsworth, 419.

'*bucketful*' of blood Ibid.

'*closer to death than to life*' Ibid.

'*To me it seemed as though my life was merely clinging to my lips*' Ibid, 420.

'*free from unpleasantness*' Ibid.

'*that gentle feeling . . . glide into sleep*' Ibid.

'*Don't read him as children do . . . read him* in order to live' Sarah Bakewell (2010/2011), *How to Live: A Life of Montaigne in One Question and Twenty Attempts at an Answer*, Vintage: London, 11.

'From being the gloomiest ... the art of living well' Ibid, 14.

'to inure yourself to death all you have to do is to draw nigh to it'. Michel de Montaigne (1991), *The Complete Essays*, translated by M. A. Screech, Penguin Classics: Harmondsworth, 424

'I felt myself oozing away so gently, and in so gentle and pleasing a fashion' Ibid, 423

'How weary, stale, flat and unprofitable ...' William Shakespeare (1988), *The Tragedy of Hamlet, Prince of Denmark*, New Penguin Shakespeare, general editor T. J. B. Spencer, associate editor Stanley Wells, Penguin: Harmondsworth, 75.

'wise men at their end know dark is right' Dylan Thomas (1979), 'Do Not Go Gentle into That Good Night', from *The Poems*, edited and introduced by Daniel Jones, J. M. Dent & Sons Ltd: London, 208.

Chapter 2 – Acceptance: Embracing Reality

'because the search for mental health ... out of season' John Sellars (2020), *The Fourfold Remedy: Epicurus and the Art of Happiness*, Penguin Random House: UK, 9.

There is a passage in Epictetus ... good clinical practice Epictetus (2008), *Discourses and Selected Writings*, translated and edited by Robert Dobbin, Penguin Books: UK, 227.

'It is not events that disturb people, it is their judgements concerning them' Ibid, 223.

'nothing is sufficient for the person who finds sufficiency too little' Epicurus (2012), *The Art of Happiness*, translated with an introduction and commentary by George K. Strodach, foreword by Daniel Klein, Penguin Books: New York, 183.

'death is nothing to us' Ibid, 132.

'so long as we are existent ... we are non-existent' Ibid, 157.

'of no concern either to the living ... themselves non-existent' Ibid.

'On this happy day ... the conversations we have had' Ibid, 84.

'exhorted his friends to remember his teachings and passed away' Ibid, 83

'he was carried into a vapour-bath, where he suffocated' Seneca (2004), *Letters from a Stoic*, selected and translated with an introduction by Robin Campbell, Penguin Books: UK, 244.

'living is the least important activity of the preoccupied man' John Sellars (2020), *Lessons in Stoicism*, Penguin Random House: UK, 50.

we should reflect on our own mortality every day Ibid, 49.

'This is our big mistake ... owned by death' Ryan Holiday and Stephen Hanselman (2022), *Lives of the Stoics*, Profile Books: London, 191.

'the act of forgetting is a form of death always present in life' Philip Roth (2001), *Shop Talk: A Writer and His Colleagues and Their Work*, Boston: Houghton Mifflin, 97.

'It will be the same after me as it was before me' Seneca (2004), *Letters from a Stoic*, selected and translated with an introduction by Robin Campbell, Penguin Books: UK, 104.

'Wouldn't you think a man an utter fool . . . no concern with either period' Ibid, 127.

'a kind of incurable sickness' Ibid, 209.

old age can be 'full of pleasure' Ibid, 58.

'How nice it is to have out-worn one's desires and left them behind!' Ibid.

'It is the final glass . . . off into oblivion' Ibid.

'You will die . . . because you are alive' Ibid, 132.

'Didn't I warn you?' Ryan Holiday and Stephen Hanselman (2022), *Lives of the Stoics*, Profile Books: London, 253.

'the mind and its functions require the bulk of our attention' Epictetus (2008), *Discourses and Selected Writings*, translated and edited by Robert Dobbin, Penguin Books: UK, 240.

'The philosopher's lecture-hall . . . when you enter it' Ryan Holiday and Stephen Hanselman (2022), *Lives of the Stoics*, Profile Books: London, 256.

Epictetus declared that the principal task . . . can't be controlled Ibid, 257.

'is the body's problem, not the mind's' Epictetus (2008), *Discourses and Selected Writings*, translated and edited by Robert Dobbin, Penguin Books: UK, 224.

'an impediment to the leg, but not to the will' Ryan Holiday and Stephen Hanselman (2022), *Lives of the Stoics*, Profile Books: London, 253.

'I must die. But must I die bawling?' Epictetus (2008), *Discourses and Selected Writings*, translated and edited by Robert Dobbin, Penguin Books: UK, 7.

'I have to die . . . dying I will tend to later' Ibid.

'Under no circumstances . . . she was returned' Ibid, 225.

'a late middle-aged man . . . the demands of life' John Sellars (2020), *Lessons in Stoicism*, Penguin Random House: UK, 40.

Freudian combination . . . morally weaker 'lower' parts Marcus Aurelius (2006), *Meditations*, translated with notes by Martin Hammond, and an introduction by Diskin Clay, Penguin Books: UK, xvii.

addressing himself as 'you' . . . observations and interpretations Ibid.

a 'fortress' Ibid, 80.

'the whole earth is a mere point in space' Ibid, 24.

the vastness of 'immeasurable time' Ibid.

'Take a view from above . . . lived after you . . .' Ibid, 89.

'how many . . . soon forget it' Ibid.

'Whatever happens to you . . . spinning from eternity . . .' Ibid, 95.

'thread of destiny' that can be traced back to 'ancient causes' Ibid, 38.

'You should meditate often . . . the unity of all being' Ibid, 53.

'is maimed ... connection and continuity' Ibid, 38.

'What does not benefit the hive, does not benefit the bee either' Ibid, 57.

'The present moment ... he does not possess' Ibid, 14.

'both the longest-lived and the earliest to die ... stands to be deprived' Ibid

There are conflicting accounts ... the most uplifting Ryan Holiday and Stephen Hanselman (2022), *Lives of the Stoics*, Profile Books: London, 49.

Chapter 3 – Turning Points: Revelations, Awakenings and Callings

'every corner of the world' Joseph Campbell (1949), *The Hero with a Thousand Faces*, Bolingen Series XVII, Third edition, The Joseph Campbell Foundation, New World Library: Novato, California, xiii.

'the call to adventure' Ibid (see Part I, Chapter 1: 'Departure: The Call to Adventure').

'The apple unbitten in the palm' Philip Larkin (2003), *Collected Poems*, Faber and Faber: London, 103.

'the awakening of the self' Joseph Campbell (1949), *The Hero with a Thousand Faces*, Bolingen Series XVII, Third edition, The Joseph Campbell Foundation, New World Library: Novato, California, 42.

'atmosphere of irresistible fascination' Ibid, 46.

What must be faced ... 'the conscious personality' Ibid.

'even though the hero returns ... they may be found unfruitful' Ibid.

'Often in actual life ... other interests' Ibid, 49.

'against the natural order of things' Douglas Adams (2021), *The Salmon of Doubt*, Pan: London.

'It seems possible that, after a certain age ... an ever-receding past' Michael Foley (2013), *Life Lessons from Bergson*, Macmillan: London, 40–1.

'chance word ... magic spring' Joseph Campbell (1949), *The Hero with a Thousand Faces*, Bolingen Series XVII, Third edition, The Joseph Campbell Foundation, New World Library: Novato, California, 5.

'I feel something start within me ... mounting slowly' Marcel Proust (1989), *Remembrance of Things Past*, Volume One (Swann's Way, Within a Budding Grove), translated by C. K. Scott Moncrieff and Terence Kilmartin, Penguin: Harmondsworth, 49.

'palpitating in the depths of my being' Ibid.

'leave the thing alone' Ibid, 50.

'in the bosom of immortal night' Joseph Campbell (1949), *The Hero with a Thousand Faces*, Bolingen Series XVII, Third edition, The Joseph Campbell Foundation, New World Library: Novato, California, 44.

if diagnosed with depression ... three to six months Whiteford, H. A., Harris, M. G.,

McKeon, G. et al (2013), 'Estimating remission from untreated major depression: a systematic review and meta-analysis', *Psychological Medicine*, Vol. 43, Issue 8, 1569–85.

'revelatory experiences' David B. Yaden and Andrew B. Newberg (2022), *The Varieties of Spiritual Experience: 21st Century Research and Perspectives* (Chapter 10: Revelatory Experiences: Voices, Visions, and Epiphanies), OUP: New York, 185–206.

'calling experiences' Ibid, 195.

those who follow vocational 'callings' Ibid, 197.

Thinking is effortful ... automatic, fast and inaccurate see Daniel Kahneman (2011/2012), *Thinking Fast and Slow*, Allen Lane, Penguin Books: Strand, London.

Charles Darwin ... 'better than a dog' Robert Wright (1994/1996), *The Moral Animal: Why We Are the Way We Are*, Abacus: London, 114.

Evidence demonstrating the superiority of intuition ... Iain McGilchrist (2021/2023), *The Matter With Things: Our Brains, Our Delusions, and the Unmaking of the World*, Volume 1, Perspectiva Press: London, 701–3.

It is discussed in academic papers ... popular psychology books Zander, T., Öllinger, M. & Volz, Kirsten G. (2016), 'Intuition and Insight: Two Processes that Build on Each Other or Fundamentally Differ?', *Frontiers in Psychology*, Sep 13; 7: 1395. See also Gladwell, M. (2005), *Blink: The Power of Thinking Without Thinking*, Penguin Books: London.

Nietzsche once wrote, 'There is more sense in thy body than in thy best wisdom' Iain McGilchrist (2021/2023), *The Matter With Things: Our Brains, Our Delusions, and the Unmaking of the World*, Volume 1, Perspectiva Press: London, 706.

The gut has between two and six hundred million neurons Ibid, 679.

In addition, the gut transmits ... to the gut Ibid.

The heart also has its own nervous system ... the 'little brain' of the heart see J. Andrew Armour (2007), 'The Little Brain on the Heart', *Cleveland Clinical Journal of Medicine*, Vol. 74, Supplement 1.

more controversially, it has also been suggested ... intuitive information see M. O. Salem (2007), *The Heart, Mind and Spirit* (https://www.rcpsych.ac.uk/docs/default-source/members/sigs/spirituality-spsig/resources/heart-mind-and-spirit-mohamed-salem.pdf?sfvrsn=207f7229_2).

'call of the soul' Lisa Miller (2021/2022), *The Awakened Brain: The Psychology of Spirituality*, Allen Lane: London, 174.

This effect has been demonstrated ... by cognitive psychologists Sio, U. N. & Ormerod, T. C. (2009), 'Does incubation enhance problem solving? A meta-analytic review', *Psychological Bulletin*, 135(1), 94–120.

'awakening experiences' Steve Taylor (2018), 'An Awakening', *The Psychologist*, 6 August 2018. (https://www.bps.org.uk/psychologist/awakening).

'awakened awareness' Lisa Miller (2021/2022), *The Awakened Brain: The Psychology of*

Spirituality, Allen Lane: London, 162.

Specific structures and areas of the brain ... became active Ibid.

'see that the world is alive talking to us' Ibid.

'achieving awareness' Ibid, 163.

'we literally see more ... What is life showing me now?' Ibid, 164.

'This awakened awareness ... life's purpose and meaning' Ibid, 164–5.

Chapter 4 – Soul Searching: The Psychology of Spirituality

family, work, education and religious community Dilip Jeste and Scott Lafee (2020), *Wiser: The Scientific Roots of Wisdom, Compassion, and What Makes Us Good*, Sounds True: Boulder, Colorado, 194.

Regular attendance of religious services ... diagnosed with cancer Ibid, 195.

There are also considerable mental health benefits ... reduced risk of suicide Ibid.

This misconception arose ... religious in nature David B. Yaden and Andrew B. Newberg (2022), *The Varieties of Spiritual Experience: 21st Century Research and Perspectives*, Oxford University Press: Oxford, 123.

Over the past thirty years ... can be disentangled Lisa Miller (2021/2022), *The Awakened Brain: The Psychology of Spirituality*, Allen Lane: London, 60.

Kendler demonstrated ... decreased risk of addiction Kendler, K. S., Gardner, C. O. & Prescott, C. A. (1997), 'Religion, psychopathology, and substance use and abuse: a multimeasure, genetic-epidemiologic study', *American Journal of Psychiatry* 154(3): 322–39.

Interpreting this kind of data ... rooted in biology Lisa Miller (2021/2022), *The Awakened Brain: The Psychology of Spirituality*, Allen Lane: London, 58.

'It was the largest protective effect ... in the resilience literature' Ibid, 52.

Miller suggests that what we call 'depression' ... continuously frustrated Ibid, 62.

it has been argued ... trends in contemporary research David B. Yaden and Andrew B. Newberg (2022), *The Varieties of Spiritual Experience: 21st Century Research and Perspectives*, Oxford University Press: Oxford, 7.

Henry David Thoreau ... dinner guests Ibid, 18.

The philosopher Ralph Waldo Emerson was William's godfather Ibid, 19.

'best friend' ... 'the most wildly melodious perfume' Linda Simon (1998), *Genuine Reality: A Life of William James*, University of Chicago Press: Chicago, 95.

'real backbone' of 'religious life' ... 'most important function' William James (1985), letter quoted in the Introduction to *The Varieties of Religious Experience: A Study in Human Nature*, edited with an introduction by Martin E. Marty, Penguin Books: London, xix.

Human beings, he says, are prone to 'world sickness' Ibid, 139 *failures, blunders and misdeeds* Ibid, 138.

'a little cooling down . . . melancholy metaphysicians' Ibid, 140.

'Can things whose end . . . our souls require?' Ibid, 139.

'Back of everything . . . all-encompassing blackness.' Ibid.

'Old age has the last word' Ibid, 140.

'every individual existence . . . helpless agony' Ibid, 163.

Tolstoy was alone in a forest, listening to 'mysterious noises' . . . Ibid, 185.

His dormant 'juvenile force of faith' was revived, and he realised that his refined and conventional life was 'no life, but a parody of life' Ibid, 185.

Tolstoy's 'crisis was the getting of his soul in order . . . its unity and level' Ibid, 186.

James quotes from St Augustine . . . 'wills' that disturbed his soul Ibid, 172.

'There are persons . . . another gets the upper hand' Ibid, 169.

The unhappy and dissatisfied . . . 'intellectual constitution' Ibid, 167.

James proposes that healthy psychological adjustment . . . 'the inner self' Ibid, 170.

For some people, this 'unifying of the inner self' . . . 'right subordination' Ibid, 170.

'sick souls' . . . 'must be twice-born in order to be happy' Ibid, 166.

'if there be higher spiritual agencies . . . remain ajar or open' Ibid, 242.

'a shifting of the emotional centre . . . harmonious affections . . .' Ibid, 273.

These correspond closely . . . with healthy ageing Dilip Jeste and Scott Lafee (2020), *Wiser: The Scientific Roots of Wisdom, Compassion, and What Makes Us Good*, Sounds True: Boulder, Colorado, 13.

from a mid- or late-life crisis . . . 'inner unity and peace' William James (1985), *The Varieties of Religious Experience: A Study in Human Nature*, edited with an introduction by Martin E. Marty, Penguin Books: London, 175.

James was fully aware of Freud's work . . . The Varieties of Religious Experience Ibid, 234.

While travelling in Switzerland . . . and 'virtue' David B. Yaden and Andrew B. Newberg (2022), *The Varieties of Spiritual Experience: 21st Century Research and Perspectives*, Oxford University Press: Oxford, 30.

James also experimented with nitrous oxide . . . accessible to him Ibid.

In his first published description . . . 'intense metaphysical illumination' Mike Jay (2024), *Psychonauts: Drugs and the Making of the Modern Mind*, Yale University Press: London, 103.

'there is an element of wisdom . . . a creed about the world' Bertrand Russell (1986), *Mysticism and Logic*, Unwin Paperbacks: London, 29.

'whatever is best in Man' . . . Ibid, 29.

In his autobiography, Russell... episode of 'mystic illumination' Bertrand Russell (1967), *The Autobiography of Bertrand Russell 1872–1914*, George Allen and Unwin Ltd: London, 146.

'Suddenly the ground... quite another region' Ibid.

'cut off from everyone and everything by walls of agony' Ibid.

'loneliness of the human soul'... 'teachers have preached' Ibid.

'became a completely different person' Ibid.

'The mystic insight... all my human relations' Ibid.

received a grant... a reservation in Alberta Scott Barry Kaufman (2022), *Transcend: The New Science of Self-Actualization*, Sheldon Press: London, 4–5.

ranked highly among these traits... a general openness to experience Ibid, 89.

ego transcendence... 'fusion of the person and the world' Ibid, 196.

Maslow shared James's view... integration and wholeness Ibid, xxxi.

In addition to peak experiences... 'unitary consciousness' Ibid, 242.

In fact, just before he died... 'sacralizing' exercises Ibid, 243.

Transcenders are more prone to sadness... the suffering of others Ibid, 233.

'I had thought that I'm at the peak... greedy & ungrateful' Ibid, 244.

'In this age so concerned with travel... human experience' David B. Yaden and Andrew B. Newberg (2022), *The Varieties of Spiritual Experience: 21st Century Research and Perspectives*, Oxford University Press: Oxford, 153–54.

'mental state of deep unity' Ibid, 72.

In both groups, entering a state of deep unity... the body and its surroundings Ibid, 72 & 242.

There is also some evidence... episodes of mystical unity Urgesi, C., Aglioti, S. M., Skrap, M. & Fabbro, F. (2010), 'The spiritual brain: selective cortical lesions modulate human self-transcendence', *Neuron*, 65(3), 244.

the English author and seeker of truth Paul Brunton (https://www.paulbrunton.org/wp-content/uploads/2023/11/A-Search-for-Paul-Brunton-New-Dawn-191.pdf).

'I find myself outside the rim... remoulded in rapture' Arvind Sharma (1993), *The Experiential Dimension of Advaita Vedanta*, Motilal Banarsidass Publishers: Delhi, 92–3.

the presence of psychedelic alkaloids... skeletal remains David B. Yaden and Andrew B. Newberg (2022), *The Varieties of Spiritual Experience: 21st Century Research and Perspectives*, Oxford University Press: Oxford, 348.

found that subjects who were given psilocybin... events of their lives Ibid, 352–3.

Another distinguished psychopharmacologist... 'default mode network' Carhart-Harris, Robin L., Leech, Robert, Hellyer, Peter J. et al (2014), 'The entropic brain: a theory of conscious states informed by neuroimaging research with psychedelic drugs', *Frontiers in Human Neuroscience*, 3 February 2014 (https://doi.org/10.3389/fnhum.2014.00020).

Roland Griffiths and colleagues . . . cancer diagnoses Griffiths, Roland R., Johnson, Matthew W., Carducci, Michael A. et al (2016), 'Psilocybin produces substantial and sustained decreases in depression and anxiety in patients with life-threatening cancer: a randomized double-blind trial', *Journal of Psychopharmacology*, 30(12): 1181–97 (DOI: 10.1177/0269881116675513).

along with a significantly reduced fear of dying Michael Pollan (2018), *How to Change Your Mind: The New Science of Psychedelics*, Penguin Books: London, 8.

Carhart-Harris and colleagues . . . Conrad Hal Waddington in the 1940s Carhart-Harris, R. L., Chandaria, S., Erritzoe, D. E. et al (2023), 'Canalization and plasticity in psychopathology', *Neuropharmacology* 226: 109398 (DOI: 10.1016/j.neuropharm.2022.109398).

'Here, we invoke the analogies . . . "rebirth"' Ibid, 4.

'We come into this world . . . to wipe clean the tape' Mike Jay (2023/2024), *Psychonauts: Drugs and the Making of the Modern Mind*, Yale University Press: London, 298.

Ecstatic worship . . . ancient Greece and Rome see Hugh Bowden (2023), *Mystery Cults in the Ancient World*, Thames and Hudson: UK.

Chapter 5 – Integration: The Essential Task

'which as it were, performs . . . existence of its own' C. G. Jung (1959/2014), *The Archetypes and the Collective Unconscious*, Second edition, translated by R. F. C. Hull, Routledge: London, 79.

Jung suggested that archetypes pattern instinctual behaviour Ibid, 44.

'A living organism, over time . . . can be read as a book' Richard Dawkins (2024), 'Our Immortal Genes', interview with Richard Pallardy, *New Humanist* (Winter), 30.

She identified several psychiatric vulnerabilities . . . several generations Yehuda, R. & Lehrner, A. (2018), 'Intergenerational transmission of trauma effects: putative role of epigenetic mechanisms', *World Psychiatry*, 17(3): 243–57. (https://pmc.ncbi.nlm.nih.gov/articles/PMC6127768/).

Psychotherapists specialising in the treatment of trauma . . . family histories see Mark Wolynn (2022), *It Didn't Start with You*, Vermilion: London.

'While epigenetic studies . . . treatment of these conditions' Nestler, E., Peña, C. & Akbarian, S. (2015), 'Epigenetic Basis of Mental Illness', *The Neuroscientist*, Vol. 22 (5) – see Abstract (https://journals.sagepub.com/doi/10.1177/1073858415608147).

'radical affirmation' Rupert Sheldrake – see https://www.sheldrake.org/research/morphic-resonance.

Jung was reading The Divine Comedy *. . . began to deteriorate* C. G. Jung (2009), *The Red Book, Liber Novus, A Reader's Edition*, edited and with an introduction by Sonu Shamdasani, preface by Ulrich Hoerni, translated by Mark Kyburz, John Peck and Sonu Shamdasani, W. W. Norton & Company: London, 31.

Philemon, an archetypal sage . . . appeared to Jung in a dream C. G. Jung (1962/82), *Memories,*

Dreams, Reflections, recorded and edited by Aniela Jaffé, translated from the German by Richard and Clara Winston, Collins Fount Paperbacks: Glasgow, 207.

Jung realised that this apparition . . . 'superior insight' Ibid, 208.

'confrontation with the unconscious' Ibid, 194.

'*I am walking alone in a dark forest . . . it begins to rain*' C. G. Jung (2009), *The Red Book, Liber Novus, A Reader's Edition*, edited and with an introduction by Sonu Shamdasani, preface by Ulrich Hoerni, translated by Mark Kyburz, John Peck and Sonu Shamdasani, W. W. Norton & Company: London, 220.

the '*style of the archetypes*' C. G. Jung (1962/82), *Memories, Dreams, Reflections*, recorded and edited by Aniela Jaffé, translated from the German by Richard and Clara Winston, Collins Fount Paperbacks: Glasgow, 202.

'*Then we saw him coming . . . the bones of the dead*' C. G. Jung (2009), *The Red Book, Liber Novus, A Reader's Edition*, edited and with an introduction by Sonu Shamdasani, preface by Ulrich Hoerni, translated by Mark Kyburz, John Peck and Sonu Shamdasani, W. W. Norton & Company: London, 161.

'*How shall I ever walk . . . to the lees?*' Ibid, 148.

'*Before me was the entrance to a dark cave . . . glowing red crystal*' C. G. Jung (1962/82), *Memories, Dreams, Reflections*, recorded and edited by Aniela Jaffé, translated from the German by Richard and Clara Winston, Collins Fount Paperbacks: Glasgow, 203.

Many artists aspire to a state . . . 'overflowing of dreams into real life' Mike Jay (2023/2024), *Psychonauts: Drugs and the Making of the Modern Mind*, Yale University Press: London, 190.

'*The archetype is not a causal agency . . .* spontaneously *organize themselves*' Bernardo Kastrup (2021), *Decoding Jung's Metaphysics: The Archetypal Semantics of an Experiential Universe*, foreword by Jeffrey Mishlove, afterword by James Hollis, IFF Books, Winchester: UK, 65.

He suggested that synchronicity . . . the nature of archetypes David Lindorff (2004/09), *Pauli and Jung: The Meeting of Two Great Minds*, Quest Books, Illinois, 107–8.

Mind and matter . . . potentially explain synchronicity Ibid, 2.

a time in which the 'magical-symbolical' . . . coexisted Ibid, 71.

'*the destiny of the occident . . . experience of oneness*' Ibid, 192.

'*Science is the best tool . . . only way of comprehending*' C. G. Jung (1931/2010), commentary by C. G. Jung in *The Secret of the Golden Flower*, translated and explained by Richard Wilhelm, The Book Tree: San Diego, 78.

the most significant problems of life are 'fundamentally insoluble' Ibid, 89.

'*Some higher or wider interest . . . stronger life-tendency*' Ibid, 88.

'*This does not mean that the thunderstorm . . . one is now above it*' Ibid.

The British composer Sir Michael Tippett . . . his own analysis Michael Tippett (1994), *Those Twentieth Century Blues: An Autobiography*, Pimlico: London, 63.

'autobiographical cure' Emilia Halton-Hernandez (2023), *The Marion Milner Method: Psychoanalysis, Autobiography, Creativity*, an open access publication by Routledge: Oxon, 2.

'as I cannot eat you ... a going concern' Donald Winnicott quoted in Emma Letley (2014), *Marion Milner: The Life*, Routledge, 97.

'Just in so far as I held myself still ... where I was going' Marion Milner (1937/2011), *An Experiment in Leisure*, Routledge, 138 – cited in Emilia Halton-Hernandez (2023), *The Marion Milner Method: Psychoanalysis, Autobiography, Creativity*, an open access publication by Routledge: Oxon.

'wide focus' and 'narrow focus' – *the former giving her access to what she described as 'back-of-the-mind thoughts'* Emilia Halton-Hernandez (2023), *The Marion Milner Method: Psychoanalysis, Autobiography, Creativity*, an open access publication by Routledge: Oxon, 34.

She spoke in a 'soft but musical voice' Brett Kahr (2024), *Hidden Histories of British Psychoanalysis: From Freud's Death Bed to Laing's Missing Tooth*, Karnac Books: Bicester, 131.

'evidently fallen in love' with her. Ibid, 132.

'From womb to tomb' Richard Stevens (2008), *Erik Erikson: Explorer of Identity and the Life Cycle*, Palgrave Macmillan: Hampshire, 43.

'integrity can balance ... marked the beginning' Ibid, 54–5.

He described three modes of experiencing the world ... a 'Borromean knot' (three interlinked hoops) Lionel Bailly (2020). *Lacan: A Beginner's Guide*. Oneworld: London, 89-90.

Chapter 6 – Circuits in Conversation: The Integrated Brain

The two hemispheres are in fact connected in several places Iain McGilchrist (2021/2023), *The Matter With Things: Our Brains, Our Delusions, and the Unmaking of the World*, Volume 1, Perspectiva Press: UK, 58.

Even though brain-wiring varies ... the vast majority Iain McGilchrist (2009/2018), *The Master and His Emissary: The Divided Brain and the Making of the Western World*, Yale University Press: New Haven and London, 11–12.

the corresponding area ... subsequently inhibited Iain McGilchrist (2021/2023), *The Matter With Things: Our Brains, Our Delusions, and the Unmaking of the World*, Volume 1, Perspectiva Press: UK, 62.

it is reasonable to suggest ... engaging with the world Iain McGilchrist (2009/2018), *The Master and His Emissary: The Divided Brain and the Making of the Western World*, Yale University Press: New Haven and London, 10.

One patient reported ... a separate personality Sergio Della Salla, 'The Anarchic Hand', *The Psychologist*, 18 October 2005 (https://www.bps.org.uk/psychologist/anarchic-hand).

Apollonian and Dionysian ... intuition and wholeness Iain McGilchrist (2009/2018), *The*

Master and His Emissary: The Divided Brain and the Making of the Western World, Yale University Press: New Haven and London, 199.

The circuitry of the left hemisphere . . . the right hemisphere Ibid, 42.

the more we rely on this interpretation . . . are dismissed Ibid, 399.

'As a result of this central semiotic problem . . . a glass' Jonathan Rosen (2023), *The Best Minds: A Story of Friendship, Madness, and the Tragedy of Good Intentions*, Allen Lane: UK, 120.

the right hemisphere . . . associated with the unconscious Ibid, 186.

Brain scans and electroencephalographic recordings . . . right hemispheric phenomenon Ibid.

The right hemisphere supports 'metaphor' . . . literal representations Ibid, 71.

the general idea of a creative reconciliation . . . optimal hemispheric cooperation Iain McGilchrist (2021/2023), *The Matter With Things: Our Brains, Our Delusions, and the Unmaking of the World*, Volume 1, Perspectiva Press: UK, 55.

'For him [Jung] . . . its role is altered' The Matter With Things: Our Brains, Our Delusions, and the Unmaking of the World, Volume II, Perspectiva Press: UK, 876.

The right hemisphere . . . 'tendency to melancholy' Iain McGilchrist (2009/2018), *The Master and His Emissary: The Divided Brain and the Making of the Western World*, Yale University Press: New Haven and London, 85.

William James asserted that melancholy . . . 'complete religious evolution' Ibid, 306.

'to begin with you try different channels . . . no longer listening to them' Iain McGilchrist (2021/2023), *The Matter With Things: Our Brains, Our Delusions, and the Unmaking of the World*, Volume 1, Perspectiva Press: UK, 34.

'An increasingly mechanistic . . . dysfunctional left hemisphere' Iain McGilchrist (2009/2018), *The Master and His Emissary: The Divided Brain and the Making of the Western World*, Yale University Press: New Haven and London, 6

'I wish I had read more of the mystics earlier in my life' Iain McGilchrist (2021/2023), *The Matter With Things: Our Brains, Our Delusions, and the Unmaking of the World*, Volume II, Perspectiva Press: UK, 1333.

'when we focus our attention . . . linked and integrated' Daniel Siegel (2010/2021), *Mindsight: Transform Your Brain With the New Science of Kindness*, Oneworld: UK, 42–3.

This is associated with a growing awareness . . . 'part of a much larger whole' Ibid, 76.

This class of meta-awareness . . . practice of mindfulness Ibid, 32.

'reflection we can observe . . . becoming lost in it' Ibid, 33.

'experience creates the repeated neural firing . . . laid down involuntarily' Ibid, 42.

Chapter 7 – Shadowlands: Negotiating Obstacles

Campbell points out . . . usually the most exciting Joseph Campbell (1949), *The Hero with a Thousand Faces*, Bolingen Series XVII, Third edition, The Joseph Campbell Foundation, New World Library: Novato, California, 81.

'There can be no question . . . effective guidance' Ibid, 86–7.

'the "negative" side of the personality . . . the personal unconscious' cited in *Fontana Pocket Readers: Jung – Selected Writings* (1986), introduced by Anthony Storr, Part 4, 'Archetypes: Shadow; Anima; Animus; the Persona; the Old Wise Man', Fontana: London, 87.

According to Jung . . . the shadow as a 'medical' problem Ibid, 89.

'the psyche of modern man' Ibid, 380.

'the normal individual . . . looking within' Ibid.

Jung asserted that the task of accommodating the shadow . . . engage his attention Ibid, 281.

Which suggests that the midpoint of life . . . transformative Anthony Storr (1997), *Feet of Clay*, HarperCollins: London, xiv.

Bhagwan Shree Rajneesh . . . addicted to Valium and nitrous oxide Ibid, 59.

'The wisest men follow their own direction . . . no prophets guiding them' Euripides, *Iphigenia in Tauris*. Cited on title page of Anthony Storr (1997), *Feet of Clay*, HarperCollins: London.

Chapter 8 – Meaning: Existence and Purpose

Sartre gave impromptu renditions . . . impersonated Donald Duck Sarah Bakewell (2017), *At the Existentialist Café: Freedom, Being & Apricot Cocktails*, Vintage: London, 14.

Beauvoir was a reckless hillwalker . . . liked wearing turbans Ibid, 13.

In the 1980s the philosopher Harry Frankfurt . . . human foible Harry Frankfurt (2005), *On Bullshit*, Princetown University Press: New Jersey. See also *Raritan* magazine, Vol. 6, no. 2.

One of the subheadings . . . 'meaning crisis' see the YouTube channel of John Vervaeke: 'Dr John Vervaeke: Creating Solutions to the Meaning Crisis' (https://www.youtube.com/user/johnvervaeke).

Camus applauds Sisyphus . . . a 'hero' of the absurd Albert Camus (1942/2000), *The Myth of Sisyphus*, Penguin Books: London, 87.

'Something has happened to me . . . not like anything obvious' Jean-Paul Sartre (1984), *Nausea*, Penguin Modern Classics: Harmondsworth, 13.

'I can no longer explain what I see . . . towards fear' Ibid, 19.

It has been described as one of the hardest books ever written. Michael Inwood (2019), *Heidegger: A Very Short Introduction*, Second edition, Oxford University Press: Oxford, 12.

'being-towards-death'... 'making sense of it as a whole' A. C. Grayling (2019), *The History of Philosophy* (Kindle edition), Penguin: London, 481.

he reportedly attended a book-burning in Freiburg Sarah Bakewell (2017), *At the Existentialist Café: Freedom, Being & Apricot Cocktails*, Vintage: London, 80.

'Don't you know that sometimes a man ... the level of his works?' Jean-Paul Sartre (1974) A More Precise Characterization of Existentialism, in Michel Contat and Michel Rybalka, eds. *The Writings of Jean-Paul Sartre*. Translated by Richard C. McCleary. Northwestern University Press: Evanston, Ill, 2: 156.

He aligned clinical practice ... Daseinsanalytic Institute in Zurich Mick Cooper (2017), *Existential Therapies: Second Edition*, Sage: London, 44.

Conversely, psychological problems ... 'close off' experience Ibid, 47.

'a seed of unrest will remain' Alfried Längle (2001), 'Old age from an existential-analytical perspective', *Psychological Reports*, 89, 211–15.

'It is the task of the person ... has to do with the self' Ibid.

'Whoever has done what he wanted ... is still waiting' Ibid.

'Whoever is able to newly find himself... the autumn sun' Ibid.

'there is compelling evidence ... meaning in life and wellbeing' Mick Cooper (2017), *Existential Therapies: Second Edition*, Sage: London, 185.

Psychologist and philosopher Joel Vos ... categories of meaning Joel Vos (2023), 'The Meaning Sextet: A Systematic Literature Review and Further Validation of a Universal Typology of Meaning in Life', *Journal of Constructivist Psychology*, Vol. 36, issue 2, 204–31.

Chapter 9 – The Subjective Hourglass: Time and the Perception of Time

'What are days for?' ... 'running over the fields' Philip Larkin (2003), *Collected Poems*, Faber and Faber: London, 98.

'What then is time?' ... 'I do not know' Dean Buonomano (2018), *Your Brain is a Time Machine*, W. W. Norton & Company: New York, 4.

'At the most fundamental level ... time as we experience it' Carlo Rovelli (2019), *The Order of Time*, Penguin: London, 169.

'Physics helps us to penetrate layers ... the fog caused by our emotions' Ibid, 174.

Although the precise way ... spatial metaphors Dean Buonomano (2018), *Your Brain is a Time Machine*, W. W. Norton & Company: New York, 183.

'Some idealization of the past ... serves a similar purpose' Melanie Klein (1963), 'On the Sense of Loneliness', cited in *Envy and Gratitude and Other Works 1946–1963*, with an introduction by Hanna Segal, Vintage: London, 311.

It became a significant diagnosis ... in 1918 Tiffany Watt Smith (2016), *The Book of Human Emotions*, Profile: London, 186.

'We always have time enough, if we will but use it aright' Johann Wolfgang von Goethe (1882), *The Autobiography of Goethe: Truth and Poetry From My Own Life*, Library of Alexandria, 394.

Some of these climbers recalled . . . 'review' their entire lives Dean Buonomano (2018), *Your Brain is a Time Machine*, W. W. Norton & Company: New York, 57-58.

'In general,' William James observed . . . 'more memories than a day' Ibid, 60.

'Let any one try . . . gone in the instant of becoming' Claudia Hammond (2013), *Time Warped*, Canongate: Edinburgh, 300.

'that interfering neurotic . . . blessedly out of the way' Aldous Huxley (2004), *The Doors of Perception*, Vintage: London, 32.

Mescalin 'delivered' him . . . 'idolatrously worshipped notions' Ibid, 20.

'That chair – shall I ever forget it? . . . aware of anything else' Ibid, 32.

'These effects of mescalin . . . cerebral reducing valve' Ibid, 13.

Estimates vary considerably . . . up to 40 per cent of cases Nahm, Michael & Greyson, Bruce (2009), 'Terminal Lucidity in Patients With Chronic Schizophrenia and Dementia: A Survey of the Literature – Brief Report', *Journal of Nervous and Mental Disease*, 197(12): 942-4 (DOI: 10.1097/NMD.0b013e3181c22583).

there are liver cells that 'know' the time of day Dean Buonomano (2018), *Your Brain is a Time Machine*, W. W. Norton & Company: New York, 33.

This is why 'sleep and circadian rhythm disruption' . . . catch-all term see Russell Foster (2022), *Life Time: The New Science of the Body Clock, and How it Can Revolutionize Your Sleep and Health*, Penguin: UK.

Although there are some features of SCRD . . . the modern world Mathew Walker (2017), *Why We Sleep*, Allen Lane: UK, 101.

'The last few years . . . the Quantified Self to live forever' Michael Foley (2013), *Life Lessons from Bergson*, Macmillan: London, 25.

the 'shadow of natural selection' Peter Medawar (1952). *An Unsolved Problem of Biology*. H. K. Lewis: London.

'our unique system of intergenerational cooperation . . . useful grandparents' Daniel Lieberman (2020), *Exercised: The Science of Physical Activity, Rest, and Health*, Allen Lane: UK, 230.

Chapter 10 – Conclusion: How it Works

There is some variation . . . remarkably stable Rudnev, M., Barrett, H. C., Buckwalter, W. et al (2024), 'Dimensions of wisdom perception across twelve countries on five continents', *Nature Communications*, 15: 6375.

'No one can build you the bridge . . . the tunnels of one's being' Friedrich Nietzsche (1874), *Schopenhauer as Educator*. Cited in Scott Barry Kaufman (2022), *Transcend: The New Science of Self-Actualization*, Sheldon Press: London, xxxviii. See also

Friedrich Nietzsche (1874), *Schopenhauer as Educator*, 106 https://archive.org/details/ NietzscheSchopenhauerAsEducatorCollins/mode.

A frequently paraphrased declaration . . . 'God-shaped hole' Jonathan Haidt (2024), *The Anxious Generation: How the Great Rewiring of Childhood is Causing an Epidemic of Mental Illness*, Allen Lane: UK, 215.

'To make God laugh' . . . 'tell him your plans' Dilip Jeste and Scott Lafee (2020), *Wiser: The Scientific Roots of Wisdom, Compassion, and What Makes Us Good*, Sounds True: Boulder, Colorado, 188.

a 'calling' to the inner life . . . 'comes to us again and again' James Hollis (2005), *Finding Meaning in the Second Half of Life: How to Finally, Really Grow Up*, Avery: Penguin Random House: New York, 21.

'The wisdom we attribute to older adults . . . changes in neurochemistry' Daniel Levitin (2021), *The Changing Mind: A Neuroscientist's Guide to Ageing Well*, Penguin Life: UK, 144.

In the 1960s, a clinical psychologist, Jerome Singer . . . guilt-laden fantasies. Singer, J. L. (1975), 'Navigating the stream of consciousness: research in daydreaming and related inner experience', *American Psychologist*, 30, 727–38.

'the unconscious made use . . . lofty symbolical significance' C. G. Jung (1959/2014), *The Archetypes and the Collective Unconscious: Second Edition*, translated by R. F. C. Hull, Routledge: London, 293.

When the great Irish writer James Joyce . . . 'where you swim, she drowns' NB: There are various accounts of what was said and the precise wording changes accordingly. For Joyce's 1934 consultation with Jung, see Ronald Hayman (2002), *A Life of Jung*, Bloomsbury: London, 325.

'The whole life of the individual . . . to die before they are born.' Erich Fromm (2002). *The Sane Society*. With an introduction by David Ingleby. Routledge: London, 25.

'fully functioning person' Carl Rogers (1959) 'A Theory of Therapy, Personality, and Interpersonal Relationships, As Developed in the Client-Centred Framework', reprinted in *The Carl Rogers Reader* (1990), edited by Howard Kirschenbaum and Valerie Land Henderson, Constable & Robinson: Great Britain, 236.

Frank Martela and colleagues published the first large-scale study comparing the predictive power of 'purpose' and 'satisfaction' Martela, F., Laitinen, E., & Hakulinen, C. (2024), 'Which predicts longevity better: Satisfaction with life or purpose in life?', *Psychology and Ageing*, 39(6), 589–98.

The feeling of 'loss of self' . . . default mode network activation Dacher Keltner (2024), *Awe: The Transformative Power of Everyday Wonder*, Penguin: UK, 36.

'Language . . . the latter one step nearer' Friedrich Nietzsche (1967), *The Birth of Tragedy and The Case of Wagner*, translated by Walter Kaufmann, Vintage Books: New York, 55–6.

'I was recuperating from a mini-breakdown . . . played by Solomon and the Hallé.' Classic FM interview – Ken Russell on Gustav Mahler See: https://www.classicfm.com/ composers/mahler/guides/classic-fm-heroes-gustav-mahler/#:~:text=I%20was%20 recuperating%20from%20a,sit%20up%20and%20take%20notice.

'Words divide, tones unite' Victor Zuckerkandl (1973), *Man the Musician, Sound and Symbol*, translated by Norbert Guterman, Princeton University Press: New Jersey, 75.

Listening to music . . . the cerebellum Daniel Levitin (2006), *This is Your Brain on Music: Understanding a Human Obsession*, Atlantic Books: London, 9 and 191.

We shiver, get goosebumps . . . sometimes, we cry Iain McGilchrist (2018), *The Master and His Emissary: The Divided Brain and the Making of the Western World*, Yale University Press: New Haven and London, 73.

The fastest-growing age group . . . centenarians Andrew J. Scott (2024), *The Longevity Imperative: Building a Better Society for Healthier, Longer Lives*, Basic Books: London, 11.

'A transpersonal sense of affinity . . . contemplative solitude' Lars Tornstam (2011), 'Maturing into Gerotranscendence', *Journal of Transpersonal Psychology*, Vol. 43, no. 2, 168.

'a tragedy that many of us live . . . the final escape from this' Ibid, 177.

Individuals who have more positive self-perceptions . . . less positive self-perceptions Andrew J. Scott (2024), *The Longevity Imperative: Building a Better Society for Healthier, Longer Lives*, Basic Books: London, 197.

'Some old people are oppressed . . . what was possible has been done' Bertrand Russell (2021), 'How to Grow Old', in *Portraits from Memory and Other Essays* (Routledge Classics), with a new foreword by Nicholas Griffin, Routledge: London, 44.

Acknowledgements

I would like to thank Richard Beswick, my UK editor at Abacus, for encouraging me to write a book about psychological adjustment in later life and Daniel Balado for copyediting my final draft.

Index

acceptance 3, 35–53, 94, 97, 158, 169, 220
'achieving awareness' 75
active grandparent hypothesis 192–3, 222
active imagination 114–15, 119, 145, 206, 207
Adams, Douglas 60
addiction 81, 153, 170, 172
afterlife 13, 79
agoraphobia 168
Agrippina 41–2
'alien hand' 134–5
Alpert, Richard 185
ALTOS 25
altruism 175, 195, 221
Alzheimer's disease 187, 207
Amis, Kingsley 44
analytical psychology 58, 84, 107, 111, 139
ancestral memory 108
answering activity 122–3
anti-ageing products 25
anti-psychiatry 209
Apollonian drive 136
archetypes 107–8, 112, 117–18, 149, 152
Arendt, Hannah 167

Arrian 46
art 115, 122, 214, 217, 224
'As Bad as a Mile' 56
ataraxia 39, 53
attention 43, 75, 123, 131–2, 138, 141–2, 145, 185
Augustine, St 86, 178
authentic choices 166
avoidant talking 31–2
awakened awareness 74, 75–6, 123
awakening experiences 73–4, 85, 87, 91, 94, 210
awe 198, 214–18, 220

Bakewell, Sarah 30
Be Here Now 185
bead memories 123
Becker, Ernest 18–19, 23–4, 29, 104
Beckett, Samuel 174
behaviourism 91
Bergson, Henri 60, 191
Bezos, Jeff 25
Binswanger, Ludwig 167–8, 169
Blake, William 95
block universe 178, 220
Boss, Medard 168, 169

brain
    cerebral cortex 74, 207
    corpus callosum 131, 133–4
    hemispheres 131–7, 138–40, 145–6
    music effect 218
    suprachiasmatic nuclei 189
Brunton, Paul 98
Buddhism 81, 96, 115, 142, 215
'bullshit' 162
Buonomano, Dean 189

calling experiences 66, 94
Campbell, Joseph 54–5, 57–9, 60–1, 63, 64–5, 66, 72, 73, 148, 158, 194
Camus, Albert 163
canalization 100
Caravaggio 224–6
Carhart-Harris, Robin 99–100
cerebral cortex 74, 207
Chekhov, Anton 14, 17
Chrysippus 53
circadian clocks 189–90, 213–14
cleromancy 201
cognitive psychology 28, 73
cognitive reserve 145
cognitive restructuring 52
cognitive therapies 38, 52
collective unconscious 107–8, 110
complacency 16, 28, 43, 55, 59–60, 61, 201
connectivity 94, 97, 158, 212, 216
the conscious 5–6, 57, 61, 70, 86, 107, 143–5, 204–5, 211, 217
    brain hemispheres 132, 138, 139, 145
    creativity 208
    dreams 113
conversion 87, 95, 217
Cooper, Mick 174–5
coping strategies 27, 49

corpus callosum 131, 133–4
creativity 114, 131, 206–9

Dalai Lama 153
Dante Alighieri 1, 2–3, 111, 148, 194
Darwin, Charles 68
Dawkins, Richard 108
daydreaming 206–7, 216–17
'Days' 177
de Beauvoir, Simone 160–1, 163
de Nerval, Gérard 115
de Quincey, Thomas 113
decision making 55, 67–8, 71, 116, 174, 196
deconstructionism 138
default mode network 7, 99, 143, 147, 207, 216
defence mechanisms 15–19, 27, 31, 34, 38, 43, 168, 201–2
dementia 129–30, 144–5, 207
The Denial of Death 18–19, 24
denial of death 11–34
depression 52, 65, 72, 74–5, 77, 80, 172, 207
    awakening 210
    old age 219
    psychedelic substances 99–100
    spirituality 81–2, 84–6, 96
Derrida, Jacques 137–8
determinism 91–2
Diogenes Laertius 38–9, 41
Dionysian drive 136
Dionysus 101
distraction 43, 85, 161, 185–6
divorce 16–17
Domitian, Emperor 45
dopamine 170
Doré, Gustave 1
Dostoevsky, Fyodor 165
Dr Strangelove syndrome 134–5
dreams 62, 91, 107, 110–11, 113–14, 117, 119, 205–6

brain hemispheres 138–9
self-analysis 122
drugs 7, 98–101, 113, 183, 186–7
   addiction 81, 153, 170, 172
   psychedelic 7, 98–101, 143–4, 147, 162, 200

ecstatic worship 101
ego 6–7, 124, 131, 139
   dissolution 101
   inflation 152
   transcendence 186
Einstein, Albert 118, 140, 179
Ellis, Albert 38
'emancipated innocence' 221
embodiment 24, 161, 165, 169, 223
emotion-focused coping 27
enteric nervous system 70, 71
entrainment 190
Epaphroditus 45
The Epic of Gilgamesh 11–12
Epictetus 37–8, 45–8
Epicureanism 37, 38–41, 53
epigenetics 109
epilepsy 134
Erikson, Erik 4, 124–5, 141
Euripides 157
evolution 12–13, 17, 48, 67, 108, 113–14, 131, 192–3, 222
evolutionary psychology 13, 209–10
exceptionalism 28
existential anxiety 24, 34, 38, 79, 99, 103, 126, 143, 163–4, 198
existential panic 142, 182
existential psychotherapy 14–15, 18, 165, 167–72, 174–5, 181
existential vacuum 170
existentialism 3, 160–5, 167–75, 211

fantasies 115
fight and flight response 13

Fischer, Roland 97
fixation 59
Flaubert, Gustave 30
'flourishing' 80
Foley, Michael 191–2
Foster, Russell 189–90
Frankfurt, Harry 162
Frankl, Viktor 169–71, 223
free association 122
Freud, Sigmund 5, 6, 13, 15, 17, 28, 55, 59, 62, 79, 88–9, 91, 106–8, 131, 198, 202, 206–7
Fromm, Erich 185, 211
fuzzy mathematics 201

Galileo 22
Gazzaniga, Michael 134, 137
generalisation 31
gerotranscendence 219–22
Getty Kouros 69
'glimmers' 215
Goethe, Johann von 182
Goldstein, Kurt 211
Grant, Cary 101
gratitude 95, 97, 202
Grayling, A. C. 166
Griffiths, Roland 99
guilt 151–2, 207
gurus 152–7, 158
gut feeling 60, 70, 71, 165

Halton-Hernandez, Emilia 121
Hamlet 33
happiness 148, 212, 219
Hartley, L. P. 181
Hegel, Georg Wilhelm Friedrich 4
Heidegger, Martin 165–7, 168
Heim, Albert 182
Heraclitus 213
heralds 57–8, 73
heroes 54–5, 57–8, 107, 148
heterogeneous personality 86
hierarchy of needs 93–5

Hollis, James 203
horizontal integration 130, 219
'How to Grow Old' 226
humanistic psychologists 92, 211
Huxley, Aldous 186–7
hysteria 5, 15, 156

I Ching 201
id 6–7
idealization 180
Idomeneus 41
immortality projects 11–34, 39, 79, 201, 213
inauthentic choices 166
indigenous cultures 63, 64, 158, 191
individuation 110–11, 116, 119–20, 126–7, 138, 139, 148, 151, 153–4, 192, 211, 215–16, 219
The Inferno 1, 2–3, 111, 148
inner consent 172, 181
inner life 203–4
insomnia 2, 152
instincts 108
integration 95, 105, 197, 204–5, 208, 212, 216–17, 219
  brain 128–46
  existential 173
  unconscious 106–27
intellectualisation 31
intrinsic cardiac nervous system (ICNS) 70–1
intuition 60, 64, 68–71

James, William 8, 14, 82–90, 91, 95, 100, 104, 126, 139, 151, 183, 184
Jaques, Elliott 2
Johnson, Bryan 25
Johnson, Samuel 16
Joyce, James 211
Jung, Carl Gustav 4, 8, 58, 104–8, 110–21, 123, 126–7, 138–9, 143–6, 148–51, 157, 192, 193, 199–202, 205–9, 211, 221–2

Kabbalah 6
Kahr, Brett 123–4
Kastrup, Bernardo 117
Keltner, Dacher 215, 217
Kendler, Kenneth 81
Klein, Daniel 25
Klein, Melanie 180
Kubrick, Stanley 134
Kundera, Milan 44
Kurzweil, Ray 19–20

Lacan, Jacques 126–7
Laing, R. D. 209, 210
Längle, Alfried 171–4, 181, 212
Larkin, Philip 56, 177, 184
Lashley, Karl 144
Levitin, Daniel 204
Lieberman, Daniel 193
'life-stages' model 4
lifeline 40
lived experience 168
logotherapy 169–70, 171–2
longevity 80, 195, 212, 218–19, 223
LSD 7, 101, 147
Lucretius 39

McCartney, Paul 208
McGilchrist, Iain 135, 136–7, 138–40, 170
mandalas 115–16
Marcus Aurelius 49–51, 89
Marsh, Henry 27
Martela, Frank 212
Maslow, Abraham 8, 92–7, 139, 142, 186, 211, 215
Maslow's hammer 96
mass hysteria 156
mass unconscious 108
materialism 8, 39, 80, 82, 93, 127, 156–7

May, Rollo 211
meaning 160–75, 223
  crisis 162–3
  longevity 212
Medawar, Peter 192
medical model of mental illness 209–10
meditation 8, 29, 74, 81, 97–8, 142, 154–6, 162, 188, 202, 217
memento mori 16, 224
mental health 8–9
  ego weakening 7
  Maslow 95
  meaning 171
  risk 4
  spirituality 79–82
  transpersonal interest 154
mental illness 80, 82, 85, 88, 100, 168, 209–10
mescalin 186–7
meta-crisis 161–2
midlife crisis 2, 16–17, 153
Miller, Lisa 72, 74–5, 81–2, 123
Milner, Marion 121–4
mindfulness meditation 81, 142, 162, 188
mindsight 142
mistakes 54–7
modernism 140
Montaigne, Michel de 29–32, 52
morphic resonance 110
multi-clock principle 189
music 217–18, 220
mystery cults 101
mysticism 90, 119, 140, 154–6
mythology 54–5, 57–9, 72, 148

narcissism 152, 157, 215
narrow focus attention 75, 123, 131–2, 138
natural selection 192–3
near-death experiences 30–2, 102–3

Nero, Emperor 41–2
nervous breakdowns 55–6, 110, 217
Nestler, Eric 109
neural connectivity 143–4
neuroplasticity 144
neurotheology 8
Newberg, Andrew 97–8
Nietzsche, Friedrich 70, 136, 141, 197, 217
nostalgia 180–1
nullity of death 40–1, 44
numinous 75, 77, 80, 147, 218

objectivity 142
openness 94, 142
Orwell, George 157

Pascal, Blaise 198
Pauli, Wolfgang 118–19, 140
peak experiences 94–5, 186, 214, 216
persona 200, 201
personality disorders 172
personhood 172, 207, 211
Philemon 111, 123
Pink Floyd 176
plateau experiences 95, 215
poly-crisis 161
post-bereavement hallucination 21
post-retirement activities 116–17
post-structuralism 137–8
pragmatism 8, 84, 89, 97, 103–4, 116, 158–9, 170, 184, 198–9, 219
problem-focused coping 27
problem-solving, disengagement 72–3
projection 150
Proust, Marcel 61, 72, 74
psilocybin 7, 99, 143, 147
psychedelic drugs 7, 98–101, 143–4, 147, 162, 200
psychoanalysis 5, 15, 31, 62, 88, 91–2, 121–3, 131, 167–8

psychological distress 72, 74, 209–10
psychopathology 100

Quantified Self 191–2

raised consciousness 89, 94–5, 97, 99, 104, 120, 144, 188, 214, 216–17
Rajneesh, Bhagwan Shree 153
Ram Dass, Baba 185
Rational Emotive Therapy 38
rationality 71, 119
reconstitution 200
The Red Book 111–13, 115
reflectiveness 194–6, 199, 219
relativity theory 179
religion 3, 79–82, 84–91, 158, 198–9, 202
   ecstatic worship 101
   psychedelics 98
   see also spirituality
repression 5–6, 15, 149, 152
revelatory experiences 66, 94
Rinpoche, Sogyal 153
Rogers, Carl 185, 211–12
Romanticism 140, 214
Rosen, Jonathan 137–8
Rovelli, Carlo 179
Russell, Bertrand 89–91, 226
Russell, Ken 217

St Jerome Writing 224–6
Sartre, Jean-Paul 160–1, 163, 164–5, 167
Sayers, Dorothy L. 3
schizophrenia 210–11
self 5, 6–7, 115–17, 126
   dissolution 200
   loss of 186, 215–16
self-acceptance 151
self-actualisation 94–5, 96, 111, 211, 222
self-analysis 121–3
Sellars, John 49

Seneca 41–5
serotonin 70
the shadow 148–51, 209
shamans 99, 147, 210, 214
shame 151–2
Sheldrake, Rupert 110
Siegel, Daniel 141, 142–3
Singer, Jerome 206–7
Sisyphus 163
sleep
   insomnia 2, 152
   see also dreams
sleep and circadian rhythm disruption (SCRD) 189–90
Sliding Doors moments 116
slow living 203, 207
social connectivity 94, 97, 158, 212, 216
social media 18, 43, 62, 150, 203
social relationships 142, 220, 221
Sperry, Roger 134
spirituality 8, 74–5, 77–105, 107, 110–11, 119, 171, 198–9, 220
split-brain patients 134–5
Stoicism 3, 29, 37–8, 41–53, 126, 162, 169, 172, 202
Storr, Anthony 153
stream of consciousness 61–2
structural models 6–7
suicide 56–7, 80, 82, 222
super-ego 6
suprachiasmatic nuclei 189
survival instinct 12–14, 32
suspended animation 19
synchronicity 117–18, 119, 200–1
Szasz, Thomas 209

Taoism 72, 114
Taylor, Steve 73–4
technology, resistance to 60
terminal lucidity 187–8
terror management theory 13–14
Thomas, Dylan 34

Index

time 176–93, 212–13
  blindness 190, 191
  dilation 183, 213
  management 181–2
  nostalgia 180–1
  novelty 183–4, 213
  perception 182–7, 213, 220
  present moment 50, 51, 177–8, 184–6, 188–9, 213
  spatial metaphors 179–80
'tip of the tongue' phenomenon 73
Tippett, Sir Michael 120–1
Tolstoy, Leo 85–6
Tornstam, Lars 219–22
transcendence 96, 97–8, 139, 142, 157
transformative experiences 30, 52, 65–6, 103–4, 170
transgenerational trauma 108–9
transhumanism 19–20, 33
transpersonal interest 154, 219–20
transpersonal psychology 8, 66, 92, 209–10, 214
transpiration 142

the unconscious 4, 5–6, 56, 57, 64, 66, 68–70, 91, 131, 143–5, 148–9, 204–5, 211, 217
  brain hemispheres 138, 139
  creativity 208–9
  integration 106–27

problem-solving 73
spirituality 87–8

ventral attention network 75
vertical integration 130–1, 219
Vervaeke, John 162–3
Vos, Joel 175

Waddington, Conrad Hal 100
Waddington landscape 100–1
Wallas, Graham 73
'Ward No. 6' 14, 17
Whitehead, Evelyn 90
whole brain emulation 19
wholeness 5–8, 10, 95, 119, 126, 136, 173, 197, 204–5, 211–12, 215–16, 220, 222
wide focus attention 75, 123, 131–2
Winnicott, Donald 121–2
Woolf, Virginia 121
world sickness 84, 86
wu wei 72

Yalom, Irvin 14–15
Yehuda, Rachel 109

Zeno 38
Zeno's paradox 26
Zuckerkandl, Viktor 218

RAISING READERS
Books Build Bright Futures

Dear Reader,

We'd love your attention for one more page to tell you about the crisis in children's reading, and what we can all do.

Studies have shown that reading for fun is the **single biggest predictor of a child's future life chances** – more than family circumstance, parents' educational background or income. It improves academic results, mental health, wealth, communication skills, ambition and happiness.[1]

The number of children reading for fun is in rapid decline. Young people have a lot of competition for their time. In 2024, 1 in 10 children and young people in the UK aged 5 to 18 did not own a single book at home.[2]

Hachette works extensively with schools, libraries and literacy charities, but here are some ways we can all raise more readers:

- Reading to children for just 10 minutes a day makes a difference
- Don't give up if children aren't regular readers – there will be books for them!
- Visit bookshops and libraries to get recommendations
- Encourage them to listen to audiobooks
- Support school libraries
- Give books as gifts

There's a lot more information about how to encourage children to read on our website: **www.RaisingReaders.co.uk**

Thank you for reading.

---

[1] OECD, '21st-Century Readers: Developing Literacy Skills in a Digital World', 2021, https://www.oecd.org/en/publications/21st-century-readers_a83d84cb-en.html

[2] National Literacy Trust, 'Book Ownership in 2024', November 2024, https://literacytrust.org.uk/research-services/research-reports/book-ownership-in-2024